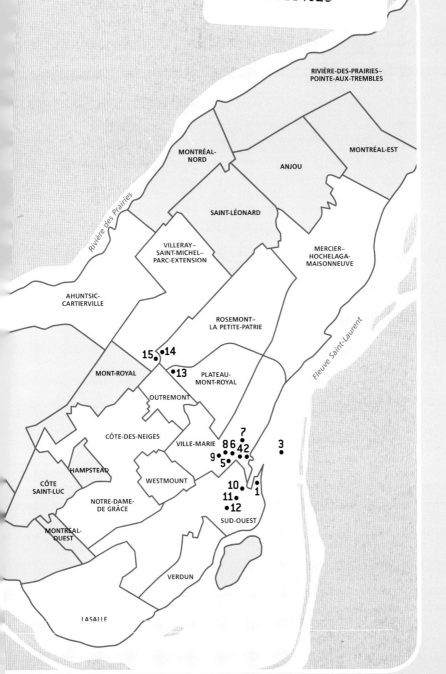

Project Editor: Agnès Saint-Laurent
Art Direction & Design: Josée Amyotte
Image Editing: Johanne Lemay
Graphic Design: Chantal Landry
Translation: Matthew Brown, Louisa Sage
Revision: Robert Ronald
Proofreading: Reilley Bishop-Stall
Photo Credits: Olivier Ruel

EXCLUSIVE DISTRIBUTOR:

For Canada and the United States:
Simon & Schuster Canada
166 King Street East, Suite 300
Toronto, ON M5A 1J3
Phone: (647) 427-8882
        1-800-387-0446
Fax: (647) 430-9446
simonandschuster.ca

Bibliothèque et Archives nationales du Québec and
Library and Archives Canada cataloguing in publication

Bouchard, Claire,

   [300 raisons d'aimer Montréal. English]

   300 reasons to love Montreal

   Translation of : 300 raisons d'aimer Montréal.

   ISBN 978-1-9880026-4-4

   1. Montréal (Québec) - Guidebooks.
I. Parent, Marie-Joëlle. II. Ruel, Olivier. III. Title.
IV. Title : 300 raisons d'aimer Montréal. English.
V. Title : Three hundred reasons to love Montreal.

FC2947.18.B6813 2017   917.14'28045
C2017-940505-5

Marie-Joëlle Parent is the author and creator
of *300 Reasons to Love New York*, the inspiration
for the "300 Reasons to Love" collection.

WARNING
As a city thirsty for new trends, Montreal is constantly
changing, which means that the lifespan of bars, restaurants and hotels varies greatly. Right up until this book
went to print, I walked through the city's neighborhoods
time and time again to ensure that the information was
up to date. However, as nothing is safe from the passing
of time, know that some establishments might have
moved or shut down. Menus, prices, fees and business
hours are provided as a guideline and are also subject to
change. Enjoy your stay!

04-17

© 2017 Juniper Publishing,
division of the Sogides Group Inc.,
a subsidiary of Québecor Média Inc.
(Montreal, Quebec)

Legal deposit: 2017
National Library of Québec
National Library of Canada

ISBN 978-1-988002-64-4

Conseil des Arts   Canada Council
du Canada   for the Arts

We gratefully acknowledge the support of the Canada
Council for the Arts for its publishing program.

We acknowledge the financial support of the Government
of Canada through the Canada Book Fund for our publishing
activities.

CLAIRE BOUCHARD

300

REASONS TO LOVE
MONTREAL

Photography
OLIVIER RUEL

Table of Contents

Preface by Marie-Joëlle Parent **6**
I Love Montreal **9**

My Top Picks **10**
  Not-to-be-Missed Events ▪ Accommodations

Cité-du-Havre, the Old Port, Parc Jean-Drapeau **17**

Old Montreal, Quartier International **31**

Chinatown, the Gay Village, Quartier des Spectacles . . . **49**

Downtown **72**

Griffintown, Little Burgundy, Saint-Henri, Verdun **91**

Westmount, Notre-Dame-de-Grâce (NDG),
Côte-des-Neiges **111**

Outremont, Mile End, Plateau-Mont-Royal 129

Hochelaga-Maisonneuve 167

Rosemont, Petite-Patrie, Little Italy, Mile-Ex 194

Parc Extension, Villeray, Saint-Michel, Ahuntsic 225

Off the Beaten Path and Day Trips 245

The Best of Montreal According to... 255

Index 280
Photo Credits 285
Acknowledgments 287

Preface

I'm extraordinarily happy to introduce *300 Reasons to Love Montreal*, the fourth volume of the collection I started with *300 Reasons to Love New York*. Little did I know then, when I started writing my first book, that the city where I grew up would eventually become part of this series.

My favorite childhood memories are directly connected to Montreal. During my school years, the city was my playground. I loved exploring the old shops on Boulevard Saint-Laurent, the obscure little concert venues, the flowered alleys, the bars of the Plateau, the cafés of Little Italy and the huge public markets. I discovered a passion for art-deco buildings, delicatessens and old barbershops.

I'll never forget my very first apartment, a tiny two-room in the heart of Mile End. My neighborhood soon became my universe. Each morning started with a stop at Fairmount Bagel before I hopped on my bike to head down to the university. Summer nights ended surrounded by friends on my balcony, sharing a bottle of wine. Life has a gentle rhythm in Montreal—that's what I miss most after having moved away.

I left Montreal over eight years ago, but the city has a permanent home in my heart. Montreal is my passport—my identity. I visit several times a year, and I always love rediscovering it with new eyes.

As soon as I met Claire Bouchard, I knew she was a true Montreal specialist—she was perfect to share the best of Montreal with the world. She spent the last few years seeking out the hidden treasures and unusual spots that will surprise even longtime Montrealers. Her Montreal is multicultural, gourmet, green, innovative and community-minded.

Originally from Quebec's North Shore, she never felt she was born in the right place, until she finally moved to Montreal to go to school in the 1990s. She never left. Even 20 years on, she's just as enchanted with the city, and her curious and adventurous spirit is as strong as ever. She lived in many neighborhoods—Mile End, the Plateau, Centre-Sud and Villeray—before finally settling in Petite-Patrie, the area that holds the most charm for her. Her neighbors are Chinese, Portuguese, Turkish and Greek. That's Montreal: a cultural mosaic.

"Montreal might not have the huge tourist attractions of New York or Paris, but it's a city that's very alive. You have to take a little time to really appreciate it. That's when it really reveals its charms," she says. I totally agree.

Marie-Joëlle Parent
Creator of the "300 Reasons to Love" collection
Author of *300 Reasons to Love New York*
and *300 Reasons to Love San Francisco*

"This city is going to drive me crazy.
This city is going to drive me completely crazy."
Xavier Caféine
From the song *Montréal (cette ville)*

I Love Montreal

I fell madly in love with it the day I moved here—a hot August day in 1995. Having grown up in a much smaller city, I suddenly had the feeling I'd been born in the wrong place. I felt good in Montreal. There was so much to do, to see, to discover, to eat. So I decided to make it my home forever. Since then, I have been exploring Montreal like a tourist in my own town, discovering neighborhoods, new places and new things to do.

I Love Montreal—a Lot

I love its **outdoor staircases**: straight, curved or spiral; its **green alleys** pulsing with life, and the perfect place to stroll for a glimpse of the "real" Montreal. I love the city's impressive **murals**—often colorful, sometimes abstract, but always alive and vibrant, which turn the city into a sort of open-air museum. I love its **four seasons**, each so distinct: the contrast between the intense summer heat waves and the deep cold of winter, the first warm days of spring and the magical light of an autumn afternoon. I love its **cultural diversity**: In the midst of a French-speaking majority, residents hailing from about 120 countries and speaking nearly 200 different languages live side by side harmoniously

and with mutual respect. I love its many **restaurants**—the city boasts more per capita than New York or San Francisco! In the tourist areas, there are 66.3 restaurants per square kilometer. With more than 5,700 eating establishments, it's not surprising that Montreal has become one of the most popular culinary destinations in the world.

I Love Montreal—with a Passion

That's why it is such a great honor for me to share what I have learned from 20 years of exploring the city, to guide you through all its diverse neighborhoods, and to help you to discover 300 reasons to love Montreal: the best cafés, the most authentic restaurants, the most beautiful terraces, not-to-be-missed activities, the most wonderful streets, and some well-kept secrets. These reasons are very personal, and certainly did not make up an exhaustive list. There are thousands of reasons to love Montreal, a heterogeneous city, constantly in motion, full of creative energy and never dull. There are so many artists to discover, new cafés popping up, new ways to see the city that you'd never noticed before, and newly green alleyways.
Myriad Reasons to Love Montreal, and to Love it like Crazy!

MY TOP PICKS

MY FAVORITE RESTAURANTS
1 Kazu: 1862 Rue Sainte-Catherine Ouest [REASON #86]
2 Le Petit Alep: 191 Rue Jean-Talon Est [REASON #268]
3 Bottega: 65 Rue Saint-Zotique Est [REASON #256]
4 Olive & Gourmando: 351 Rue Saint-Paul Ouest [REASON #24]
5 Thaïlande: 88 Rue Bernard Ouest [REASON #146]

THE NICEST STREETS
1 Rue Demers, between Avenue Henri-Julien and Avenue de l'Hôtel-de-Ville [REASON #158]
2 Rue de Castelnau Est, between Avenue de Gaspé and Rue Drolet [REASON #269]
3 Rue Sainte-Hélène [REASON #19]
4 Avenue Laval, between Avenue Duluth Est and Rue Sherbrooke Est [REASON #174]
5 Avenue McGill College [REASON #73]

THE BEST POUTINES
1 La Banquise: 994 Rue Rachel Est [REASON #178]
2 Brutus: 1290 Rue Beaubien Est [REASON #236]
3 Ma Poule Mouillée: 969 Rue Rachel Est [REASON #178]
4 Broue Pub Brouhaha: 5860 Avenue De Lorimier [REASON #232]
5 Chez Claudette: 351 Avenue Laurier Est [REASON #178]
   Honorable mention: Frite Alors! (there are many locations)

THE MOST DISTINGUISHED MICROBREWERIES
1 Dieu du Ciel!: 29 Avenue Laurier Ouest [REASON #156]
2 Isle de Garde: 1039 Rue Beaubien Est [REASON #238]
3 Brasserie Harricana: 95 Rue Jean-Talon Ouest
4 Ma Brasserie: 2300 Rue Holt
5 L'Amère à Boire: 2049 Rue Saint-Denis [REASON #47]

THE BEST CHEAP-EATS RESTAURANTS

1 Bombay Mahal: 1001 Rue Jean-Talon Ouest [REASON #266]
2 Romados: 115 Rue Rachel Est [REASON #169]
3 Chez Bong: 1021 Boulevard Saint-Laurent [REASON #32]
4 La Maison de Mademoiselle Dumpling: 6381 Rue Saint-Hubert [REASON #245]
5 Pho Bac: 1016 Boulevard Saint-Laurent [REASON #36]

THE MOST ENCHANTING PARKS

1 Mount Royal Park, the Plateau [REASON #165]
2 Parc des Rapides, LaSalle [REASON #115]
3 Parc Jean-Drapeau, Sainte-Marie [REASON #10]
4 Parc La Fontaine, the Plateau [REASON #181]
5 Parc Sir-Wilfrid-Laurier, the Plateau [REASON #181]
6 Parc Jarry, Villeray
7 Westmount Park, Westmount [REASON #117]
8 Parc René-Lévesque, Lachine [REASON #299]
9 Parc-Nature de l'île-de-la-Visitation, Ahuntsic [REASON #285]
10 Parc Pratt, Outremont

THE MEALS I DREAM ABOUT

1 Tuna and salmon tartare bowl at Kazu: 1862 Rue Sainte-Catherine Ouest [REASON #86]
2 The La Vong fish at Y Lan: 6425 Rue Saint-Denis [REASON #251]
3 Steak-capicollo sandwich at Café Milano: 5188 Rue Jarry Est [REASON #282]
4 Lamb at Le Petit Alep: 191 Rue Jean-Talon Est [REASON #268]
5 Chicken at Romados: 115 Rue Rachel Est [REASON #169]
6 Margherita pizza at Bottega: 65 Rue Saint-Zotique Est [REASON #256]
7 Cajun chicken, mango and guacamole sandwich at Olive & Gourmando: 351 Rue Saint-Paul Ouest [REASON #24]
8 The #25 (vermicelli and sautéed lemongrass beef) at Pho Bac: 1016 Boulevard Saint-Laurent [REASON #36]
9 Kaeng Choochee curry at Thaïlande: 88 Rue Bernard Ouest [REASON #146]
10 Gorgon (gorgonzola and hazelnuts) pasta sauce at Diabolissimo: 1256 Avenue du Mont-Royal Est [REASON #182]

THE BEST CAFÉS (FOR THE COFFEE)

1 Pourquoi Pas Espresso Bar: 1447 Rue Amherst [REASON #39]
2 Café Myriade: 1432 Rue Mackay [REASON #88]
3 Tunnel Espresso Bar: 1253 Avenue McGill College [REASON #88]
4 Café Pista: 500 Rue Beaubien Est [REASON #249]
5 Café LaRue & Fils: 244 Rue de Castelnau Est [REASON #269]

THE MOST CHARMING CAFÉS FOR LOUNGING

1 Crew Collectif & Café: 360 Rue Saint-Jacques [REASON #23]
2 Le Falco: 5605 Avenue de Gaspé [REASON #151]
3 Tommy: 200 Rue Notre-Dame Ouest [REASON #22]
4 Café Sfouf: 1250 Rue Ontario Est [REASON #43]
5 Le Butterblume: 5836 Boulevard Saint-Laurent [REASON #149]

MURALS WORTH MENTIONING

1 *L'Esprit d'Été:* Boulevard Rosemont, between Avenue Christophe-Colomb
and Rue de La Roche [REASON #243]
2 *Germaine* (tribute to Michel Tremblay): Rue Saint-Dominique, between
Rue Villeneuve Est and Avenue du Mont-Royal Est [REASON #173]
3 *L'Air du Temps:* Rue Sanguinet, at the corner of Rue Émery [REASON #49]
4 *Más - Penser à Prendre le Temps:* Avenue Papineau, at the corner of Rue de
Fleurimont [REASON #243]
5 *Comme un Jeu d'Enfants:* Avenue Papineau, at the corner of Rue Jarry Est
[REASON #284]

THE QUINTESSENTIAL BRUNCH

1 Pâtisserie Rhubarbe: 5091 Rue De Lanaudière [REASON #187]
2 La Récolte: 764 Rue Bélanger [REASON #241]
3 Chez Régine: 1840 Rue Beaubien Est [REASON #233]
4 Le Sain Bol: 5095 Rue Fabre [REASON #190]
5 LEMÉAC: 1045 Avenue Laurier Ouest

PERSONAL INSTAGRAM ACCOUNTS TO FOLLOW FOR DISCOVERING MONTREAL

@archimontreal
@montrealismes
@amelipstick
@yesmini_
@dani.e.l

NOT-TO-BE-MISSED EVENTS

Throughout the year, Montreal is home to about 100 festivals and events: musical, culinary and cultural. Here is a list of my favorites.

Les Rendez-vous du cinéma québécois (end of February): Ten days that showcase the richness of Quebec cinema, where industry professionals and film fans meet [rvcq.quebeccinema.ca].

MONTRÉAL EN LUMIÈRE (last week of February, first in March): In the middle of winter 1.3 million people celebrate Montreal at this festival that combines culture, cuisine and family activities [montrealenlumiere.com].

Les Premiers Vendredis (Fridays): Street food trucks gather at Olympic Stadium on the first Friday of the month, from May to October [cuisinederue.org].

C2MTL (end of May): Three days of meetings that merge creativity with the world of business and encourage collaboration and the development of new business solutions. Passes are very expensive, but the conferences, hosted by world-class leaders, are always very inspiring [c2montreal.com].

Tour de l'Île and Tour la Nuit (first weekend of June): Thousands of cyclists tour the city streets on a variety of road courses (23K for Tour la Nuit; 30, 50 or 100K for Tour de l'Île) [velo.qc.ca].

Mural Festival (mid-June): In the heart of Boulevard Saint-Laurent, the Mural Festival celebrates urban art by hosting internationally renowned artists, whose creations are made live on the spot [muralfestival.com].

Montreal International Jazz Festival (first week of July): The biggest jazz festival on the planet, with two million festival-goers [montrealjazzfest.com].

Montréal Complètement Cirque (early July): Eleven days of colorful performances in the streets, in parks and in theaters [montrealcompletementcirque.com].

Montreal Fireworks Festival (L'International des Feux Loto-Québec) (July Saturdays and some Wednesdays): This one's my favorite. A fireworks competition between countries from all over the world. The view from the Jacques Cartier Bridge is spectacular—and it's free [laronde.com].

Fantasia (end of July): A mandatory destination for fans of genre films that are rarely shown in North America [fantasiafestival.com].

Osheaga (last weekend in July or first in August): Emerging bands rub shoulders with the biggest artists from around the world [osheaga.com/en].

Heavy Montréal (last weekend in July or first in August): The premier destination for fans of rock and heavy metal music [heavymontreal.com].

POP Montreal (second or third week of September): Five days and 450 bands. This is the most popular event for fans of independent music and new talent [popmontreal.com].

MTL à TABLE (November): For 10 days, 150 restaurants offer a three-course menu for $21, $31 or $41. A great way to discover new restaurants [tourism-montreal.org/mtlatable].

Accommodations

Montreal is one of the safest cities in the world: No neighborhood is off limits. Among the city's many great hotels, allow me to suggest a few of the more noteworthy.

Hotel Renaissance: In the heart of downtown, this luxurious hotel highlights urban art and local talent. The frescoes in each room have been painted by hand, and the illustrations in the toilets, corridors, lobby, restaurant and conference rooms were all created by local artists. The rooftop terrace is worth a visit [renmontreal.com].

Hotel Le Place d'Armes: The first boutique hotel in Old Montreal, it is located in the prestigious Place d'Armes, where Old Montreal meets the Quartier International. With its magnificent neoclassical facade, with rounded corners, it is one of the most beautiful buildings in Old Montreal (see Reason #20) [hotelplacedarmes.com].

Ritz-Carlton: This legendary hotel is the only one in Quebec to receive a Five Diamond rating by the CAA and the AAA (Canadian and American Automobile associations). The house restaurant, Maison Boulud, is renowned, and there is also an elegant Dom Pérignon Champagne Bar. Luxury, opulence and historical charm, all under one roof (see Reason #81) [ritzcarlton.com/en/hotels/canada/montreal].

Hotel Le St-James: Another splendid facade. Established in the Merchants' Bank building (see Reason #21), dating back to 1870, Hotel Le St-James is the best place to spot international celebrities passing through the city [hotellestjames.com].

Hotel ALT: With its fixed year-round rate, regardless of the room, the ALT is definitely the best value for money of the options listed here. The first hotel to be located in the Griffintown area (see Reason #89), it offers no-frills accommodations with modern design and has a fantastic view of downtown Montreal [althotels.com].

Montreal's layout is on a grid, making it very easy to navigate. The numbering of street buildings on the south-north axis ranges from zero (Rue de la Commune) to 10800 (Boulevard Gouin). Addresses in the 5000 range are located near Avenue Laurier. For the east-west axis, Boulevard Saint-Laurent—also known as The Main—represents zero, and the numbering starts from one on either side. This means it's very important to check whether an address is "Est" (East) or "Ouest" (West), which indicates "east of Boulevard Saint-Laurent" or "west of Boulevard Saint-Laurent."

Cité-du-Havre, the Old Port, Parc Jean-Drapeau

The south end of the city, bordered by the St. Lawrence River (*Fleuve Saint-Laurent*), offers the most memorable panoramic views of Montreal. An important testament to the economic and social development of the country, today this area is also a popular destination for tourists, and a picturesque leisure area for residents. It is enjoyed year-round as a place to go for a stroll and to relax or to do a variety of activities, including extreme sports, in a charming location with easy access to the river.

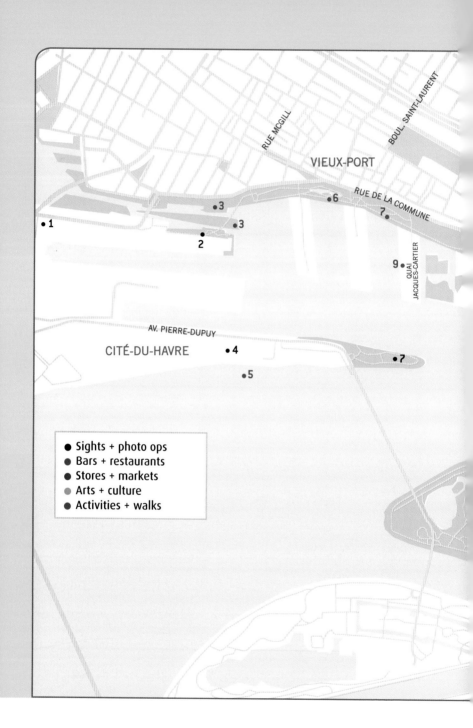

VIEUX-PORT

RUE MCGILL

BOUL. SAINT-LAURENT

RUE DE LA COMMUNE

QUAI JACQUES-CARTIER

●1

●3

●3

●2

●6

7●

9●

AV. PIERRE-DUPUY

CITÉ-DU-HAVRE

●4

●5

●7

- Sights + photo ops
- Bars + restaurants
- Stores + markets
- Arts + culture
- Activities + walks

RUE SAINT-DENIS

AUTOROUTE VILLE-MARIE

RUE SAINTE-CATHERINE E.

BOUL. RENÉ-LÉVESQUE E.

AV. PAPINEAU

QUAI
L'HORLOGE • 8

FLEUVE SAINT-LAURENT

• 13

CH. DU TOUR-DE-L'ISLE

11
•

PARC JEAN-DRAPEAU
• 12

• 10

• 10

ÎLE SAINTE-HÉLÈNE

CH. MACDONALD

• 10

ÎLE NOTRE-DAME

The Iconic Sign

1 The red neon **Farine Five Roses** sign has been standing as a beacon since 1948. It almost came down when the Five Roses brand was sold to a U.S. company—there seemed to be no reason to keep it there, and the neon lights were shut off in 2006. But numerous groups sprang to its defense. In 2013, it was announced that the iconic sign would stay. The sign has truly become a part of Montreal's urban landscape, and plays an essential role in its pop culture. Each letter in the sign stands about 15 feet (five meters) tall, and the lights blink on and off at 22-second intervals. In the 1960s the sign contained four words: *Farine Five Roses Flour*. When Bill 101 (the law that made French the official language of Quebec) came into effect in 1977, the word "Flour" was removed [950 Rue Mill].

A Walk Through the Past

2 It may be a little hard to get to, but a walk at **Pointe-du-Moulin** is worth your time. The pier is mostly made of material dug up during the construction of the Lachine Canal. To get there, take the footbridge at the south end of Rue McGill. Once you're at the pier, you'll get a close-up view of the gigantic **Silo No. 5**, a cluster of grain elevators that's about 1,300 feet (400 meters) long. It's a reminder that Montreal was once the hub of the grain trade in North America. The future of the abandoned building complex remains a question mark, but it's currently protected as a heritage site. Finish your walk with a look at one of Montreal's best-kept secret artworks: **La Grande Fonte** (A), an impressive 50-foot (15-meter) sculpture by Montreal artist Robert Roussil.

River Relaxation

3 **Bota Bota** (A) is a floating spa in an old ferry docked in the Old Port (*Vieux-Port*) [Old Port, Rue de la Commune Ouest]. The location is amazing; there's a spectacular view of Old Montreal from the whirlpool on the top deck. It's also the nicest spot in the city for manicures and pedicures. Add to that its slick modern look—it has won a number of design and architecture awards—and Bota Bota is a shoe-in for top relaxation destination in the city. Try it in the depths of winter or on a hot summer day; it's a totally different experience. If you can, visit on a weekday, as it can be (overly) busy on weekends. For a post-spa snack, try **Muvbox** [Place du Génie, Old Port] for clam chowder, or a lobster roll from the Gulf islands—Îles de la Madeleine. When the restaurant in a container opens its doors each year, it's a sign that spring has arrived and vacation time is just around the corner. Open from May to October.

Roadwork is constant in Montreal, to the point where the orange traffic cone has become a symbol of identity.

Creative Cubes

4 Built for Expo 67, **Habitat 67** was the first modern building to be granted historic status (2009) by the provincial government. Extravagant, slightly controversial and outrageously cutting edge for its time, Habitat 67 was celebrated around the world and gained international recognition for its creator, architect Moshe Safdie. Astonishingly, Safdie was only 24 years old when he designed the building; it was his master's thesis for an architecture program, and the first building he ever designed. Quite a fairy-tale story [2600 Avenue Pierre-Dupuy].

3A

Surfing in the City

5 More and more river surfers are lining up to ride the **Habitat 67 standing wave** on the St. Lawrence River. Easily accessible and surprisingly powerful, the perpetual wave is caused by fast-moving water flowing over the river's rocky bottom. In May, it can get as high as six feet (two meters). There's another option in LaSalle, to the west. Known in French as the **Vague à Guy** (Guy's wave), it's a better choice for beginner surfers, because the water there is calmer. The two sites are surfed an estimated 20,000 times a year [Parc de la Cité-du-Havre, behind Habitat 67].

DECALADE
.com

An Extreme Experience at the Old Port

6 If you're a thrill seeker, pluck up your courage for the **Decalade** challenge: Rappel down the outer walls of the Conveyor Quay Tower. As you descend, you face the ground—it makes you feel like you're the hero of *Mission Impossible*. If you're afraid of heights, this experience might not be for you. The starting point, the top of the abandoned tower, is 160 feet (50 meters) above the ground. As you get ready, contemplating the 12-story drop below with your feet dangling over the edge, a rush of adrenalin hits you like a tidal wave. Excitement guaranteed [Quai des Convoyeurs, Old Port].

Fishing with Jean

7 Jean Desjardins, guide and owner of **Pêche Vieux-Montréal**, has been navigating the St. Lawrence for 35 years. He's still amazed by the great fishing the river has to offer. "There are so many fish that I have to give it a try every time I go out—sometimes a few times an hour!" He can bring up to four clients on his boat at one time, helping them try their luck with the sturgeon, bass, pike and walleye that lurk right in city's midst. Catches are generally released back into the water (after a souvenir photo, of course), but if you want to eat them you can bring them home (recent studies show that fish in the St. Lawrence are healthy and perfectly edible). Half-day or full-day trips, starting from the Old Port, take place in winter and summer alike. In winter, a hovercraft will take you fishing on ice or open water. You'll have to book ahead: [pechevm.com].

Experienced and beginner anglers will both find that the tip of **Parc de la Cité-du-Havre** is a peaceful spot to cast a line. The smallest of Montreal's major parks, it also offers a great view of Old Montreal and the Jacques Cartier Bridge—it's really worth seeing. Parking is free [3400 Avenue Pierre-Dupuy].

Montreal Beach

8 Since 2012, Montreal has had its own urban beach: **Clock Tower Beach**, at the end of Quai de l'Horloge. On hot summer days, city-dwellers can relax, drink in hand, on its 22,000 square feet (2,000 square meters) of white sand. Access to the beach costs $2. Purists argue that it's not a real beach, and it's true that swimming is prohibited due to the strong currents (if it's swimming you want, see Reason #12). But it's still worth the trip. As you unwind at the easternmost point of the Old Port, you get a view of Montreal in all its splendor: the river, downtown, the Jacques Cartier Bridge and Île Sainte-Hélène in the background. Don't forget to take a look at the clock tower; built in England, it has pretty much the same mechanism as London's Big Ben does.

Cross the Water to Parc Jean-Drapeau

9 There are a number of ways to get to Parc Jean-Drapeau: via the Jacques Cartier Bridge, by bus or by Metro. But if it's between May and October and you're on foot or bike, take the **river shuttle** from the Old Port—it's so much more pleasant. For a dollar more than the price of a Metro ride, you can relax in the sun on the upper deck and enjoy the 10-minute trip with a great view of the city [Navettes Maritimes du Saint-Laurent, Quai Jacques-Cartier]

8

The Park in the Heart of the River

10 **Parc Jean-Drapeau** is a remnant from two events that changed Montreal permanently: Expo 67 (the World Exhibition in 1967) and the 1976 Summer Olympics. It's one of my favorite spots in or around the city—I feel like I'm on vacation as soon as I get there. Covering one square mile, the park is made up of two islands, **Sainte-Hélène** and **Notre-Dame**. The latter was built from scratch; the process took just nine months, using earth that was removed during the digging of the Metro tunnels.

Île Sainte-Hélène is where you'll find **La Ronde** amusement park, and the hyper-popular **Osheaga** and **Heavy Montréal** music festivals. Other events are held there as well, like **Fête des Neiges**

(Snow Festival), **Week-ends du Monde** and **Piknic Électronik** (see Reason #11).

Île Notre-Dame should be known as "Sports-Lovers' Paradise." The gigantic **Olympic Basin**, over a mile (2.3 kilometers) long, is the biggest artificial rowing basin in North America. Local associations use it for training in rowing, kayaking, paddle-surfing and dragon boating. When the F1 isn't in town, the **Circuit Gilles-Villeneuve** becomes a spectacular racetrack for cycling and in-line skating. Its surface is beautifully smooth, and it offers a panoramic view of the Old Port—and cars are completely absent. But watch out: You'll move really quickly. After an activity-filled day, nothing beats a swim at **Jean-Doré Beach**, with clean water and a 2,000-foot (600-meter) stretch of sand.

A Different Kind of Picnic

11 **Piknic Électronik** takes place every Sunday from May to September at Parc Jean-Drapeau, in front of the impressive stainless steel sculpture by Alexander Calder, *L'Homme*. When the weather's good, join the 100,000 people who go there every summer to move their bodies to great dance, techno, electro and house music. It's a unique outdoor event and a great place to bring friends and family. The concept was created in Montreal in 2003, and was exported in 2012: It now takes place in Barcelona, Melbourne, Sydney, Dubai, Lisbon, Paris, Cannes and Santiago. The party doesn't happen if it's raining [right near Jean-Drapeau Metro station].

Swimming at the Foot of the Biosphere

12 Île Sainte-Hélène is home to one of the nicest outdoor aquatic complexes in Canada. Just a few steps from the Metro, the **Parc Jean-Drapeau Aquatic Complex**, built for the 2005 World Aquatics Championships, has three pools. The gigantic 164-foot (50-meter) recreational pool has a gradual incline, and its bottom is covered in a protective mat, so it's perfect for young children. Several lanes are reserved for laps. Located right at the foot of the **Biosphere**, it's hard to find a better spot for a great workout [130 Chemin du Tour de l'Isle].

11

12 13

The Jacques Cartier Bridge Time Capsule

13 Whenever I leave the city for a few days and return via the **Jacques Cartier Bridge**, I remember how much I love Montreal. It's quite a view: the Biosphere, the **Lévis Tower**, the **Quai de l'Horloge** and the downtown skyscrapers on one side; La Ronde, the Olympic Stadium and different bell towers on the other. And right in the middle of this panorama stands the magnificent Mount Royal (see Reason #165) with the famous cross at its summit.

In 2017 the Jacques Cartier Bridge will be illuminated by a kaleidoscopic light show created by Moment Factory, an internationally-known Montreal-based company. It's commonly thought that the finials (ornaments) that top the four towers at the cantilever section of the bridge are replicas of the Eiffel Tower. Sadly, it's just a myth. These "miniature towers" are merely ornaments, an aesthetic touch that was part of the original plans. They're bigger than you might think from looking at a photo: each is 13 feet (four meters) tall and weighs around six tons.

A time capsule was placed in the bridge's cornerstone, which was buried in one of the pillars when construction of the bridge began in 1926. The container holds 59 items, including newspapers from August 7, 1926, coins from 1925, aerial photos of the harbor and a geographical map of the city. Unfortunately, no one knows exactly where the stone was placed.

Old Montreal, Quartier International

This area, with buildings and streets imbued with centuries of history, bears witness to the most important milestones in the development not only of the city, but of the whole country. Old Montreal (*Vieux-Montréal*) is rich in collective memories and architectural marvels; to explore it thoroughly requires visiting it over and over again, not just once. The most photogenic area in the city, Old Montreal never ceases to delight with its charm from days gone by, and to surprise with its continual renewal.

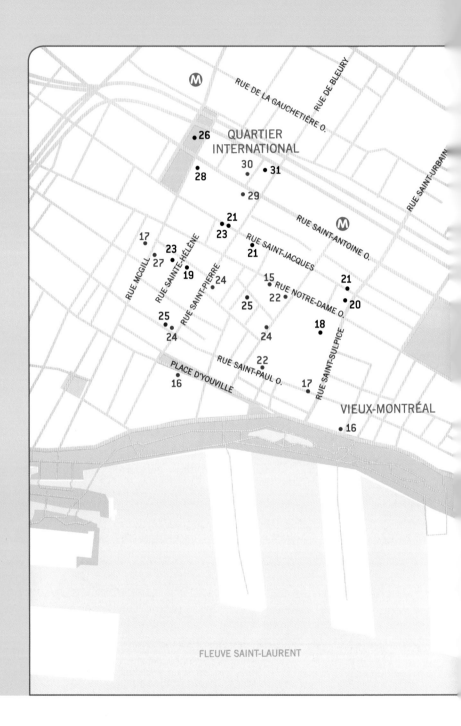

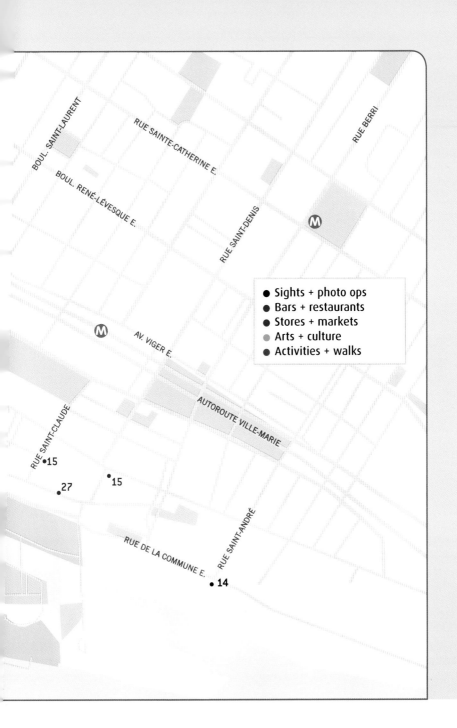

RUE SAINT-LAURENT

RUE SAINTE-CATHERINE E.

RUE BERRI

BOUL. SAINT-LAURENT

BOUL. RENÉ-LÉVESQUE E.

RUE SAINT-DENIS

Ⓜ

- Sights + photo ops
- Bars + restaurants
- Stores + markets
- Arts + culture
- Activities + walks

Ⓜ AV. VIGER E.

AUTOROUTE VILLE-MARIE

RUE SAINT-CLAUDE
•15
•27 •15

RUE DE LA COMMUNE E.

RUE SAINT-ANDRÉ

• 14

Explore the Moving Road

14 The poetic name of **Belvédère du Chemin-Qui-Marche** comes from a First Nations expression associated with the St. Lawrence River: *Chemin-Qui-Marche* meaning "moving road." Located at the east end of Old Montreal, the 550-foot (165-meter) long linear park is a great place to relax, daydream and stroll around. Starting from Rue Saint-André, walk the wooden terrace that overlooks the train tracks, and admire the panorama. You can learn about Montreal's past from the benches; each one is engraved with details of a historic event, from 1535 to today [at the corner of Rue de la Commune Est and Rue Saint-André].

A Club That's not a Club

15 Don't let the name fool you; **Le Club Chasse et Pêche** (A) [423 Rue Saint-Claude] isn't a private hunting and fishing club. It's actually one of the best restaurants in the city. The restaurant's stone walls are steeped in history. It has elegant decor, attentive service, flawless fine cuisine—everything you need for a perfect night. The classic dish at Chasse et Pêche is its take on surf and turf: lobster tail confit with white butter and a beautiful piece of Kobe beef. The scallops with lemon confit are a truly memorable starter. Everything is succulent, from start to finish.

If you want to further explore the gourmet restaurants of Old Montreal, you won't be disappointed by the inventive, accessible and perfectly balanced cuisine at **400 Coups** [400 Rue Notre-Dame Est], which highlights local and seasonal ingredients. The delicate dishes and the magnificent terrace at **Accord** [212 Rue Notre-Dame Ouest] also deserve mention. Wine lovers will feel right at home with its impressive selection of privately imported organic and natural wines. You're guaranteed to come up with a perfect food-wine pairing—a match made in heaven.

16A 17A

A Carnivore's Paradise

16

You don't have to drive 2,000 miles (3,000 kilometers) to find authentic barbecue; Montreal has some that's worthy of the best BBQ joints in Texas or Louisiana. A stop at **Lattuca Barbecue** (A) [15 Rue de la Commune Ouest] is sure to satisfy a meat lover completely. The restaurant is like its chef, John Lattuca: simple, friendly and unpretentious. For example, rolls of brown kraft paper serve as napkins. I recommend ordering the Trinity platter so you can try the ribs, brisket and pulled pork. The meat is incredibly juicy and tender. This style of cooking can take up to 14 hours, so Lattuca only cooks a predetermined amount each day—the restaurant closes when they run out. It's a good idea to reserve a table.

If you prefer a more high-end restaurant, **Gibbys** [298 Place D'Youville] is considered one of the best steakhouses in the city. Lodged in a 200-year-old building called Écuries D'Youville ("écuries" means "stables"), this reputable restaurant has stone walls and exposed beams. The portions are generous, the meat perfectly grilled and the house salad (of all things) is divine. Reservations are recommended here as well.

The Mozzarella Bar

17

Mangiafoco (A) [105 Rue Saint-Paul Ouest] describes itself as a mozzarella bar. That won me over right away. What could possibly be more appealing to my epicurean side? The menu has Neapolitan pizza, antipasti and salads. And of course, there's a range of fresh mozzarellas (burrata, buffalo, smoked and truffle) served on platters with a choice of sides: marinated artichokes, grilled asparagus, pancetta, house-made gravlax, prosciutto, porchetta and so on. A bit farther west is another great Italian restaurant: **Nolana** (B) [444 Rue McGill]. Long, narrow and lined with windows, it offers fresh pasta and wood-oven-cooked pizzas. The *polpetta di carne* (meatballs, tomato sauce and Parmesan) is fantastic, as is the fresh, crunchy green bean salad. For pizza, the margherita is an excellent classic, and the mushroom and ricotta is sublime.

17B

Experience the Power of the Organ

18 Renowned for its opulent interior, **Notre-Dame Basilica** (A) is one of the most beautiful examples of Gothic Revival architecture in North America. Visit on Wednesday, Thursday or Friday during the summer for one of the **Prenez Place à l'Orgue** concerts; it will add a whole new dimension to your visit. Hosted by Pierre Grandmaison, organist at the basilica since 1973, the workshops let you delve into the heart of this enormous instrument and experience its awesome power. It has 7,000 pipes that range from a fraction of an inch to over 30 feet (9 meters) high. Sit just a few feet away: you'll get goose bumps when the low notes sound.
You can also enjoy the incredible acoustics from the balcony, and of course there's the majestic beauty of the space [110 Rue Notre-Dame Ouest].

A Street from Long Ago

19 The diminutive **Rue Sainte-Hélène** (between Rue Notre-Dame Ouest and Rue le Moyne) has only two blocks of houses, but it will transport you to another time. Twenty-two gas lanterns provide soft, romantic light at night—it's a delightful 19th-century scene. The surrounding buildings were built between 1858 and 1871. They're ornately decorated, and the architectural consistency between them is really impressive. It's no surprise that this little street—named in honor of Hélène Boullé—the wife of French explorer Samuel de Champlain—has become a top shooting location for period films.

20 B

Right beside it is the **Aldred Building** (A) [501 Place d'Armes]. Built in 1931, it marks the major shift in architectural styles toward modern and art deco. Although it's nowhere near as big, the Aldred was inspired by New York's skyscrapers from the same period, like the Empire State Building and the Chrysler Building. Its unique design makes it a distinctive figure on Montreal's landscape. The building is open to the public, and has fun art-deco touches, like the bronze panels with swallows perched on power lines in the hallways.

The **Life Association of Scotland Building** (B) [701 Place d'Armes], at the corner of Rue Saint-Jacques, is the height of elegance. Built in 1870, the building has rich ornamentation and rounded corners. The fourth floor, originally the top floor, is lower in height than the other floors. Three stories were added to the building 50 years after it was built. **Le Place d'Armes Hôtel & Suites** has occupied the building since the start of the 2000s. Visit the rooftop terrace for a memorable aperitif.

A Trio at Place d'Armes

20 Three of the most prestigious buildings in the city are found at Place d'Armes. With its distinctive architecture, my favorite is the **New York Life Insurance Building** [511 Place d'Armes]. Built in 1889 and made with Scottish red sandstone, the eight-story tower was Canada's first skyscraper. After New York Life sold the building to the Quebec Bank in 1909, the entrance was rebuilt—hence the inscription "The Quebec Bank Established 1818" over the main door. Be sure to take a look at the ornamentation on the facade and the carved arabesques in the entrance archway.

20 A

Banks from Another Era

21

In the second part of the 19th century, Rue Saint-Jacques was home to the headquarters of the largest financial institutions in Canada—it was basically the country's version of Wall Street. While most of the major banks eventually moved out of Old Montreal, the area retains its magnificent architectural heritage.

Across from Place d'Armes is the **Bank of Montreal** building (A) [119 Rue Saint-Jacques], built in 1847. With its six huge columns, a triangular pediment in front and a dome at the top, it looks like an ancient Greco-Roman temple—you can't miss it. The building is open to the public. When you enter, you're transported to the banks of the olden days: marble countertops, an enormous main hall and ceilings decorated with gold leaf. The Bank of Montreal still occupies the building; there's also a small museum that explores the 19th-century banking world (admission is free).

The **Canadian Bank of Commerce** building (B) [265 Rue Saint-Jacques] has monumental architecture with a beaux-arts influence and an imposing granite colonnade—it charms visitors instantly. It was built in 1909, and the bank sold the historic jewel in 2012. It now houses

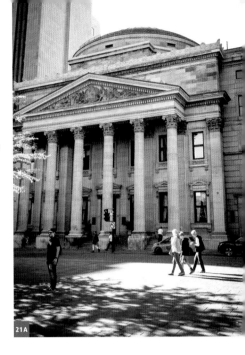

21A

Théâtre St-James, a private venue for receptions and concerts.

When the former **Merchants' Bank** building (C) [355 Rue Saint-Jacques] was built, from 1870 to 1873, it had only four floors. Thirty years later, the bank decided to remove the roof and add four stories to the original building. A last level was built at the end of the 1920s. The majestic facade bears witness to the building's transformations over the years. Today, the building is home to the popular **Hotel Le St-James**.

21B 21C

Little Cafés that are Worth a Visit

22 Lodged in an 1874 building, **Tommy** (A) [200 Rue Notre-Dame Ouest] has a lovely interior design: rich Victorian woodwork and retro furniture, white walls and lush green hanging plants. The three levels inside make the perfect place to linger for hours, a fresh juice or a latte in one hand and a book in the other. If you like third-wave coffee and latte art, you'll love the beverages for takeout at **Le Petit Dep** (B) [179 Rue Saint-Paul Ouest]. This original business with an unmistakable mint-green facade is also a micro-depanneur ("depanneur" is the Quebecois word for convenience store). Stock up on penny candy, prepared dishes, gourmet products and local beers.

A Breathtaking Latte

23

In the first half of the 20th century, a race was on to build the tallest building in the British Empire. The Royal Bank Tower, completed in the spring of 1928, held this prestigious title for a few months, until Toronto's Royal York Hotel beat it by three feet the following year. Today the Royal Bank Tower is an office building for local businesses. The **Crew Collectif & Café** on the ground floor will take your breath away. Walk through the monumental hall to the staircase that leads to the former bank. The room has dizzyingly high vaulted ceilings decorated with gold. A collective of self-employed workers took over the superb space so they could use it and its meeting rooms in exchange for a monthly membership or hourly rental fee. At the center of this truly inspiring work area is a café to satisfy your caffeine and snack needs. Stop in for a look; it's worth seeing [360 Rue Saint-Jacques].

23 A

23 B

A Healthy Lunch That's Quick and Delicious

24 I fell in love with **Olive & Gourmando** (A) [351 Rue Saint-Paul Ouest] the moment I set foot in the restaurant. Everything, from the bread to the ketchup to the desserts to the ricotta, is homemade. Try the Cajun chicken sandwich with guacamole, tomato and mango, and the vegan and gluten-free #24 salad, an Asian-inspired dish with soba noodles, pickled daikon, peanuts and mint. My mouth waters just thinking about it. A few steps away is another café that opened more than 25 years ago, but that strangely remains somewhat of a secret: **Titanic** [445 Rue Saint-Pierre]. The menu offers over 20 sandwiches that are packed with toppings. And the macaroni and cheese, grilled vegetable antipasti and carrot cake are also definitely worth the trip. With a decor that conjures up a California vacation, **Venice MTL** [440 Rue Saint-François-Xavier] has been charming customers since the day it opened. The food is top-notch: salads, poke bowls, tacos and toast, all original and bursting with flavor. The menu also has gluten- and lactose-free, vegan and vegetarian options, and colorful healthy ingredients: kale, avocado, edamame, coriander, lime and ginger. Open Monday to Saturday from 11 a.m. to 11 p.m.

Chic Boutiques

25 Up for some shopping? **Espace Pepin** [350 and 378 Rue Saint-Paul Ouest] is a unique shop: part fashion and lifestyle boutique and part workshop for the artist and co-owner Lysanne Pepin. It offers a vast collection of men's and women's designer clothes, shoes, accessories, jewelry and select decorative objects. A second boutique, offering "everything for the home," recently opened its doors right nearby. It also has a restaurant with a vegetarian lunch menu. It's like being at home—but a thousand times prettier. If I could, I'd buy all my clothes from **Boutique Room Service Loft** (A) [465 Rue Saint-Jean]. It has men's and women's collections, and each piece is carefully selected for its quality, its timeless appeal and its material: silk, wool, linen, cotton and cashmere. There's no pretention—the focus is on simplicity and good taste. These are clothes you'll wear for years to come. To finish off your day, check out the prominent Quebec designers who have set up shop in Old Montreal: **Denis Gagnon** [170 Rue Saint-Paul Ouest], **Philippe Dubuc** [417 Rue Saint-Pierre] and **Rad Hourani** [231 Rue Saint-Paul Ouest].

24A 25A

An Authentic Parisian Metro Stop

26 At Square Victoria, you can see a jewel of the Montreal Metro art collection: an authentic subway entrance from the Paris Metro circa 1900. It's an internationally known symbol of the Metro system in the City of Light, the birthplace of the art-nouveau style. Built by French architect Hector Guimard, it's the only authentic Parisian subway station entrance outside of Paris [Square-Victoria–OACI Metro station, Saint-Antoine exit].

Montreal Happy Hour

27 In summertime, when the work day is through, it's hard to beat the luxurious terrace at **Boris Bistro** (A) [465 Rue McGill] for a "cinq à sept"—Quebec's version of happy hour. The spacious terrace is one of the most beautiful in the city. It's nestled inside an inner courtyard, behind a facade that's been preserved from a building that burned down in a fire years ago. Lovers of sparkling wine should definitely visit **La Champagnerie** [343 Rue Saint-Paul Est]. There are more than a hundred available brands, with about a dozen by the glass. You'll find Prosecco, cava and champagne from all over and for every budget. The more adventurous can even try their hand at sabering a bottle. If you've also got an appetite, the food is great.

In Montreal, we wait in line for the bus, and we get on one at a time by the front door.

A Gift from Berlin

28 The City of Montreal received an unusual gift from the German capital for its 350th anniversary: a **section of the Berlin Wall** (A), which fell in 1989. It's on display at the **World Trade Center Montreal** (Centre de Commerce Mondial). Take some time to examine both sides of the fragment and read the information on the signs. When you stand on the east side, try to imagine the full 96 miles (155 kilometers) of that momentous and tragic wall, sometimes called the Wall of Shame. On the other side, you'll see colorful graffiti made by West Berliners. It's a powerful reminder that liberty triumphs in the end. Also in the World Trade Center, visit the majestic **Amphitrite Fountain** and the 2,150-square-foot (200-square-meter) black granite reflecting pool [747 Rue du Square-Victoria].

The Green Fairy

29 **Sarah B**, the bar at the InterContinental Montreal hotel, has something special to offer: it specializes in absinthe—sometimes called the green fairy. Banned in many countries, this spirit contained methanol, a neurotoxic compound. At various times it has been thought to cause epilepsy, tuberculosis and dementia. Drinking the green fairy involves a ritual with a number of implements: water, a glass, sugar and a perforated spoon. The aromas are complex and vary from one kind to another: anise, fennel, mint, coriander, verbena. Named after French actress Sarah Bernhardt, the bar is plush and the lighting is low. You can book one of the two rooms for your group if you want some privacy. Drink cautiously: Some types of absinthe are almost 90-percent alcohol [360 Rue Saint-Antoine Ouest].

Normand Laprise:
The Pioneer

30

Montreal's status as one of the world's major culinary destinations is due in large part to chef Normand Laprise. He was the forerunner, the pioneer, the mentor, who paved the way and trained many of the city's now-renowned chefs, including Martin Picard of Pied de Cochon, Frédéric Morin of Joe Beef, and Charles-Antoine Crête of Montreal Plaza.

With his restaurant **Toqué!**, which opened in 1993, Laprise was one of the first to adopt a philosophy that focused squarely on the ingredients, and to resolutely opt for Quebec products—from hormone- and antibiotic-free meat, to local vegetables and wild herbs and mushrooms. Now at the helm of the best restaurant in province, Normand gets all of his ingredients from Quebec farmers, breeders and fishermen. He builds solid relationships with them, while working to obtain the best possible ingredients. And he has the utmost respect for the products, from the beginning to end, using the least amount of resources possible. Indeed, in addition to promoting local sourcing, Normand Laprise is also devoted to eliminating food waste.

How would I describe his cooking? Inventive and highly refined, Normand's creations are exceptional at showcasing the high-quality ingredients he works with. A member of Relais et Châteaux, with a four diamond rating from the AAA and CAA, Toqué! is a restaurant for truly special occasions. For the full experience, choose the tasting menu, which changes daily based on available ingredients. If you drop by for lunch, consider a beet and goat cheese salad, followed by chicken breast with a carrot purée and fingerling potatoes. With extremely high-quality service—exceptional these days—and a bold wine list, Toqué!, in my opinion, should be experienced at least once—no, twice—in a lifetime.

A man of great integrity, Normand Laprise has graciously accepted the Ordre National du Québec and the Order of Canada for his contribution to the development of Quebec cuisine.

Among his reasons for loving Montreal are **Claude Cormier's artworks**, which can be found in different parts of the city (including the pink balls [see Reason #38] and Clock Tower Beach [see Reason #8]); the stationery **Nota Bene** for high-quality Japanese and Scandinavian paper products; and the **Place des Festivals** (see Reason #52) on a hot summer afternoon, with the laughter of children—including his girls—who have fun playing in the water. In winter, he's drawn to **Luminothérapie**, a creative light therapy installation that mirrors the personality of Montreal. And, finally, the people! "They are the basis of our culture, with their big and bold ideas. Montreal is a city of entrepreneurs from all walks of life."

31B

31A

A Riopelle Masterpiece

31 Jean-Paul Riopelle, who was born in Montreal in 1923 and died at the age of 78, was one of Canada's most illustrious painters. In 2004, a public square was built in his honor in the heart of the International District. The masterpiece at **Place Jean-Paul-Riopelle** is without question the sculpture-fountain created by the artist, entitled *La Joute* (A). It consists of 29 cast bronze sculptures representing animals and mythic figures, all gathered around the "Tower of Life." In the evening from mid-May to mid-October, you can see quite a spectacle: mist, water and fire combine to form a dramatic ring of fire—make sure you witness it. At the south entrance is **Le Grand Jean-Paul**, a life-sized sculpture of Riopelle at age 45. It was made by Roseline Granet, a friend of the painter. On the east side, you can't miss the **Palais des Congrès de Montréal** (B) [1001 Place Jean-Paul-Riopelle]. The building's facade consists of huge panels of colored glass that create a kaleidoscope effect. Try to visit on a sunny day so you can see the play of light inside.

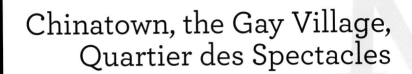

Chinatown, the Gay Village, Quartier des Spectacles

To the east of the city center are three adjoining districts, each with its own distinct personality: Chinatown (*Quartier Chinois*), the Gay Village and the Quartier des Spectacles (entertainment district). These three lively neighborhoods are bustling with activity, and are rich in culture and entertainment. Formerly the red-light district, over the years the area has been transformed into a creative hub, and a major economic driver for the city. Welcome to the cultural heart of Montreal.

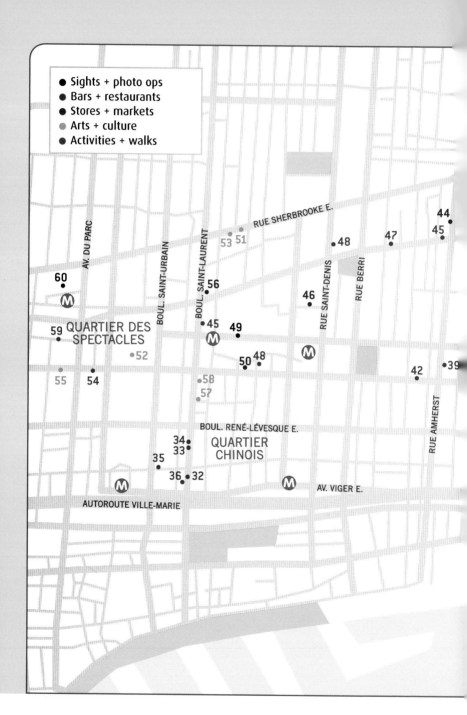

- Sights + photo ops
- Bars + restaurants
- Stores + markets
- Arts + culture
- Activities + walks

RUE SHERBROOKE E.

AV. DU PARC

BOUL. SAINT-URBAIN

BOUL. SAINT-LAURENT

RUE SAINT-DENIS

RUE BERRI

RUE AMHERST

44
45
47
48
53 51
60
56
46
59 QUARTIER DES SPECTACLES
45
49
52
50 48
55 54
42 •39
58
57

BOUL. RENÉ-LÉVESQUE E.

34
33 QUARTIER CHINOIS
35
36 • 32

AV. VIGER E.

AUTOROUTE VILLE-MARIE

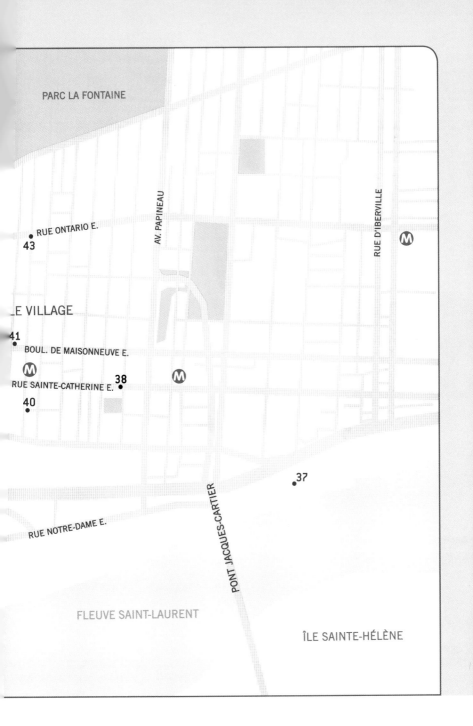

PARC LA FONTAINE

AV. PAPINEAU

RUE D'IBERVILLE

RUE ONTARIO E.

43

Ⓜ

LE VILLAGE

41

BOUL. DE MAISONNEUVE E.

Ⓜ

RUE SAINTE-CATHERINE E. 38

Ⓜ

40

37

RUE NOTRE-DAME E.

PONT JACQUES-CARTIER

FLEUVE SAINT-LAURENT

ÎLE SAINTE-HÉLÈNE

ORANGE
ROUGE
RESTAURANT

午餐
11H30 14H30   17H30 22H30
M M J V   M M J V S

32B

32A

Delectable Tacos

33

It's strange but true: You'll find the best taqueria in town...in Chinatown. **La Capital Tacos** (A) is located just below the north **arch of Chinatown**, the entranceway to the neighborhood at the corner of Boulevard René-Lévesque and Boulevard Saint-Laurent. I recommend the *chicharron de queso*, a crunchy cheese roll cooked on a griddle, and beet salad with lime vinaigrette. I'm a fanatic for tacos *al pastor* (marinated pork, pineapple and cilantro); I always order them at a new Mexican restaurant to gauge its quality. At La Capital Tacos, they're exceptional. Two things make them stand out: The pineapple is lightly grilled, and it's served with avocado sauce. [1096 Boulevard Saint-Laurent]

Pearls of Asia

32

With paneled wood walls, you might think you're in a small-town legion hall. In fact, **Chez Bong** (A) [1021 Boulevard Saint-Laurent] is one of the best Korean restaurants in town. The dishes are popping with flavor, and the bibimbap is served in a hot stone bowl. **Orange Rouge** (B) may be the most high-end restaurant in Chinatown; it's also one of the only restaurants whose owners aren't from Asia. Amidst its black walls and swanky decor, you'll find reinvented Asian cuisine: chrysanthemum salad, fried rice with soft-shell crab and squid and albacore sashimi with kimchi crème fraîche. Such creative dishes! [106 Rue de la Gauchetière Ouest]

33

Weather has a big impact on the everyday lives of Montrealers. Because it is so varied, it's no surprise that the weather website MétéoMédia is the fourth most visited information site in the province. (meteomedia.com/ca/meteo/quebec/montreal)

Eat Passport-Free

34 From the street, the bar **Le Mal Nécessaire** [1106 Boulevard Saint-Laurent] is pretty inconspicuous, except for the green neon pineapple lighting the stairwell leading down to the bar. It's merely a taste of the fantastic tiki atmosphere that waits for you inside. Some of the cocktails are served in a fresh pineapple or coconut—you can almost feel the warm Polynesian breeze. If you're hungry, you can order Chinese dishes from the restaurant upstairs.

Desserts from Another Land

35 The pleasant aroma of bread and sugar greets you when you arrive at **Pâtisserie Harmonie**, tucked right in the heart of Chinatown. When you enter, you'll feel transported. All the desserts are Chinese—I hardly recognized any of them. There are multitudes of red bean and coconut sweet breads, and sesame- and tea-flavored rice paste balls. Go crazy; the treats are about a dollar per pastry. They're lovely to look at, delicious and marvelously soft—like biting into a cloud [85 Rue de la Gauchetière Ouest].

On the Go: Top Picks for Chinatown

36 To warm your bones or lift your spirits, there's no better dish than the "Spécial", a soup with beef at **Nouilles de Lan Zhou** (A) [1006 Boulevard Saint-Laurent]. Savory clear broth, thin slices of beef, and best of all, the incredible texture of their homemade noodles. I always reach the bottom of the bowl too soon—the tragedy of loving a soup too deeply!

The Vietnamese restaurant **Pho Bac** [1016 Boulevard Saint-Laurent] is a bit of a hole in the wall. People love it for the pho soup, but I like to go for the bò bún #25, a bowl of rice vermicelli, lettuce and marinated vegetables topped with lemongrass sautéed beef. It's the best in town. As if that weren't enough, the dish comes with imperial rolls. Cash only.

Noodle Factory [1018 Rue Saint-Urbain] leaves me happy and satisfied every time I go. I have a weakness for their homemade dumplings, fried or Hunan style (topped with an exquisite peanut sauce), and the slightly spicy Singapore-style noodles. Tea is free, and children are welcome. Cash only.

Ephemeral Village

37

The **Village au Pied-du-Courant** is a temporary installation set up each year from June to the end of September. The festive gathering place is set up on a vast expanse of sand beside the St. Lawrence River, just east of the Jacques Cartier Bridge. It's filled with hammocks, boccie courts, plastic ball rooms, fun and original furniture, food trucks, bars, etc. Bring friends and family along; it's a great place for kids. It's also a great spot to watch the Montreal Fireworks Festival (l'International des Feux Loto-Québec), which takes place at La Ronde in July. Admission is free, but there's a fee for the stands (cash only). It's a great example of urban revitalization and citizen initiative. Open from Thursday to Sunday, and on Wednesday during the fireworks festival [2100 Rue Notre-Dame Est].

Candy Pink

38

From May to September, Sainte-Catherine street, between Saint-Hubert and Papineau, is pedestrian-only. Garlands of **pink balls** (*Les Boules Roses*) are strung up to mark the area. The 170,000 pink resin balls and netting suspended over the street on thin cables is really an art piece, designed by landscape architect Claude Cormier. The effect is striking: a pink ribbon stretching for half a mile. The raising of the pink balls coincides with the opening of dozens of terraces, which bar and restaurant owners set up at the start of each summer season.

Find Calm on Sainte-Rose

40 To escape the hustle and bustle of Rue Sainte-Catherine, take refuge on **Rue Sainte-Rose**, a charming narrow residential street south of the popular and busy main artery. This hidden treasure of the Gay Village is largely a pedestrian street, and even becomes a park at certain points. Start your walk at Rue Beaudry and head east. You'll see low townhouses, modest working-class homes from another time, with skylights, covered entrances and wrought iron fences. At the end of your walk [to No. 1671], just before Avenue Papineau, look for a pretty stone house—with gabled dormers—that was built in 1870.

Top-Notch Baristas

39 For one of the best coffees in town (and my personal favorite), head to **Pourquoi Pas Espresso Bar** [1447 Rue Amherst]. They only serve single-origin coffee, bought direct trade. Two beans are on the menu each day, with their origin and particular aromas marked for customers: You might find notes of orange, cocoa, lemon, jasmine and more. Many customers come from far away for the homemade coconut-almond milk. You'll also be happy to learn that their baristas excel in latte art—get ready to Instagram.

Exotic Food in the Village

41 Discover Vietnamese street food at **Red Tiger** (A), a trendy and affordable little pub with vibrant colors. The cocktails are impressively original, and each dish is tastier than the last. My favorites: green papaya salad with homemade beef jerky (you choose the spice level); satay chicken brochettes with coconut; beef carpaccio with crispy shrimp chips; and five-spice braised pork ribs. The dishes are surprising and authentic [1201 Boulevard de Maisonneuve Est].

Even on the grayest days, it's warm and pleasant at **Agrikol**, a Haitian restaurant with a festive tropical atmosphere. The rhythms on the stereo will make you think it's Friday night in Port-au-Prince. If you're there with a group, get the Ti Ponch, with a quarter, half or full bottle of white rum, which you pour yourself with cane syrup and lime. On the food side, a small, simple menu offers typical dishes: malanga acra, marinated pork and truly addictive plantains. They don't take reservations [1844 Rue Amherst].

Opened more than 30 years ago by the Martinez family, **La Guadalupe Mexicaine** serves the best margaritas in the city, hands down. Don't miss a chance to try the *mole poblano*, chicken with a rich, oily chocolate sauce, prepared with 30 spices and five kinds of dried peppers. Everything is homemade [2345 Rue Ontario Est].

The Sauciest Cafés

42 Welcome to the most eccentric café in town. With its slogan *Chaque graine est unique* ("Each seed is unique"—*graine* is a slang word for a particular male body part...), **La Graine Brûlée** (A) [921 Rue Sainte-Catherine Est] isn't afraid to make an impression. The decor, full of loud colors, is a bit like a village fair. It's a popular spot for students to work on their laptops and enjoy a light meal (soups, wraps, grilled cheese, vegetarian chili and hot dogs). There's even a play area with cushions, a television and Super Nintendo. The owners also push the boundaries of good taste to the limit with a line of cups, stationery and T-shirts that incorporate risqué messages that are guaranteed to make you blush; they're hilarious.

Rage [1436 Rue Amherst] is another spot you'll be sure to remember: It's an axe-throwing facility (you read correctly!). In this indoor throwing range, you can blow off steam while improving your concentration and precision. Let your inner warrior out to play. For ages 13 and over.

43 A

42 A

Small Delights on Ontario

43 With its white walls, elementary school furniture and abundant decorative plants, **Café Sfouf** (A) [1250 Rue Ontario Est] exudes simplicity. The menu offers Lebanese-inspired savory and sweet toast; opt for the sublime goat cheese, pistachio and honey. For dessert, try the sfouf, a semolina cake spiced with turmeric and topped with pine nuts. Kids are more than welcome: They get toast at half price. And, there's parking for strollers and a play area for the very little ones.

Next door, you'll find one of the best Italian bakeries outside of Little Italy. **Arte e Farina** [1256 Rue Ontario Est] mostly does takeout orders, but you can also sit at the counter for pizza, focaccia, biscotti and more. There's a wide selection of desserts (the stuffed donuts are fabulous) and other tasty Italian items, cooked to perfection.

45 A

Sixties Design on Amherst

44

For retro furniture and somewhat colorful and eccentric accessories, **Spoutnik** is your destination of choice. You'll find a great selection of light fixtures, wall decorations and small furniture pieces in a range of styles. It's a true trip to the 1960s! [2120 Rue Amherst]

44

The Culinary Arts of Quebec

45

"Explosive," "heavenly," "I'm in love"—rapturous phrases like these are a common sight in reviews of **Le Mousso** (A), a restaurant that opened at the end of 2015. Take a look at the Instagram account of the young chef and owner, Antonin Mousseau-Rivard. The dishes on display are so beautiful and elegant they're moving. The wonder isn't limited to the visual; Mousseau-Rivard astonishes the taste buds, too. The restaurant takes Montreal gastronomy to a new level. Using almost exclusively Quebec ingredients, Mousseau-Rivard transports customers with his modern, inventive and audacious cuisine. Tasting menu only, with seven to 10 courses, depending on the season; fixed price. Let the chef take over. You're in good hands [1023 Rue Ontario Est].

Bouillon Bilk [1595 Boulevard Saint-Laurent] is another restaurant that's universally loved. Tucked between two electronic stores, it's a little hidden gem, with minimalist decor and bold dishes. The service is attentive and the mixture of flavors is always well balanced, offering surprises at every turn. The food at **Cadet** [1431 Boulevard Saint-Laurent], a little brother to Bouillon Bilk, is equally outstanding. I had a broccoli and spätzle dish that was absolutely divine—yes, I used the words "broccoli" and "divine" in the same sentence. That's how good it is.

The Tea Masters

46 "We drink tea to forget the noise of the world;" so said Lu Yu, author of *The Classic of Tea*. I really do feel at peace when I visit **Camellia Sinensis**. I like the sophistication, the professionalism, the advisors and the vast selection of teas (more than 250). Since 1998, the four tasters have traveled throughout Asia, seeking out the best raw teas, which they alone distribute in North America. My favorites are Dragon Pearls, a green tea lightly scented with jasmine, and Genmaicha with Matcha and Sencha, which has grilled and puffed rice [351 Rue Émery].

Beer from Here

47 **Le Cheval Blanc** (A) [809 Rue Ontario Est] became the first licensed brewpub in Montreal in 1987, well ahead of the microbrewery trend that has overtaken the city. Its atmosphere hasn't changed; it remains an unpretentious place, one you're always happy to return to. The tavern only sells beers brewed on-site. The white beer (*blanche*) is their best-known classic, but do try some other special drafts as well, like the Double Bonheur, a nitrogen-carbonated IPA, or the Berliner Cerise, a sour wheat beer made with Quebec cherries. **L'Amère à Boire** [2049 Rue Saint-Denis], another top-notch brewery, has been satisfying the hop needs of students, beer enthusiasts and passersby since 1996. The menu has Czech, German, Danish and English beers, including the popular Cerná and Stout Impérial.

48A

The Mystery Bar

48 It's an inspired marketing strategy: open a bar with a secret address. To find out where **Le 4ᵉ Mur** is located, you have to sign up on their website and become a member. The bar is a speakeasy, based on Prohibition-era bars in the United States, where customers had to keep their voices low when ordering (hence the name *speakeasy*). I won't reveal the location here. The bar is renowned for its cocktail menu, its cozy atmosphere and its roaring-twenties decor. Sign up online and show up to try one of their impressive signature cocktails, like the "I Love Negroni" [le4emur.com].

Feeling nostalgic for Tetris, Ms. Pac-Man and Mortal Kombat? **Arcade MTL** [2031 Rue Saint-Denis] is a bar that's totally devoted to retro arcade and video games. The entry fee gives you access to over a dozen 1980s arcade games, a pinball machine and a few other consoles that are wonderfully far out of date. Sip a cocktail while you play. You must be 18 to enter.

In summertime, the terrace at **Le Sainte-Élisabeth** (A) [1412 Rue Sainte-Élisabeth] is one of the most impressive in the city. The buildings that surround it form a vast enclave, completely blanketed in vines about 10 feet (three meters) high. In the fall, when the leaves are turning red, it's truly spectacular.

Murals and Motivation

49 If you like murals, make a point of visiting Habitations Jeanne-Mance, a housing project that's home to 1,700 people from 70 different countries. There you can admire the 13 murals that were created thanks to the arts organization MU ("mue" is a French term that means "rejuvenation through the shedding of an old skin"), to help strengthen community spirit and add color to the neighborhood. One must see **L'Air du Temps** (A); it can be seen from the corner of Rue Sanguinet and Rue Émery. The incredibly detailed mural depicts the urban landscape in a previous era. I love the touch of humor at the bottom of the image: orange traffic cones, which are so representative of the state of road infrastructure in Montreal today. There's another great mural on the chalet in Parc Toussaint-Louverture: **Entre Ciel et Terre** was made in collaboration with youth living in the housing project.

Not far from there, at the corner of Avenue du Président-Kennedy and Rue Jeanne-Mance, is the **oldest mural** in Montreal, painted by Jacques Sabourin and Claude Dagenais in 1972.

49A

Hats Through the Ages

50 A true institution, hat-maker **Henri Henri** has been topping men's heads since 1932. Inside the store, time seems to have stopped in the 1930s—the original furniture and decor is still in place. During the 1950s and 1960s, the store took the phrase "hat trick" literally, offering a free hat to any hockey player who scored three goals in a single game at the Forum, then the home arena of the Montreal Canadiens. Stylish headwear was provided to legends like Maurice Richard, Bobby Hull and Phil Esposito. Catering mainly to men but with a selection for women as well, Henri Henri offers hats and accessories in all different styles: hustler, aviator, tweed, felt, fur, straw, Western—they even have panama hats and bowler hats [189 Rue Sainte-Catherine Est].

Dinu Bumbaru: Mr. Heritage

51

With a degree in architecture and the author of several publications, Dinu Bumbaru is the policy director for Heritage Montreal, and has been the organization's spokesperson for many years. His more than 500 interviews given in Montreal, Canada and abroad have earned him the nickname of "Mr. Heritage."

Since being established in 1975, **Heritage Montreal** has greatly contributed to the enhancement and protection of the architectural, historical, natural and cultural heritage of Greater Montreal. This nonprofit organization played a key role in the development of the **Old Port**, in protecting **Mount Royal**, and in safeguarding the **Milton-Parc area**, the **Monument-National**, the **Jean-Talon train station**, and the **Guaranteed Pure Milk bottle** (see Reason #79), to name just a few. Heritage Montreal is currently involved in deciding the future of **Silo No. 5** (see Reason #2), having saved it from demolition in 1996.

Over 40 years, the organization has done a tremendous job, but so much still remains to be done. "Heritage is not just a few monuments here and there," explained Bumbaru. "Of course we have great churches and places of worship with splendid architecture, but we also have an urban landscape enhanced by the work of craftspeople: the ornate work of blacksmiths on staircases, the metal moldings made by tinsmiths, the brickwork, stonework and woodwork... Unfortunately, these erode over time."

For Bumbaru, Montreal is distinguished by its "walkability," by the clusters of neighborhoods: interesting spaces that are great for strolling. Pointe-Saint-Charles is a good example. This modest neighborhood offers magnificent views of the city and the mountain; from there, a walk along the Lachine Canal will lead you to Verdun or Little Burgundy. "The art of building in modest neighborhoods is fascinating. It should not be forgotten that it's not only the grandiose houses that define a city's heritage, but also the diversity of its residential architecture."

52 A

A Hotbed of Culture

52 **Quartier des Spectacles** covers about one-third of a square mile (one square kilometer). It's bordered by Rue Saint-Hubert to the east, Rue City Councillors to the west, Rue Sherbrooke to the north and Boulevard René-Lévesque to the south. The neighborhood encompasses the Quartier Latin and includes the grounds of **Place des Festivals** and the **Promenade des Artistes** on Boulevard de Maisonneuve Ouest, and **Place Émilie-Gamelin** on Rue Berri. With 80 different cultural venues, 28,000 seats in 30 theaters and 450 culture-focused businesses, the area packs quite a cultural punch. Over 100 shows take place each month, and 40 festivals a year. With the biggest interactive fountain installation in Canada, Place des Festivals is an essential destination. The area covers 65,000 square feet (6,000 square meters), and can hold up to 25,000 people for a big show. With seven million visitors each year, Quartier des Spectacles adds a real spark to the city in winter and summer alike. It's a direct connection between Montreal's creativity and the international scene.

Classical Music for the People

53 The **Chapelle Historique du Bon-Pasteur** is one of Montreal's best-kept musical secrets. The building has exceptional acoustics for music lovers, and religious architecture that has been maintained as it was in the 19th century. The 150-seat room is dedicated to music in all its forms, but it's used mainly for recitals and chamber music performances. Considered by many musicians to be an essential and invaluable springboard for their careers, the Chapelle Historique du Bon-Pasteur stays true to its mission of making culture accessible to all: Admission is free to most concerts [100 Rue Sherbrooke Est].

Against the Current

54 With an amazing location that has a view of Place des Festivals, **Anticafé** isn't exactly a café (as its name suggests). It's distinctly different: a space that's open to all, with Wi-Fi and free coffee, tea and cookies that you serve yourself. To enjoy it, you pay an hourly fee of a few dollars ($3 for the first hour, $2 for additional hours, with a maximum cost of $9 per day). The huge 12-room spot is a temporary home to students, workers, travelers and passersby. It feels harmonious and friendly, a bit like a youth hostel. It's a spot to work with colleagues, visit with friends, play games, read or study. You'll feel right at home [294 Rue Sainte-Catherine Ouest].

Twenty-Five Art Galleries Under the Same Roof

55 **Le Belgo** (A) [372 Rue Sainte-Catherine Ouest] has a number of workshops, art studios and dance schools. It also has no less than 25 art galleries, and the highest concentration of contemporary artworks in Canada. Each gallery has its own schedule, but most are open Wednesday to Saturday from 12 p.m. to 5 p.m. Walk down the various corridors to discover exciting new art and talk to the gallerists. If you're still hungry for modern art afterward, go to the **Musée d'Art Contemporain** [185 Rue Sainte-Catherine Ouest]—it's the top modern art destination in Quebec.

56 A

The Height of Eccentricity

56 It's undoubtedly the most eclectic place in Montreal: a vintage store, café-bistro, cabaret and costume store, all in one. With its graffiti-covered facade (don't let the shabby exterior put you off), **Eva B.** (A) is a decidedly alternative operation. It attracts students, artists and fashionistas looking for retro clothing, collectibles or Halloween costumes. The cabaret space is a place to showcase the talents of underground artists from the theater scene, the music world and the visual arts community. You'll probably find what you're looking for—and you'll definitely find things you never expected [2015 Boulevard Saint-Laurent].

For a post-shopping pick-me-up, stop at **Nougat & Nectarine** (B). The bakery offers pleasure for the eyes and taste buds that far outweighs the guilt of indulging. It specializes in cakes and cupcakes, and also has mouthwatering pastries and a breakfast and lunch menu. If you're there at the right time, the open kitchen lets you watch the pastry chefs at work, carefully constructing towering wedding cakes that they decorate elaborately [2115 Boulevard Saint-Laurent].

56 B

57 A

Improv for Sport

58

It's a little-known fact, but improvisation games were invented right here in Montreal, in 1977, by actors Robert Gravel and Yvon Leduc. They wanted to experiment with new forms of theater and to get away from the elitist side of the art. Their solution: an amalgam of theater and ice hockey. The concept went on to become popular in over 30 countries. The **Ligue Nationale d'Improvisation** is the most well-known improv games organization. It holds matches on Sunday and Monday evenings at **Club Soda** [1225 Boulevard Saint-Laurent]. The **Ligue d'Improvisation Montréalaise** (A) is popular for its experimental approach. It holds events every Sunday at **Lion d'Or** [1676 Rue Ontario Est]. **Théâtre Sainte-Catherine** [264 Rue Sainte-Catherine Est] hosts a free improv workshop in English on Sundays, and **Lundis d'Impro** ("Improv Mondays") in French the next day. For **LALIG**—another improvisation company— matches, check out **Abreuvoir** [403 Rue Ontario Est] on Mondays.

The Digital Mecca

57

A hub of creativity, the **Société des Arts Technologiques** (SAT) is a nonprofit organization known around the world for its role in developing digital technologies, such as immersive experiences, augmented reality and all kinds of art related to new technologies. The **Satosphère**, a massive dome for the projection of 360-degree immersive audiovisual works, can hold 350 spectators. The SAT has helped the uninitiated discover digital culture since it was founded in 1996. It always has something interesting to see. Upstairs, the **Labo Culinaire** (A) has a seasonal menu and natural wines; the terrace is magical in the summer. Visit the website for a complete schedule [1201 Boulevard Saint-Laurent].

58 A

Zébulon Perron: The Zébulon Touch

59 Is there a Zébulon touch? It would seem so. All the restaurants, bars and cafés that feature **Zébulon Perron**'s unique interior design consistently become hot spots: **Buvette chez Simone**, **Grinder**, **Philémon Bar**, **Hachoir**, **Impasto** and **Tommy**, to name a few.

The singularity of Perron's work has inspired the Montreal design aficionado over the past few years to the point that he has become the most coveted interior designer in town. His designs are characterized by a certain simplicity and naturalness, as well as a warm and convivial feel. Large communal tables bring strangers together, encouraging socializing. He incorporates wood, glass, metal and retro furniture—an eclectic mix that works. Another strength of his work is the use of repurposed materials, giving new life to objects, which are used in innovative and unexpected ways; for example, the interior of a tanning bed becomes a lamp with interesting reflective properties, and worn stainless panels beautifully adorn the backsplash of a bar.

When I asked him about his reasons for loving Montreal, without a moment's hesitation he named **Mount Royal**. "Few cities can boast of having a forest in their center. It is beautiful, no matter the season." He then hastened to add **Mile End**, where he grew up, "Mile End reflects everything I like about Montreal: It has a diverse population: young, old, students, hipsters... It's multicultural, and Francophones and Anglophones live nicely side by side, which is important to me because I come from a bilingual family." Lastly, he listed the quality of the

restaurants in Montreal: "**Joe Beef**, **Le Vin Papillon**, **Le Filet**, **Nora Gray**, **Foxy**, **Montréal Plaza**, **Impasto**... The list is too long! There is talent in Montreal. We're lucky to have all these things."

Just recently, he added another string to his bow by becoming co-owner of a bar and a restaurant, for which he, of course, created the interior design. A phenomenal success since it opened, **Furco** [425 Rue Mayor] attracts downtown professionals for a well-deserved happy hour. The name comes from the building, which used to be the Canadian Fur Company warehouse. The interior is magnificent: immense windows; raw materials; a happy combination of concrete, wood and leather. Its little brother, **Café Parvis** [433 Rue Mayor], located just behind St. James United Church, has been praised by Montrealers in the know since the day it opened. It has a more organic decor, with a Mediterranean feel. I go there often—perhaps too often—for lunch. The menu features Roman pizzas, which have a thicker and crisper crust than the Neapolitan variety, and amazing salads.

60 A

Public Art takes the Metro

60 A true art gallery, the Montreal Metro system contains dozens of murals, stained glass windows, mosaics and sculptures installed in most of its 68 stations. Some notable examples: the Place-des-Arts station features *Histoire de la Musique à Montréal* (1967) (A), an illuminated stained glass mural by the famous illustrator Frédéric Back. It depicts key moments in the city's musical history and pays tribute to some of its great musicians.

At the Berri-UQAM station, overlooking the Green line, *Hommage aux Fondateurs de la Ville de Montréal*, created in 1969 by Pierre Gaboriau and Pierre Osterrath, represents the city's three founders: Jérôme le Royer de la Dauversière, Jeanne Mance and Paul Chomedey de Maisonneuve. A little historical anecdote: Gaboriau, son of Robert LaPalme, who was the artistic adviser for the Metro at the time,

considered the figurative approach imposed by his father to be outdated, and against the artistic currents of the time. In playful defiance, he included several elements of abstract art in his work.

The **glasswork surrounding the entrance of the Champ-de-Mars station**, considered artist Marcelle Ferron's masterpiece, is the most well-known and acclaimed work in the Metro system. When the sun is shining, the 60-meter-long by nine-meter-high (200 by 30 feet) stained glass casts a brilliant colored pattern of light onto the platform.

"Meet me at the puck." "The puck" is what Montrealers have nicknamed the circular, two-meter-wide black granite bench near the ticket booth at the Berri-UQAM station. It resembles an ice hockey puck, and is a popular meeting spot. Often overlooked is the fact that in its center is the **plaque commemorating the inauguration of the Montreal Metro** (B), dated October 14, 1966.

60 B

Downtown

Tucked in between Mount Royal and the St. Lawrence River, Montreal's city center is exceptionally distinctive: Skyscrapers cohabit alongside historical buildings, boutiques and church steeples—an eclectic landscape particular to Montreal, rendered in a mixture of styles and cultures. A center for businesses, the main hotels, universities and office buildings, the downtown (*Centre-Ville*) area is also a shopping paradise. This densely populated area is home to Rue Sainte-Catherine, the liveliest street in the province, and to the famous network of underground malls.

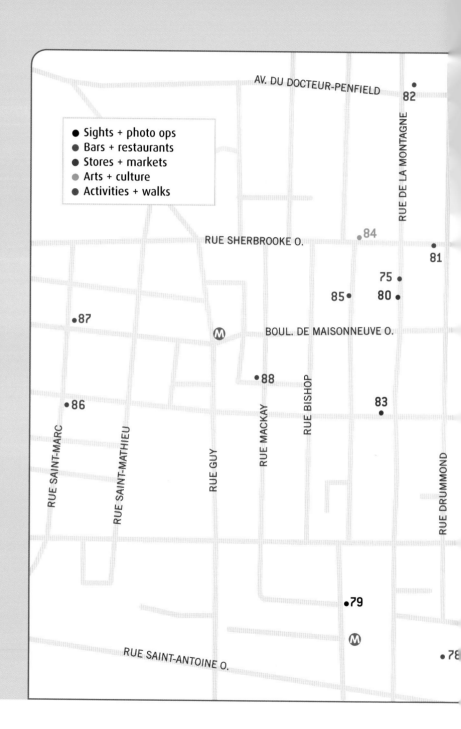

AV. DU DOCTEUR-PENFIELD

82

RUE DE LA MONTAGNE

- Sights + photo ops
- Bars + restaurants
- Stores + markets
- Arts + culture
- Activities + walks

RUE SHERBROOKE O.

84

81

75

85   80

87

Ⓜ   BOUL. DE MAISONNEUVE O.

88

RUE BISHOP

86

83

RUE SAINT-MARC

RUE SAINT-MATHIEU

RUE GUY

RUE MACKAY

RUE DRUMMOND

79

Ⓜ

RUE SAINT-ANTOINE O.

78

CENTRE-VILLE

RUE UNIVERSITY

RUE MAYOR

RUE PEEL

AV. MCGILL COLLEGE

AV. UNION

RUE SAINTE-CATHERINE O.

RUE MANSFIELD

SQUARE
DORCHESTER

BOUL. RENÉ-LÉVESQUE O.

PLACE
DU
CANADA

BOUL. ROBERT-BOURASSA

AV. VIGER O.

70

63

73

74

62

71

64

66 69

72

61

77

76

68

65

61A 62

Wine Heaven

62 **Vinum Design** is a boutique specializing in accessories for wine tasting and conservation. It has more than 800 products for professionals and newcomers alike, including the widest selection of glasses in town. Their specialists will guide you in choosing the perfect glass for any occasion. You'll also find carafes, decanters, corkscrews, and a wine-cellar design and construction service for those of us who dwell in Montreal [1480 Rue City Councillors].

The City Under your Feet

61 For most Montrealers, it's only a vast network of corridors that connect downtown buildings. But **The Underground City** (A) (*La Ville Souterraine*, also RÉSO) is really worth exploring. The complex stretches for 20 miles (32 kilometers), and 500,000 pedestrians move through it daily, protected from the weather above. With 190 points of entry, this network of tunnels and galleries is the largest underground complex in the world, connecting 2,000 stores, 63 buildings, including 10 university buildings nine major hotels, eight Metro stations and five transportation terminals.

Throughout The Underground City, you'll find artworks that are worth the trip below street level. One of the highlights is Jean-Paul Mousseau's **ceramic tile circles** at the Peel Metro station. Try to spot the artist's name on each of the 37 colorful pieces. Another great piece is *Nature Légère*, a huge forest of pink trees by Claude Cormier at the Palais des Congrès. Doing an art tour in The Underground City is the perfect activity for a cold or rainy day. Companies like Kaléidoscope and Guidatour organize guided tours, and the blog *Mes Quartiers* (see Reason #214) has a guide for making your own itinerary.

Jazz Nights

63 In the years following World War II, Montreal's world-renowned jazz clubs helped local jazzmen like Oscar Peterson and Oliver Jones become legends. Today, the city's jazz scene is alive and well. For a night you'll remember, head to **Maison du Jazz** (A) [2060 Rue Aylmer], a bar-restaurant with great ambiance and chic decor. **Upstairs** [1254 Rue Mackay] is a smaller venue with a more laid-back vibe and some of the best live jazz in Quebec. Both spots have concerts every night of the week.

63A

Shopping Comes First, in Fair or Foul Weather

64 If you've got shopping in your blood, downtown is the place to be. Thanks to The Underground City, you can move from one mall to another without setting foot outside. In poor weather, my preferred route starts at **La Baie d'Hudson** (A) (Hudson's Bay) [585 Rue Sainte-Catherine Ouest], McGill Metro station. Next I visit **Promenades Cathédrale** [625 Rue Sainte-Catherine Ouest], then on to the **Eaton Centre** [705 Rue Sainte-Catherine Ouest], **Place Montréal Trust** [1500 Avenue McGill College], **Simons** [977 Rue Sainte-Catherine Ouest], and lastly **Les Cours Mont-Royal** [1455 Rue Peel]. This indoor journey will leave you at the Peel Metro station; you'll have passed near 375 stores and restaurants along the way. Side note: The **Barbie Expo**, the biggest show of its kind, is also on the route. Over 1,000 dolls are on display to be lovingly admired on the second floor of Les Cours Mont-Royal. Admission is free.

Calaveras and Guacamole

65 The Mexican restaurant **Escondite** (A) [1206 Avenue Union] is so vibrant it's practically electric—in its decor and ambiance as well as its food. There are plenty of *calaveras*—elaborately decorated skulls—and colorful frescoes and wide sombreros. The vibe is playful and kitsch, yet chic. As for the food, definitely try the Nachos 2.0: small tortillas stuffed dumpling-style with Monterey Jack, then fried and served with flawless guacamole and pomegranate seed *pico de gallo*. The combination of flavors and textures is absolutely sublime. The crispy cod tacos with avocado crema and cabbage slaw is another dish that must be tasted to be believed. The owners have two other restaurants in the neighborhood, and both follow the same winning recipe: lively decor plus great food. **La Habanera** [1216 Avenue Union] is a Cuban restaurant, and **Biiru** [1433 Rue City Councillors] is Japanese. All three restaurants are for customers 18 and over.

64A 65A

Relax Beneath the Skyscrapers

66

Downtown Montreal is charmingly bustling and vibrant but sometimes you need a quiet place to enjoy a takeout meal, away from the chaos of the main streets. Just behind **Christ Church Cathedral**, **Raoul Wallenberg Square** (A) was built in honor of a Swedish diplomat and World War II hero. Wallenberg helped save tens of thousands of Hungarian Jews by assisting them in fleeing Budapest during the Nazi occupation. With its fountain, flower-filled spaces and many benches, the garden is a peaceful oasis among the skyscrapers [1444 Avenue Union].

Dorchester Square has gone through several incarnations. Once a cemetery, it was transformed into an immense park called Dominion Square, with two very differently designed sections. To the north, it was precisely and symmetrically divided; to the south, winding lanes were created, inspired by picturesque English gardens. The south part became Place du Canada in 1967. Surrounded by the most illustrious downtown buildings, the 118,000-square-foot (11,000-square-meter) park is without question one of the city's loveliest.

The **McGill University Campus** is a tranquil, verdant paradise. Go through the Roddick Gates, at the north end of Avenue McGill College, and follow the example of the students and professionals you see around you: Relax in the shade of a tree, have a picnic with friends, or just lie in the sun. You deserve it [845 Rue Sherbrooke Ouest].

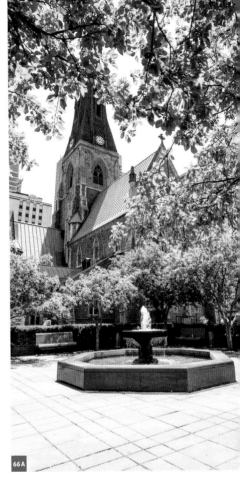

66 A

Built in 2002 on a former parking lot, **Domtar Garden** is a peaceful spot next to the Quartier des Spectacles. The park is divided into two sections. The north part is based on a typical forest in eastern Canada, with oak, sugar maple and birch trees. The south part is more urban, with a natural stone terrace and rows of plants [corner of Rue Bleury and Boulevard de Maisonneuve Ouest].

A New Breed of Taxi

67 Founded by Montreal businessperson Alexandre Taillefer, **Téo Taxi** (Téo is a French acronym for "optimized ecological transportation") is a taxi service for the 21st century. Its entire fleet of vehicles is 100-percent electric. You order a taxi using a mobile app, which tells you the wait time, helps you locate the assigned car and provides an estimate of the cost of the trip. You also use the app to pay by credit card. The cars are clean and in excellent condition—they even have Wi-Fi [teomtl.com].

Montreal's Heights

68 Opened in 2016, the **Au Sommet** (A) observatory at Place Ville Marie is 600 feet (185 meters) high, or 46 stories. A glass enclosure with a modern, minimalist design offers a 360-degree panorama of all the city's major attractions: the river, Mount Royal, the bridges, the Olympic Stadium and more. You can even enjoy the view from outdoors on the 44th floor terrace. Give yourself enough time to visit the **#MTLGO** (B) exhibition, which features 55 portraits of Montrealers. And why not eat at the highest-altitude restaurant while you're at it? **Les Enfants Terribles** offers a contemporary take on Quebec cuisine, which you can enjoy with an incredible vista [3 Place Ville Marie].

68 A

Montreal's Beloved Jeweler

69 The legendary **Maison Birks**—the largest and most prestigious jeweler in Canada—was founded in Montreal in 1879. It has occupied the same four-story building with rounded corners at Square Phillips for 125 years, and five generations of the Birks family have worked there [1240 Phillips Square].

The Urban Forest

70 Each year during the summer, the **McCord Museum**, which is dedicated to Canadian history, shuts down the small Rue Victoria and turns it into **The Urban Forest** (A). Fun and creatively designed, it's a good spot to hang out, take part in a group yoga session or enjoy a free concert. The dynamic McCord Museum is also popular for its fascinating temporary exhibitions on all kinds of subjects. They also hold events in the evening, with food, DJs, drinks and activities related to the exhibition themes. They're always good times [690 Rue Sherbrooke Ouest].

68 B

City Cycling

72

In my humble opinion, **BIXI** may be the best thing that's happened to Montreal in the last decade. On April 15 of each year, thousands of BIXI-riders (myself included) eagerly await the seasonal arrival of the bike-sharing service. BIXI has become more than just a mode of transportation; it's become an icon, an emblem for the city itself. Launched in May 2009, the BIXI network now has 5,200 bikes and 460 stations in the Montreal area. The name BIXI comes from the words "bike" and "taxi." The sophisticated 100-percent-Quebecois design, has been exported around the world: Boston, London, Melbourne, New York, Toronto, Washington and other cities all use the bikes.

A one-way 30-minute-or-less BIXI ride is $2.95. Unlimited use over 24 hours costs $5. It's $14 for three-days, $30 for a 30-day membership, $55 for half a season and $89 for the year. BIXIs aren't really meant for long weekend rides; they're more like transit vehicles. Trips are no more than 45 minutes long; you get charged for extra minutes after that. But whether you feel like a quick ride or you just want to get from point A to point B, BIXI is a great option: healthy, affordable and green. You couldn't find a better way to get around the city [montreal.bixi.com].

If the Shoe Fits

71

In 1972, young Aldo Bensadoun, son of a shoe salesperson and grandson of a shoemaker, opened the first **ALDO** store in downtown Montreal. There's no way he could have known that through his passion he would end up building a shoe empire. The ALDO Group is a world leader in the shoe and fashion industry. Today the company has over 3,000 points of sale worldwide, employs more than 20,000 people and welcomes more than 200 million customers in its stores each year. It's a fantastic Montreal success story [aldoshoes.com].

73A

Art on the Avenue

73

Avenue McGill College (A) is without question the nicest downtown street. It's especially lovely in the spring when the apple trees are flowering and the tulips are blossoming, but it still charms in the winter, when the trees are strung with lights. The wide avenue also offers works of art that are worth discovering. At the south end of the street is Place Ville Marie. Outside the complex is a plaza, where Gerald Gladstone's sculpture-fountain **Female Landscape** is perfectly placed: As you gaze at it, you get a fabulous view of Mount Royal as a backdrop.

The sculpture **The Illuminated Crowd** by the Franco-British artist Raymond Mason will definitely move you. Located in front of 1981 Avenue McGill College, it features 65 people of all races, backgrounds and conditions. It evokes humanity's fragility.

Each summer, the McCord Museum holds an **open-air photo exhibition** on the west side of the avenue. Passersby can discover shots from the museum's impressive archives: It holds more than 1.3 million photos documenting the social history of Montreal.

Sushi Sensation

74

The biggest draw at **Shô-Dan** is the remarkable specialty sushi creations made by the chef: the Kiss Roll (shrimp tempura, avocado, sisho, soy leaf and flambé red tuna), the Hamachi (flambé yellow tuna, ponzu sauce, sesame seeds), the Majesty (lightly breaded and fried royal crab, lemon honey sauce) and more. In fact, they have a wide selection of delicacies that I would walk over hot coals for. Shô-Dan is a huge restaurant, covering three floors. It's my favorite spot for a meal with a large group [2020 Rue Metcalfe].

74

A Downtown Building with a Secret History

76 In my opinion, the most impressive downtown building is the **Sun Life Building**. The beaux-arts-style building is made with 60,200 blocks of granite and decorated with 114 columns. Not many Montrealers know that the building played a major role in "Operation Fish" during World War II. Fearing a Nazi invasion, the UK had its gold reserve and negotiable foreign securities secretly packed up in crates labeled "Fish" and shipped them to Canada. After being covertly unloaded in Halifax on July 1, 1940, the gold was moved to Ottawa, and the securities were transferred to a vault on the third level of the basement of the Sun Life Building. The 5,000 employees working there had no idea of what was happening. By the time the perilous operation was completed, some $2.5 billion (the equivalent of CAD $37 billion today) had been transferred from the UK to Canada. It was the largest amount of wealth ever transported [1155 Rue Metcalfe].

A Shot of Elegance

75 Hidden in a shop with the same name, which specializes in custom-made clothing for men, the **Cloakroom** bar is a jewel of the Montreal cocktail scene. They make classic cocktails from different ages, as well as custom cocktails made according to each customer's taste. Soft lighting, mirrors, black walls—everything is designed to create atmosphere that's simultaneously cozy, elegant and sexy. Go on weekdays if you can; there are only 25 seats, and the wait can be long on Friday and Saturday [2175 Rue de la Montagne].

Street Eats

77 **Food trucks** completely disappeared from the Montreal landscape for more than half a century, mainly for food safety reasons. In 2012, with the growing popularity of food trucks in major North American cities, street cuisine was reintroduced (hurray!), with certain conditions. From April to the end of October, some 40 trucks rotate among 30 authorized sites (some are downtown). They offer a range of cuisines, from the gourmet Europea Mobile to the exotic Traiteur Guru. Even the legendary Montreal cuisine restaurant Au Pied de Cochon has gotten in on the act. Check out the official Montreal street food calendar to find out where the trucks are located on any given day [camionderue.com].

Youppi!: the Canadiens Mascot and Symbol of the City

78 In wintertime, Montrealers are 100-percent dedicated to hockey. People arrange their lives around **Montreal Canadiens** games, and it's a central subject in every conversation. A trip to see a Habs (a nickname derived from *habitants*, the French farmers who first settled in Quebec) game at the **Bell Centre** is a fantastic experience for anyone lucky enough (and with the financial means) to score tickets. If you go see a game, you'll encounter Youppi!, one of the most beloved mascots in professional sports. Youppi! first appeared at the Olympic Stadium during a baseball game between the Montreal Expos and the Chicago Cubs on April 14, 1979. Ten years later, the mascot became the first in North America to be thrown out of a Major League Baseball game: The crime was having gotten too rambunctious on top of the visiting Dodgers dugout. The Dodgers manager, Tommy Lasorda, was not amused, and complained to the umpires. Youppi! was a symbol of the Expos up until the team played their last game, in September 2004. One year later, on September 16, 2005, the news was announced: The charismatic creature would be adopted by the Canadiens. It was the hockey team's first mascot in its almost 100-year history.

Top Designs

80 **Marie Saint Pierre** heads one of the leading fashion houses in Quebec, a label known for its femininity, timelessness and top-quality material. All the pieces are conceived, designed and produced in Montreal. Saint Pierre created her first ready-to-wear collection in 1980. Thanks to her savoir-faire and cutting-edge creations, she's still at the top of her game more than 30 years later [2081 Rue de la Montagne].

The Huge Milk Bottle

79 Another Montreal icon is the **Guaranteed Pure Milk bottle**, a water tower in disguise. It stands almost 33 feet (10 meters) tall, weighs six tons and holds 66,000 gallons (250,000 liters). The reservoir was completely restored in 2009 thanks to Heritage Montreal (see Reason #51) and other partners, including the Quebec federation of milk producers, who wanted to preserve it as a symbol of the important role the dairy industry played in Montreal's development [1025 Rue Lucien-L'Allier].

MAISON
MARIE SAINT PIERRE

82A 82B

Keep Calm and Drink Tea

81
For a truly British afternoon, visit the **Ritz-Carlton** for high tea. Scones, Devonshire tea, little gourmet sandwiches (especially the classic cucumber) and pastries are served on fine porcelain dishes carried on a three-level tray. Afternoon Tea is held twice a day, from 1:00 p.m. to 4 p.m., and from 4:30 p.m. to 7 p.m. in the Palm Court, an opulent hall that's elegantly furnished and decorated. For special occasions, order Royal Tea, accompanied by champagne [1228 Rue Sherbrooke Ouest].

Gilded Neighborhood

82
Only as big as the name suggests, the **Golden Square Mile** was the neighborhood of choice for Canada's business elite between 1850 and 1930. An incredible 70 percent of the country's wealth was concentrated there at one time. The area is bordered by Avenue des Pins, Boulevard René-Lévesque, Rue Guy and Rue University. Many of the prestigious homes have been demolished, but some beautiful ones remain. Here are five of my favorites, all of which now belong to McGill University. The red-sandstone **Charles Rudolph Hosmer House** (A) [3630 Promenade Sir-William-Osler] was built in 1901. The French-château-style **James Ross House** (B) [3644 Rue Peel], also known as Chancellor Day Hall, was built in 1892. **Lady Meredith House** [1110 Avenue des Pins Ouest], 1897, is the height of elegance. **Duggan House** [3724 Rue McTavish], 1861, is a neo-Gothic mansion; it's said to be haunted by the ghost of Scottish-born Simon McTavish, fur trader and founder of the North West Company. **Thomson House** [3650 Rue McTavish], completed in 1935, was the last home built in the gilded neighborhood.

81

83 A

The Grande Dame of Sainte-Catherine Street

83 That's the nickname for **Ogilvy**, a high-end clothing store founded in 1866. It's renowned for its vast selection of ready-to-wear brands, including some of the world's most famous.

The **animated Christmas window display** (A) is eagerly awaited each year by the throngs of passersby; it's part of the city's holiday tradition. From mid-November to the first week of January, the display delights young and old alike, with over 100 mechanical moving parts and small handmade stuffed animals in an enchanted landscape. Another Ogilvy tradition is a parade through the store by their own **bagpipe player**, every day between noon and 1 p.m. On the sidewalk in front of the store you're likely to find the busker **Cyrille Estève**, aka **Spoonman**, who's been entertaining passersby with the rhythms of his wooden spoons for 20 years [1307 Rue Sainte-Catherine Ouest].

Enjoyment for your Eyes and Ears

84 Canada's most visited art museum, the **Montreal Museum of Fine Arts** (*Musée des Beaux-Arts*) [1380 Rue Sherbrooke Ouest] should definitely be on your to-do list. Another treasure you should also make a point of seeing, one that's lesser known, is **Bourgie Hall** (A) (*Salle Bourgie*) [1339 Rue Sherbrooke Ouest]. The museum concert hall has 20 beautiful Tiffany stained glass windows—the largest collection of its kind in the country—lit up with a permanent backlighting system so you can appreciate them fully. The 460-seat room in the restored heritage church hosts some of the most interesting music performances in the city.

Give in and Sing

85 I admit it: I love karaoke. Since I wasn't lucky to be born with the vocal chords of Celine Dion, I stick to embarrassing myself mainly in front of people I know. That's why I like going to **Bar K Karaoke** [2110 Rue Crescent], which has colorful private rooms. The staff is friendly—and the great prices just make the experience that much more enjoyable. **Pang Pang Karaoké** [1226 Rue Mackay] is another bar with private rooms, along with amazing huge sofas, disco balls and multicolored lights—the decor is just like what you'd find in South Korea. The rooms can hold between two and 22 people.

84 A

A Taste of Tokyo

86 **Kazu** is the only restaurant I'll actually stand in line for—even in winter. It is very small, so you may have to wait up to 45 minutes to try the amazing dishes. But it's worth it. The chef, Kazuo Akutsu, offers Japanese cuisine that's a far cry from typical "North-Americanized" Japanese restaurants. Kazu astonishes with its originality, delicacy and flavors. I recommend the shrimp burger and the tuna and salmon bowl (tartare). Wash it all down with a cold beer or a bottle of sake. It's not great for large groups; go alone or with one companion. The service is very fast, making it the ideal spot to eat quickly—but magically—before you go catch a movie. *Kanpai*! [1862 Rue Sainte-Catherine Ouest].

Get your Broom Ready

87 The oldest still active sports club in North America is right here in Montreal. Surprisingly, it's not a hockey club, but rather a curling club. The **Royal Montreal Curling Club** was founded in 1807, when the city had a mere 12,000 inhabitants. The arena has three curling sheets, which can be rented for a two-hour period for a corporate event or to have fun with friends. The fee includes equipment and training from an instructor, who is a club member [1850 Boulevard de Maisonneuve Ouest].

Serious Little Cafés

88 For a coffee without equal, visit **Myriade** (A) [1432 Rue Mackay]. Myriade was the café that initiated the specialty coffee revolution in Montreal. For them, coffee is a science: Everything is measured and controlled, from the quality of the grains to the grind to the temperature of the water. Every cup you get just seems to get better. There's another caffeine cache hidden in the underground hallway connecting the Eaton Centre and Place Ville Marie: **Tunnel Espresso Bar**. This tiny counter serves takeout coffee of the highest caliber. Go underground; it's worth it. [1253 Avenue McGill College, tunnel level]

Griffintown, Little Burgundy, Saint-Henri, Verdun

The history of the districts southwest of the city center has been profoundly influenced by the Lachine Canal, from its construction in 1824 to the end of commercial navigation on its waters during the 1970s. Life in Griffintown, Little Burgundy (*Petite-Bourgogne*), Saint-Henri (known collectively as the Sud-Ouest—"southwest") and Verdun is full of contradictions: Proximity to the city center contrasts dramatically with easy access to water and nature. Formerly working-class neighborhoods are quietly gentrifying, and the restaurants are among the most desirable (and expensive) in town.

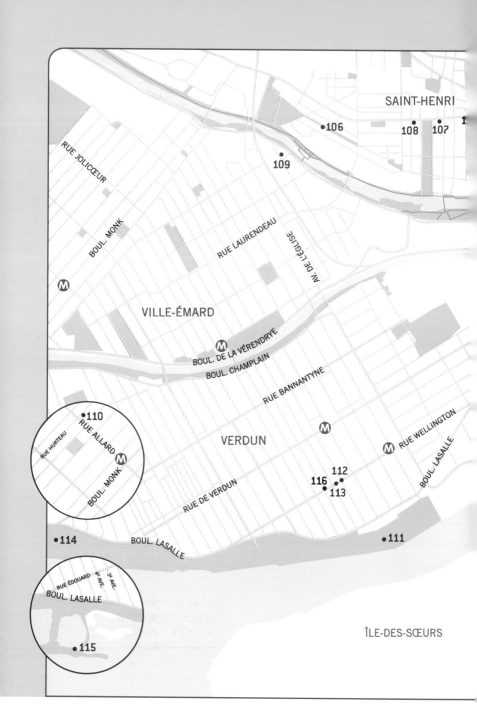

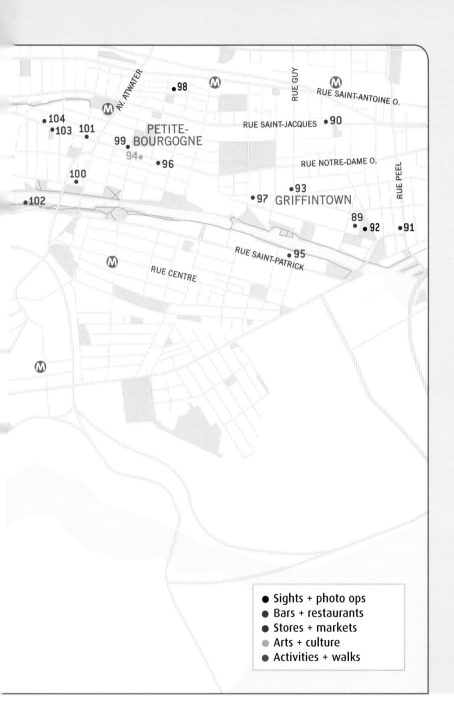

•98

AV. ATWATER

RUE GUY

Ⓜ RUE SAINT-ANTOINE O.

104
•103 101
•

RUE SAINT-JACQUES •90

99 PETITE-
BOURGOGNE

94•
•96

RUE NOTRE-DAME O.

100

RUE PEEL

•102

•93
•97 GRIFFINTOWN

89
• •92 •91

Ⓜ

RUE SAINT-PATRICK
•95

RUE CENTRE

Ⓜ

● Sights + photo ops
● Bars + restaurants
● Stores + markets
● Arts + culture
● Activities + walks

Dynamic Neighborhood

89

Griffintown is bordered by Rue Notre-Dame to the north, the Lachine Canal to the south, the Bonaventure Expressway to the east and Boulevard Georges-Vanier to the west. With its many factories and manufacturing companies, and the construction of the Lachine Canal, Griffintown was the cradle of Montreal's industrial revolution. Formerly a working-class neighborhood, its inhabitants— mainly Irish immigrants at the beginning of the 20th century—lived in extreme poverty. In the 1960s, the City of Montreal razed the area in order to establish an industrial zone. The construction of the Bonaventure Expressway in the heart of the neighborhood did nothing to help the area thrive, and by 1971, it had fewer than 800 inhabitants.

In recent years, Griffintown has seen a major transformation: More than 10,000 housing units have been built or are under construction—the towering condo buildings have dramatically altered the horizon. This revitalization was sparked by two major developments: the relocation of the École de Technologie Supérieure (ETS) to Rue Notre-Dame in the 1990s, and the Lowney real estate project, which transformed the former Cherry Blossom factory (the chocolate confection with the cherry in the center) into upscale urban condos in the early 2000s. And the Bonaventure Project, which will replace the elevated stretch of the Bonaventure Expressway with an urban boulevard at ground level, will finally put an end to the physical and psychological barrier that has long kept this neighborhood isolated. One of the most pleasant ways to experience Griffintown is on a walking tour that takes you from Rue Peel to the narrow side streets near the banks of the Lachine Canal, capturing two centuries of history, and the latest in innovations.

Sicilian Marvels

90

With its black leather-padded banquettes, candlelight glow and elegant 1960s-style wood decor, **Nora Gray** won me over instantly. The restaurant serves chic Southern-Italian cuisine (mainly Sicilian), adapted to seasonal local produce. The fresh pasta has a texture that's simply perfect. If it's on the menu when you visit, order the roasted squash stuffed with homemade goat ricotta, and the cavatelli with wild mushrooms. Delicious [1391 Rue Saint-Jacques].

Unlike in Europe, most restaurants and shops in Montreal are open on Sundays. However, several are closed on Mondays and a few on Tuesdays. Always check the opening hours before you head out.

Nadine Jazouli:
Living the Dream, One Flower at a Time

91 After studying law and spending 13 years as an account manager at an advertising agency, **Nadine Jazouli** arrived at a crossroads. Although she liked her job, the long hours at work, the feeling of being locked up in an office tower and the birth of her first son, prompted her to take a break to rebalance her life. Her first maternity leave allowed her to take a step back, explore and, finally, express her creativity through her longtime passion for flowers in a small workshop she built in the basement of her home. After a few gigs doing floral arrangements for weddings and private events, she founded **Prune les Fleurs**.

In February 2016, the self-taught florist was asked to open a Prune les Fleurs counter at **Must Société** [186 Rue Peel], a new boutique/concept store in Griffintown. This opportunity added momentum to the new direction Nadine had begun a few years before—and with that, her passion officially became her profession.

The success of Prune les Fleurs lies in the meticulous selection of flowers and in the opulent, lush and organic arrangements that celebrate their natural beauty. Every month, the store hosts workshops in which participants practice arranging flowers and greenery, learn the basic techniques for making organic-looking bouquets, give free reign to their imagination and, at the end, go home with their creation.

Now a mother of three boys, Nadine is part of a new generation of entrepreneurs forging the way in Montreal, breaking down barriers and innovating business concepts, while staying focused on balance and family life. Born in Montreal, Nadine adores her city, which she lovingly describes as "colorful." She particularly appreciates the people who live here, and the freedom they enjoy.

The Upscale Bistro and Italian Market

93 With a chic, industrial look, staggeringly high ceilings and gorgeous chandeliers, this 6,000-square-foot (555-square-meter) space is magnificent. Located next to the restaurant of the same name, **Le Richmond Marché Italien** combines a bistro, takeout counter and Italian market—it's one of Griffintown's little treasures. The bistro menu has around 30 dishes, salads and lunch sandwiches, meticulously prepared antipasti, fish and meat, and pizzas in the evening. The market has over 2,000 specialty products, local or imported from Italy, all selected with care: pasta, sauces, cheese, olive oil, balsamic vinegars, coffee, spices, and more. The takeout counter delights the eyes as well as the taste buds with a wide selection of colorful salads and quality sandwiches. You can also get lamb shanks, short ribs, vegetables and other prepared dishes [333 Rue Richmond].

A Glimpse into the Past

92 The intersection of the streets Rioux, Basin and de la Montagne form a triangle. That's where you'll find **Parc du Faubourg-Sainte-Anne,** where the foundations of Saint Anne's Church can still be seen. In the mid-19th century, Saint-Anne's was the heart of the Griffintown Irish-Catholic community. It was demolished in 1970, and only part of the foundations remain. You'll notice that the park benches face the same direction as the pews once did; it's a charming touch. Also be sure to take a look at the old working-class houses along Rue de la Montagne, with the Farine Five Roses sign in the background (see Reason #1) [corner of Rue Basin and Rue de la Montagne].

Urban Revival

94

Built in 1912, the **Corona Theatre**—then called the Family Theatre—was the main gathering place for Little Burgundy residents, showing silent films and vaudeville performances. With its imposing arch and its cross motifs, the facade is typical of pre-war cinemas. With the popularity of theaters diminishing over the years, the Family Theatre closed in 1965. The building was abandoned for decades, finally undergoing major renovations and reopening in 1998. Today the Corona Theatre hosts local artists and international stars. Its success sparked a neighborhood revival that has been continuing for a decade now; it's the hub of development on Rue Notre-Dame Ouest [2490 Rue Notre-Dame Ouest].

Social Climbing

95

Allez Up is the most popular climbing center in Montreal. Different courses at various levels of difficulty provide a great adventure/workout for beginners and devotees alike. They're impressively high and modified often to keep regular clients interested. The outdoor courses, on 125-foot (38-meter) former grain silos (the highest artificial climbing structures in Canada) add an extra challenge. It's a climbers' paradise for kids and adults. Open until midnight on weekdays and 10 p.m. on Saturdays and Sundays [1555 Rue Saint-Patrick].

Pastry Perfection

96

The boutique-restaurant **Patrice Pâtissier**, owned by renowned pastry chef Patrice Demers, is a necessary stop for anyone with a sweet tooth. Buy pastries to go, or sit down for a light lunch or Sunday brunch—you'll win either way. The chocolate, caramel and banana cream puff is mind-blowing, as are the cannelés, the maple financiers and the lemon, chamomile and honey *petits pots*. So many morsels that are as beautiful as they are delectable [2360 Rue Notre-Dame Ouest].

A Tasty Haunt on William Street

97 **Le Fantôme** [1832 Rue William] is one of the best restaurants in Griffintown. A small candlelit bistro that seats 30, it has understated decor and courteous, attentive service. The menu changes each week based on market availability. The focus is on fresh, seasonal and local produce, and the result is sublime. Choose between the six- or eight-course tasting menu, depending on how hungry you are.

The restaurant's name is based on an old Griffintown legend. The story goes that on June 27, 1942, at the corner of William and Murray, a woman's ghost appeared—she was searching for her missing head. Her name was Mary Gallagher, a prostitute, who was savagely decapitated with an axe by her friend Susan Kennedy, also a prostitute, 63 years earlier in 1879. Susan was furious that clients preferred Mary's charms to her own. The legend has it that the headless ghost of Mary returns to the intersection every seven years, looking for her head. If you're into hunting ghosts, the next appearance is supposed to be June 27, 2019.

Little Burgundy Beauties

98 I recommend strolling down **Rue Coursol** to see its colorful little Victorian houses, and the equally colorful brick triplexes, which are surprisingly uniform. The architecture is delightful: straight staircases, wrought iron, magnificently decorated wooden doors, cornices and skylights. Thanks to the care of the owners over the years, many of the original elements in this old working-class neighborhood have remained intact.

Rue Notre-Dame: A Gastronomic Paradise

99B

99C

99 Ever since the opening of **Joe Beef** (A) in 2005 [2491 Rue Notre-Dame Ouest]—ranked as one of the 100 best restaurants in the world—**Rue Notre-Dame Ouest** has become a foodie's dream. Several establishments here approach perfection, in terms of food as well as ambiance. Getting a table at some of them can be tough, so be sure to make a reservation.

Liverpool House (B) [2501 Rue Notre-Dame Ouest], Joe Beef's more festive and brightly lit little brother, has become the favorite haunt for locals. It's a good Plan B, for when Joe Beef is too busy. Have no fear: It has "Plan A" quality.

With the same owners as Joe Beef and Liverpool House, **Le Vin Papillon** (C) [2519 Rue Notre-Dame Ouest] is simply magical. The small wine bar has vintages that would make any wine lover swoon. As for the menu, vegetables and freshness are the priority (it isn't vegetarian, however). The food is exceptional. If I had to choose, this would be my favorite of the Joe Beef siblings. The only drawback is that they don't take reservations—it's first come, first served. Each member of this trio of restaurants also has an intimate garden terrace.

Foxy [1638 Rue Notre-Dame Ouest] is the new spot run by the duo responsible for the always amazing Olive & Gourmando (see Reason #24). The house specialty is wood-oven-cooked pizza. Its primary role is to cook the mouthwatering pizzas, but the oven is also used for bread, meat and vegetables. Irresistible.

With immaculate white decor and a huge garden on the back terrace, the restaurant **HVOR** (D) [1414 Rue Notre-Dame Ouest] uses local and seasonal products to offer an unforgettable gastronomic experience. They only have tasting menus, so be sure to arrive with an appetite.

Also on Rue Notre-Dame Ouest, but in Saint-Henri, **Tuck Shop** [N° 4662] could be described as friendly-chic. It's a winner in every category: ambiance, service and menu. In order to showcase the freshest products possible, the menu changes daily, based on market arrivals. That makes it hard for me to offer suggestions—just get ready for the magic that takes place every night. I guarantee a truly enjoyable experience.

99A 99D

248

A Day at the Market

100 One of the best-known attractions in the south-west, **Atwater Market** (A) opened in 1933. With its high clock tower, there's no mistaking this art-deco-style building. With a range of great stalls open year-round, it is particularly renowned for its many butcher shops and cheese shops. The charcuterie **Terrines & Pâtés**, on the main floor, sells the best duck leg confit in the entire city. For a gift or simply to treat yourself, visit **Les Douceurs du Marché** for its vast selection of local and imported products. Explore the Atwater Market on a sunny day; it's right by the Lachine Canal, so you'll also be able to stroll around and see the area [138 Avenue Atwater].

The **Canal Lounge** is the first floating café-bar in Montreal. Typical of what you'd see in Paris or Amsterdam, it's a former barge. Beautifully decorated with fresh flowers, it's the perfect spot to end the day. The Canal Lounge is moored at the Atwater Quay from May to October; no reservation necessary [22 Avenue Atwater].

100 A

The Ageless Diner

101 **Greenspot** [3041 Rue Notre-Dame Ouest] is a Saint-Henri institution that opened its doors in the 1940s. It's truly an authentic diner (Quebecers call them *casse-croûtes*), the kind they don't make anymore: jukeboxes on the tables, paper *welcome/bienvenue* place mats, faux-leather booths, milkshakes and so on. Every little touch adds enjoyment. People love the succulent homemade fries, the hot dogs that are buttered just so, the well-topped club sandwich and the poutine (the poutine menu is about three feet long). If you're really interested in Quebec nostalgia, you might order a hamburger steak or a "hot hamburger"— so comforting and tasty.

The City of Montreal is the result of the merger of several other municipalities. Don't be surprised to see numbered avenues repeated in different areas. For example, there is a 1re Avenue (1st Avenue) in Rosemont, another in Verdun, another in LaSalle, another in Lachine... When in doubt, ask for the postal code to make sure.

Seeing Montreal by Bike

102

With over 450 miles (730 kilometers) of **bike paths**, Montreal is without question a cycling-friendly city. Municipal governments have also promised to add 30 miles (50 kilometers) of new paths to the network each year. For a wonderfully scenic outing, head to the **Lachine Canal Bike Path**, or to the paths that stretch along the banks of the St. Lawrence River or the Rivière des Prairies.

When *Time* magazine ranked the world's best urban bike paths in 2009, the paths along the Lachine Canal (the oldest in Montreal and the most-used in Canada) and the St. Lawrence River took third place. Here's a great route that's 14 miles (22 kilometers) long. Start from Parc J.-Albert-Gariépy in Verdun. Bike along the shoreline of the St. Lawrence River. Go through Parc des Rapides, the Parc du Canal-de-l'Aqueduc, Parc René-Lévesque in Lachine, and then ride alongside the Lachine Canal until you get to the Atwater Market. Give yourself a little over an hour for the trip—a perfect day.

A Taste of the Middle East

103

Some restaurants enchant you from the first bite. **Sumac** (A) [3618 Rue Notre-Dame Ouest] is one of them. This small neighborhood restaurant transports you with its Middle Eastern cuisine (mainly Lebanese but also Syrian, Israeli and Egyptian). You order at the counter and then wait at your table for the feast to arrive. Go in a group, if you can, so you can share more of their house specialties. Some good choices are the garlic labneh, cooked salad, fries with humus, falafel and chicken shawarma, enhanced with s'rug, a homemade condiment made with cilantro, garlic and green chili.

Nearby, you'll find **Rasoï** (B) [3459 Rue Notre-Dame Ouest], the most eye-popping Indian restaurant in town (the ceiling is painted with an immense colored fresco). Naan bread pizza with cheese and fresh figs, lamb Madras poutine, barbecue tandoori chicken, venison samosas—it's full of surprises. Those seeking a more traditional meal will also find classic Indian dishes like aloo ghobi and butter chicken. I love the tandoori tikka paneer: fresh cheese with a tofu-like texture, cooked in a tandoori oven, served with coriander and tamarind chutney.

103 A

The Little Kiosk that Got Big

104

The Winnicki brothers first became known for their Malaysian and Singaporean street food kiosk, **Satay Brothers**, at Atwater Market. That place was a hit, which allowed them to open an actual restaurant (A) [3721 Rue Notre-Dame Ouest]. The dishes are made with lemongrass, coconut milk, cilantro, papaya, chili, hoisin and ginger—an explosion of flavors. The whole menu is worth tasting, if you can manage it: satay skewers, pork steam buns, green papaya salad, spicy laksa soup with coconut milk, and more. The kiosk at Atwater Market is open from May to October, and the restaurant is open year-round.

A pioneer of Montreal street food, **Grumman '78** [630 Rue de Courcelle] had the first food truck in the city. Increased demand meant that the owners had to transform their prep kitchen (their "headquarters") into a restaurant that's open all year long. The place is fun and can get pretty animated, especially on nights when there's a hockey game. The fish or banh mi pork tacos cannot be resisted—they're heavenly. The menu and taco selection is based on what's available...and the mood of the chefs.

106 A

A Pantry for All

105

Saint-Henri's **Marché La Pantry** wears a number of hats: neighborhood grocery store, bakery, sandwich shop and ice cream shop. Their breakfast sandwich with organic sausage is sure to start your day on the right foot. The homemade strawberry pop tarts, donuts and abricotines will satisfy your sugar addiction. Decadent sandwiches topped with vegetables fresh from the garden are made with homemade bread. The owners also grow several varieties of fruits and vegetables that have almost disappeared, like the legendary Montreal melon (see Reason #121), and they make their own honey. The soft-ice-cream window is totally Instagram-worthy [4211 Rue Notre-Dame Ouest].

104 A 105

107 A

Going Green

106

The concept of a woonerf, or a living street, originated in Netherlands: it's basically a hybrid of a park and a "green alley." **Woonerf Saint-Pierre** (A), in Saint-Henri, was the first of its kind in Montreal. It was built in 2012 in a spot formerly occupied by a raw sewage collector. Today it's a pleasant area over half a mile long, where pedestrians, cyclists and vehicles happily share the environment (the maximum speed is 6 mph (10 km/h). There are benches, lounge chairs and plenty of light. With almost two acres of greenery, many trees and shrubs, Woonerf Saint-Pierre has become a unique place for people to gather, a botanical haven and a playground. It starts at Rue Saint-Rémi and Rue Sainte-Émilie.

The first railway built on Montreal soil, in 1847, connected Griffintown and Lachine, passing through Saint-Henri. The seven miles (11 kilometers) of railway has been dismantled, and a stretch of it has been replaced with a long linear park that's great for cycling or walking. The scenic, wooded **Parc du Premier-Chemin-de-Fer** stretches from Lionel-Groulx Metro station to Place Saint-Henri. To get there from Lionel-Groulx, go to Avenue Greene, between Rue Saint-Jacques and Rue Delisle. If you're starting from Saint-Henri Metro, the park begins at the famous fire station 23 (523 Place Saint-Henri].

A Ray of Sunshine on Notre-Dame Ouest

107

My favorite thing in any city is those little hidden treasures you stumble upon by accident—especially places that are authentic and wonderfully inexpensive. **Tacos Frida** (A) [4412 Rue Notre-Dame Ouest] is a great example. In this tiny Mexican restaurant, the Perez family stays busy cooking tacos (only $2.50 each) as fast as customers can devour them. Shredded chicken, grilled beef, marinated pork: everything is mouthwatering. The vegetarian options— cactus and mushroom—are also excellent. Everything comes with a perfect guacamole. I also suggest you end with a churro, still warm from the deep fryer. To walk off your meal, **Sir George-Étienne Cartier Square** is a good destination. The park is bordered by old trees and has a pretty sculpture fountain that was installed in 1912.

An Italian Duo

108

The sandwich master of the south-west is the Italian café **Campanelli** (A) [4634 Rue Notre-Dame Ouest], hands down. The sandwiches, made to order, are original and topped generously. I would walk miles for the meatball and provolone. The pizzeria **Adamo** [4629 Rue Notre-Dame Ouest] has the same owner, and it too is the real deal. They do takeout only; opt for a whole pizza or a slice, right out of the oven (pro tip: eat it folded in two, New York style). The toppings are varied: pesto, rapini and ricotta, spicy pineapple, pepperoni, mozzarella and basil. In short, it has something for everyone.

An Upside-Down Burger

110

The hamburgers at **Dilallo** [2851 Rue Allard] have long been beloved by locals. Opened in 1929, the diner became famous for its Buck Burger (when it was created, it cost exactly that: a buck), topped with cheese, capicola and homemade hot peppers. They add their own twist to the classic burger: it's served upside down. That's the only way to eat a burger, said the founder, Luigi Dilallo. Each hamburger is still prepared using the family recipe, a cunning blend of beef, pork, veal and spices. If you're wondering why memorabilia for hockey legend **Mario Lemieux** adorns the walls, it's because the "Magnificent One" was born and raised in the neighborhood. There's another Dilallo restaurant in Little Burgundy [2523 Rue Notre-Dame Ouest] and a restaurant-bar in the Saint-Michel neighborhood.

Montreal-Made Gin and Vodka

109

With the opening of so many restaurants focusing on local products, micro-distilleries eventually followed suit and began making 100-percent local spirits. **Cirka** is a distillery on the Lachine Canal that produces "Vodka Terroir" and "Gin Sauvage," made with Quebec corn. From wort to bottling, the spirits are manufactured at their facilities on Rue Cabot. The result is a vodka with mild aromas of licorice and caramel, and gin with floral and coniferous notes. This booze has a lot of personality. The distillery is open for visits, and you get a great view of the stills, some of which reach 23 feet (seven meters) high. Note that you can't buy any products on-site; for that, go to an alcohol outlet (check online—at saq.com—first to see whether they're in stock) [2075 Rue Cabot].

You need a master's degree in urban planning to decipher Montreal parking signs. When in doubt, ask a local.

113A

The Beaten Path

111

Verdun residents will confirm it: The best thing about the neighborhood is indisputably its proximity to the river. Verdunites take advantage of the nine-mile (15 kilometers) developed riverbank all year long, taking walks and bike rides during warmer weather, and walking, skiing and snowshoeing in the winter. To make the most of it, go as close to the shore as you can, and take the beaten path (Verdunites call it the *trail du bas*), with its wild vegetation, frogs and ducks. The silence is mesmerizing; you feel like you're somewhere exotic, far from the big city. You can find the trail easily from the marina [5150 Boulevard LaSalle].

Copette Marshmallows

112

If you're on Rue Wellington on a Sunday, you'll notice a wonderful aroma wafting in the air. There's no need to wander around following your nose: The source is **Fromagerie Copette & Cie**. They make heavenly homemade waffles, caramelized to perfection—tender but with a delicious crunch. Trust me: They're worth the trip. The Fromagerie has attentive service and a great cheese selection, mostly from Quebec producers. All that and they also offer helpful advice—definitely worthy of a full recommendation [4650 Rue Wellington].

A Great Restaurant (Just Between You and Me)

113

L'In-Time (A) [4619 Rue Wellington] is a gem that you'll want to keep hidden from the rest of the world. Seating about 20, its warm atmosphere is perfect for a romantic evening. Bonus: You can bring your own wine. The simple and unpretentious menu offers pasta and mussels, along with classics like garlic escargot and salmon tartare. The service is always attentive, and the chef-owner personally cares about the happiness of his guests. It's friendly, pleasant, high-quality and affordable. Let's keep it between ourselves, okay? Cash only.

On the same street, **Wellington** [3629 Rue Wellington] is another bring-your-own-wine spot. It offers a classic French-bistro menu: homemade boudin, mussels and fries, duck breast and beef tartare. Everything is made well, but the fried veal liver deserves special mention.

112

114

Everyone in the Pool

114 The first public outdoor pool in Montreal, and the largest in Canada when it was built, the **Natatorium** opened with plenty of fanfare in July 1940. The art-deco-style aquatic complex has a huge pool that can hold 1,150 swimmers and a heated wading pool for toddlers. Admission is free. At the floating dock behind the Natatorium, you can rent kayaks and paddleboards for a unique ride on the river [6500 Boulevard LaSalle].

Nature in the City

115 To get away from it all without even leaving the city, nothing beats **Parc des Rapides**, a big 75-acre park that's open year-round. Guides are on hand to answer any question you might have about the flora and fauna and the area's history. It's the perfect spot to see the Lachine Rapids, but it's also a popular migratory bird sanctuary. Over 225 species can be seen from the walking trail, including the largest colony of herons in Quebec, after the one at Lac Saint-Pierre. There are 66 species of fish, turtles, foxes, mink and moles, and rare plants in the area. If you arrive on bicycle (the best way), you will have to lock it up at the entrance of the park [corner of Boulevard LaSalle and 7th Avenue in LaSalle].

115

116A

An Oversized Bookstore

116 Occupying a 6,500-square-foot (600-square-meter) building, **La Librairie de Verdun** (A) [4750 Rue Wellington] adds a twist to the traditional concept of independent bookstores by including the lovely kitchen accessories store **Réunion** and **Café de la Troisième** under its roof. The bright and airy space invites you to lounge and read for hours, and the knowledgeable booksellers can offer great guidance. The fantastic children's literature section is fun and inviting.

Saint-Henri is home to **Crossover Comics** [3560 Rue Notre-Dame Ouest], a bookstore devoted to comics. With their vast selection, you're sure to find something you'll love, whether you're a neophyte or a connoisseur. Focusing mainly on North American comics, they also have rare books from around the world, and a host of other items, like superhero T-shirts and figurines—some are even life-sized.

116A

Westmount, Notre-Dame-de-Grâce (NDG), Côte-des-Neiges

First stop, Westmount, a little English town within the city. Then on to Notre-Dame-de-Grâce (known by most Anglophones as "NDG") and Côte-des-Neiges. The latter two form a borough with the biggest, and youngest population, with its thousands of students, and also the most multicultural population, comprising 75 different ethnic groups. This is a lively area that benefits from an exceptional location on the west side of Mount Royal.

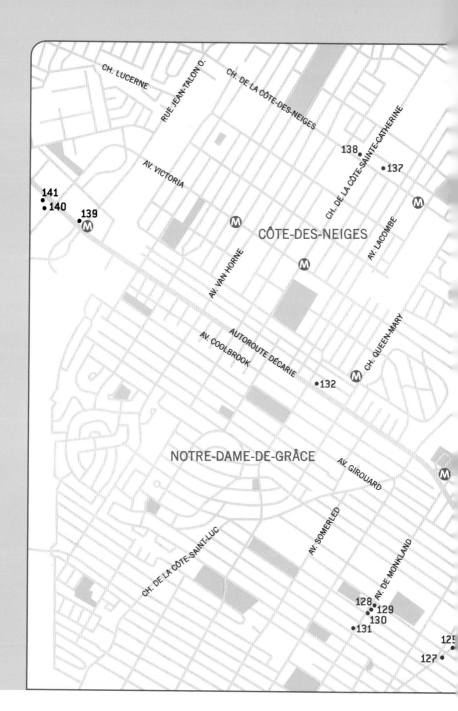

CH. LUCERNE

RUE JEAN-TALON O.

CH. DE LA CÔTE-DES-NEIGES

CH. DE LA CÔTE-SAINTE-CATHERINE

AV. VICTORIA

138

• 137

141
• 140
139

CÔTE-DES-NEIGES

AV. LACOMBE

AV. VAN HORNE

AV. COOLBROOK
AUTOROUTE DÉCARIE

CH. QUEEN-MARY

• 132

NOTRE-DAME-DE-GRÂCE

AV. GIROUARD

AV. SOMERLED

AV. DE MONKLAND

CH. DE LA CÔTE-SAINT-LUC

128
• 129
130
• 131

125

127 •

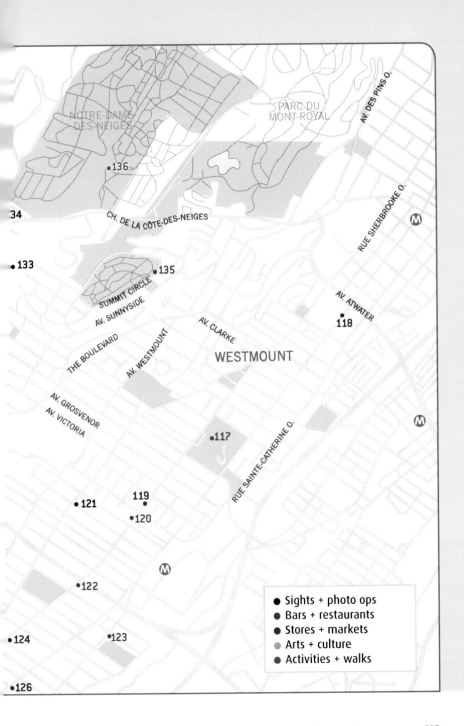

NOTRE-DAME-DES-NEIGES

PARC DU MONT-ROYAL

AV. DES PINS O.

•136

34

CH. DE LA CÔTE-DES-NEIGES

RUE SHERBROOKE O.

Ⓜ

•133

•135

SUMMIT CIRCLE
AV. SUNNYSIDE

AV. ATWATER

118

THE BOULEVARD

AV. WESTMOUNT

AV. CLARKE

WESTMOUNT

AV. GROSVENOR
AV. VICTORIA

•117

RUE SAINTE-CATHERINE O.

Ⓜ

•121

119
•
•120

Ⓜ

•122

•124

•123

● Sights + photo ops
● Bars + restaurants
● Stores + markets
● Arts + culture
● Activities + walks

•126

117A

English Charm

117

I was on the Boulevard de Maisonneuve bike path, when I first saw **Westmount Park** (A). When I passed Avenue Melville, I found myself in a scene worthy of *Dead Poets Society*. Lush green space, a bucolic lake, young people playing soccer and the neo-Gothic bell tower on the **Westmount Park United Church** [4695 Boulevard de Maisonneuve Ouest]—it was like a chunk of the English countryside in the heart of the city. At the north end of the park is **Westmount Public Library** [4574 Rue Sherbrooke Ouest]. Built in 1899, it was the first municipal library in Quebec.

A Japanese Pub that's a Guaranteed Party

118

The izakaya **Imadake** is perfect for a fun evening out with a group. It has a young crowd, a fantastic atmosphere and small dishes that make a big impression. On the menu: miso black cod, octopus balls, beef tataki (briefly seared), shrimp tempura and ramen, all very reasonably priced. This pub exudes good times, and every element adds to the festive vibe. Let your hair down and do a sake bomb (a sake shooter, balanced on chopsticks); your job is to pound on the table until the shooter falls into a glass of beer, then down the whole thing in one go [4006 Rue Sainte-Catherine].

Some cynics claim that "Montreal" is an Indigenous word meaning "city where you can never turn left." Fifteen minutes of driving in Montreal, and you might start to believe it.

119A

Decadent Salads

120

Mandy's, owned by sisters Rebecca and Mandy Wolfe, serves gourmet salads that are big and filling. Packed with fresh ingredients, bursting with flavor and popping with color, they make no pretense of being low in calories. And who cares? You can build your own salad if you like, but personally I prefer the ones prepared by Mandy, like the Wolfe Bowl, with lettuce, arugula, kale, brown rice, cherry tomatoes, walnuts, avocado, Parmesan, grated carrots, toasted sesame seeds and tamari vinaigrette. The decor, envisioned by Rebecca, is a brilliant blend of styles ranging from rustic to vintage to chic. Tasty and tasteful [5033 Rue Sherbrooke Ouest]. There are also two other locations: downtown at 2067 Rue Crescent and in Mile End at 201 Avenue Laurier Ouest.

Great Gifts

119

On Rue Sherbrooke Ouest you'll find two charming shops with a great selection of decorative items and original gifts. Candles, tableware, glasses, bags and wallets, frames, bedding, tons of cushions and even some cashmere clothing: You'll find them all at **Ben & Tournesol** (A) [4915 Rue Sherbrooke Ouest]. You'll be welcomed by the store's mascots, a friendly (and huge) Leonberger, and a tiny chihuahua. Bring your own dog, if you like—all are welcome. The word *quincaillerie* means "hardware store," but **Quincaillerie Hogg** [4855 Rue Sherbrooke Ouest] has more than just tools and building materials. With their great service and wide range of products, it's the go-to spot for everything around the home: kitchen items, decorations, gifts of all kinds, linens and even crackers and marmalade all the way from Great Britain.

120

121A

Melons and Houses from Another Era

121 At the turn of the 20th century, what is now the NDG neighborhood was known as the *verger de Montréal* (Montreal's orchard). At that time, the **Montreal melon**, a fruit with green flesh and a light nutmeg flavor, was a luxury item that was exported to the United States. The Décarie family was one of its biggest producers; they grew it on the land now occupied by a highway named after the family. Led by Mayor Jean Drapeau, Montreal started growing into a major international metropolis in the 1950s. As urbanization swallowed up the farms, the Montreal melon slipped into oblivion. Years later, a journalist became fascinated with the story and tracked down seeds of the famous melon in an Ohio seed bank (although there's no way to be sure of their authenticity). A few traces of the neighborhood's agricultural past can still be seen, particularly in country homes like the **Maison Descaris** (A) [5138 Chemin de la Côte-Saint-Antoine]. Nicknamed the *maison rose* ("pink house"), it was built in 1698, making it one of the oldest in the city. Another relic is the **Maison Joseph-Décary** [3761 Avenue de Vendôme], built in 1869; it once faced Chemin de la Côte-Saint-Antoine. You'll notice that the spelling of the family's name varies. That's because each of the three Décarie brothers opted for their own spelling to distinguish themselves from their siblings—mainly they wanted to avoid mixing up the mail.

It is completely acceptable, even recommended, to avoid food waste; ask for a doggy bag when your restaurant serving is bigger than your appetite. You can take the leftovers with you—for your dog or for yourself.

The Secret's in the Sauce

123 When you taste an Italian sub from **Momesso**, you'll understand why it's still consistently packed 40 years after it opened. The Italian sausage submarine alone is worth the trip (the meat comes from a local butcher). The grilled chicken sub definitely holds its own as well. It's the homemade hot sauce that really takes things over the top: It's absolutely delicious, adding a splash of pure magic to an already fantastic sandwich. You can buy containers of it to take home [5562 Chemin Upper Lachine].

A Classic of Quebecois Cuisine

122 The menu at **Chalet Bar-B-Q** has one thing only: chicken, thigh or breast, in salad form or as a hot sandwich. This rotisserie's longstanding secret (it opened 75 years ago) is its consistency: They stick with what they do best. Roasted slowly over maple charcoal in a brick oven, the chicken is tender and juicy, with crispy skin. Everything comes with tasty homemade fries, coleslaw and an addictive barbecue sauce. The best part: The decor hasn't changed since 1944 [5456 Rue Sherbrooke Ouest].

A Tiny Treasure

125

The tiny Japanese restaurant **Jardin Iwaki** is the hidden treasure of NDG. There's just one chef, one server and a dozen seats. They have a fixed seven-course menu (you don't get to pick the dishes), and the food is exceptionally high quality—and it's all very affordable. Little Japanese morsels, soba noodle salad, tuna tataki, miniature okonomiyaki (Japanese omelet), etc. The chef's delicate and balanced creations are enchanting, arriving one after another at a relaxing rhythm. It's perfect for a romantic dinner. Reservations required [5887 Rue Sherbrooke Ouest].

Hops and Hot Sauce

124

Any self-respecting bon vivant should make it a goal to visit **Épicerie 1668**. The shop has a fantastic selection of Quebec craft beers and a wall of hot sauces—an impressive selection from all over, ranging from mild to mega-hot. The deli counter makes decadent sandwiches, like the generously-topped roast beef and homemade smoked pork [5854 Rue Sherbrooke Ouest].

Beau Kavanagh:
From Blues Guitarist to Antiques Dealer

126

Beau Kavanagh professes to have always loved "old things." As the son of an antiques dealer and a member of a blues band, he traveled all across North America and Europe, picking up little treasures along the way: vintage clothing, collectible guitars and retro amplifiers. His passion for collecting soon extended to antique furniture and lamps, and his apartment was no longer big enough to store everything. It was then that he decided to open a shop.

Now in his thirties, **Beau** selects his treasures using intuition and taste—he chooses things that catch his eye. He refuses to box himself in, instead preferring a mix of styles, from antique to retro, to industrial. Whether it's an old poster, a neon clock, a metal lamp or a mid-century teak cabinet, anything that goes into his store must speak to him. And that perfectly describes **Encans Kavanagh** [6059 Boulevard de Maisonneuve Ouest], a collection of furniture, decorative objects, collectibles, unique clothes and all manner of things that **Beau** is passionate about. The merchandise is always changing, but it's always a reflection of his particular aesthetic. The store also hosts auctions once or twice a month, with Beau as the auctioneer. On these nights, they find takers for about 300 rare items, objects of very high quality or collectibles unearthed by Beau and his business partner, Angus Tasker.

The young antiques dealer, who was born and raised in Montreal, particularly appreciates the diversity of his city; he explains, "Immigration shaped the city, and brought with it treasures from all over the world. It's amazing what you can find in the apartments of immigrant families! Antique hunting is exciting in a city like Montreal."

127 | 129A

The Green Sheep

127

The cute takeout restaurant **Mouton Vert** serves vegetarian and vegan dishes that are freshly prepared and overflowing with local and organic produce. The friendly owner, Maggie Barakaris, originally from Greece, concocts falafel sandwiches, cabbage rolls, salads, pizzas and stuffed peppers—all healthy and delicious. On the sweet side, it's essential to try the baklava. The restaurant has a few tables, and the small terrace out front—with potted plants and herbs—is quite lovely in the summertime [6000 Rue Sherbrooke Ouest].

Wonderful Peppers

128

Serving Taiwan-inspired Szechuan cuisine, **Gia Ba** is the best Chinese restaurant in the neighborhood. Highlights include Yu Xiang eggplant, twice-cooked fish, Taiwanese steam pork burger, beef with Chinese broccoli and sweet and sour Chinese cabbage with Szechuan peppercorns. Everything is tasty, well seasoned and pleasantly spicy [5766 Avenue de Monkland].

The Search for Good Scones

129

It can be difficult to find a good scone. The little biscuits harden quickly and should be eaten fresh, the day they were made. There are two spots on Monkland that get them right. **Gryphon d'Or** (A) [5968 Avenue de Monkland] is a tearoom that serves scones during decadent brunches or tea service. They also serve delicious, comforting meals. The café **MELK** [5612 Avenue de Monkland] bakes muffins, cookies and other treats daily, as well as their reputable scones (apple, cranberry-chocolate, pecan-apricot and more). They're the perfect accompaniment for an excellent coffee, made with beans from the Vancouver roaster 49th Parallel.

128

130A

Mexico in the Spotlight

130

You could pass by it a dozen times without noticing it. Hidden away in a basement, the Mexican restaurant **Amaranto** (A) [5974 Avenue de Monkland] has an authentic family atmosphere. I recommend the *agua de Jamaica*, water with hibiscus flower—pleasantly sweet and acidic at the same time. Also try the avocado soup, an original creation with chicken stock, puréed avocado, lime, pomegranate seeds and fried tortilla strips. It's a strange combination, but a good one. The guacamole is perfect, as are the chorizo tacos. If you still have room, stop by **Che Churro** [6543 Avenue Somerled], a pastry shop that makes crunchy dulce de leche churros. The owners could not be friendlier.

Monkland, Italian Style

131

For foodies like myself, the two-in-one concept at the specialty boutique **Garde-Manger Italien** (A) and **Bistro Amerigo** [6127 Avenue de Monkland] is a godsend. On the deli side, there are plenty of carefully selected imported products like olive oil, balsamic vinegar, pesto, tomato sauce, panettone, etc. You may want to take the opportunity to buy some freshly cooked dishes and fresh products like Italian cheeses, cold cuts, meatballs and arancini. Perfect picnic fare. You can also sit on the bistro side and eat classic dishes, unpretentious and cooked to perfection. You will feel like you've been whisked away to Italy.

After, cross Avenue de Monkland to go to **Café de' Mercanti** [n° 6128], where locals get their daily dose of caffeine, Italian style. Sip your beverage (espresso, cappuccino, macchiato or Americano) at the bar, and indulge in a *dolci*: cannoli, biscotti, croissant or another pastry. In the summer, gelato or affogato (ice cream and espresso) is definitely worth considering.

131A 132

An Old-School Deli

132

With booths and pink walls, **Snowdon Deli** has a touch of retro, and it's the perfect setting to devour huge smoked meat sandwiches. For the ultimate experience, order the "old-fashioned" with homemade fries, dill pickle and (essential to make the perfect combination of the flavors, according to the owner) a cherry Coke. The smoked meat is so tender it literally melts in your mouth. Opened in 1946 by Abe and Joe Morantz, Snowdon Deli has remained a family affair; a third generation of Morantzes work there today. Some regulars have been coming to the deli for over 60 years. Loyalty like that is the best gauge of quality [5265 Boulevard Décarie].

The Highest Bell Tower

133

Each year, some two million people visit **Saint Joseph's Oratory** (A), the largest church in Canada. It is majestically set on the hillside of Mount Royal. The cross, located on top of the large dome, is the highest point in Montreal. The **stairs,** which lead from Chemin Queen Mary to the doors of the basilica, have two parallel flights of 283 concrete steps. They are separated by a central flight of 99 wooden steps, which are reserved for pilgrims who wish to climb them on their knees. Don't worry: A shuttle service is also available for visitors. The site is home to the magnificent **Garden of the Way of the Cross,** and the woods surrounding the oratory became a **nature reserve** in 2014. A visit is guaranteed to leave you feeling rejuvenated [3800 Chemin Queen Mary].

133

A Tribute Following a Tragedy

134

Nef pour Quatorze Reines (*Nave for Fourteen Queens*) is an artwork created in 1999 by Rose-Marie Goulet as a tribute to the victims of the École Polytechnique massacre that rocked Montreal on December 6, 1989. Set between two rows of trees, the memorial is made up of seven circular arcs symbolizing the waves of shock that resulted from the awful event. The names of the 14 women killed that night at Université de Montréal are inscribed in such a way that you have to stop in order to read them, creating a moment of remembrance. The powerful sculpture symbolizes the values of non-violence and respect. It's a moving and personal tribute to each of the women, ensuring that they will never be forgotten.

134

135 A

The Summit Forest

135

Summit Woods (A), a mature forest bordered by Summit Circle, is astonishingly unknown—perhaps because it's harder to get to than other parks in the city. Since there's no Metro station nearby and the steep ascent would make biking quite a challenge, you might consider going by car. The park is located at one of Mount Royal's three summits. There are 10 entry points along Summit Circle, but the **Westmount Lookout** [36 Summit Circle] is a good place to park. Then explore the many footpaths that wind through the native flora, including great towering oaks, accompanied by birdsongs. When you leave the woods, pass by the street **Surrey Gardens** and by **Summit Crescent**, until you reach a cul-de-sac; there you can get a close-up view of Saint Joseph's Oratory from the back.

136 A

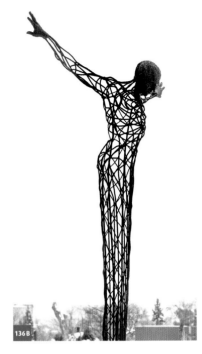

136B

A Taste of Thailand

137 With its flavors and aromas from Thailand and Cambodia, the food at **Tuk Tuk** (A) [5619A Chemin de la Côte-des-Neiges] is captivating. This friendly bring-your-own-wine restaurant stimulates all the senses, and it's easy on the wallet. Try the mango salad with chicken and shrimp, or the Larb Tuk Tuk, a salad with minced and seasoned beef or chicken, seasoned with lime juice and green onion, which you eat using lettuce leaves. For a main course, try the "Cha du Chef," a top-notch Cambodian stir-fry with beef, chicken and shrimp. The fish amok, with a rich lemongrass and coconut milk sauce, is a must. Save room for the Borbor Tnaot, a tapioca, coconut milk and palm fruit pudding.

Another affordable Thai spot is **Talay Thaï** (which translates as "the Thai River"). The shrimp Tom Yum soup, with lemongrass, lime and cilantro, is particularly tasty. Customers are addicted to the pad Thai (their most popular dish), and the Panang Nuer, slices of beef in red curry and coconut milk, topped with a savory peanut sauce [5697 Chemin de la Côte-des-Neiges].

Quiet and Contemplation

136 Built in 1854, the **Notre-Dame-des-Neiges Cemetery** (A) is the largest in Canada and the third largest in North America. The enchanting area, on one of the hillsides of Mount Royal, is the burial site for many famous Quebecers: Maurice Richard, Doug Harvey, Sir George-Étienne Cartier, Robert Bourassa, Jean Drapeau, Nick Auf der Maur, and Calixa Lavallée, composer of "O Canada." Stroll through the grounds and you'll see hundred-year-old trees adorning winding paths, and some incredible funeral artworks, like the sculpture *Le Saut de l'Ange* (B) by Édith Croft. At the north end of the cemetery, a small entrance leads to the **Chemin de Ceinture**, a pedestrian path built recently, and a **stone promontory** overlooking Université de Montréal and offering an impressive view of North Montreal and the surrounding region [4601 Chemin de la Côte-des-Neiges].

137A

Metro Geometry

139

Created by Pierre Granche, **Système** is a huge geometric sculpture that hangs in Namur Metro station. Stretching in every direction, it's so vast it fills the mezzanine, and even supports the station's lighting system. You can't miss the piece, which is made up of 28 aluminum modular units, each made up of 12 hexagons and six squares. With its futuristic look and its original 3-D composition, it's one of the city's most compelling subjects to photograph. Observant visitors will notice that the geometric form also appears on the floor pattern.

Finding the Best Pho

138

The Côte-des-Neiges neighborhood lays claim to the best pho (*soupes tonkinoises*) in the city. There are two things that make a good pho (pronounced "fuh"): the beef broth (delicious, not fatty, with subtle and balanced flavors of star anise, cinnamon, clove and cardamom), and the freshness of the ingredients. For a big hearty soup that's amazingly flavorful, I recommend **Phở Lien** (A) [5703 Chemin de la Côte-des-Neiges], **Nguyen Phi** [6260 Chemin de la Côte-des-Neiges] and **Sen Vàng** [5690 Avenue Victoria].

Orange Kitsch

140

A kitsch icon representing Montreal of yesteryear, the orange sphere at **Gibeau Orange Julep** is 40 feet (12 meters) in diameter—the equivalent of a three-story building. Hermas Gibeau founded the restaurant in 1932 (although the sphere dates from 1966), to sell his famous "orange juice," made with fresh oranges and milk. In fact, the recipe was created as a way to make juice using fewer oranges. You really go to Orange Julep for the strange architecture more than for the fast food served there. Note that there's nowhere to eat inside; they serve takeout, although you can enjoy your hot dog, poutine and juice at one of the many picnic tables if the weather's nice [7700 Boulevard Décarie].

Jane Heller:
A Montreal Poet

141

Take a look at the Orange Julep through the eyes of Montreal photographer Jane Heller (1964-2014). Imbued with nostalgia and instantly memorable, it's part of **Monumentalove**, a series of 12 photos that pay homage to the most celebrated architectural landmarks in the city: the Farine Five Roses sign, Habitat 67, the Jacques Cartier Bridge and so on. With original composition, tight framing and unique processing, these photos magnify the monuments that Montrealers no longer notice and highlight details that escape attention. They also reveal the photographer's love for the city and show the essence of Montreal identity.

When I found out I would be writing this book, I immediately wanted to do a portrait of Jane Heller, because of the impact her series had on my perception of Montreal. When I tried to find out how to contact her, I learned that she had died from breast cancer. A single mother of a 10-year-old girl, Heller had the gift of seeing beauty in everything around us, and the ability to immortalize passing moments, to capture shadow and light, humor and sadness.

As relevant and inspiring now as it ever was, her work transcends her life. That's why her family and friends took over her online shop, with the proceeds being put in a trust for her daughter, Beatrice. You can find decorative items, prints and postcards from the collection—timeless and artistic souvenirs of Montreal that are light years beyond the trinkets found in your average gift shop [monumentalove.com].

139

Outremont, Mile End, Plateau-Mont-Royal

At just 1 ½ square miles (3.9 square kilometers), residential Outremont is Montreal's smallest neighborhood. Plateau-Mont-Royal (the Plateau)—which includes the Mile End neighborhood—extends from the foot of Mount Royal's east side. It has the highest population density in Montreal, with 32,000 inhabitants per square mile (12,350 per square kilometer). One of Quebec's main cultural and artistic centers with tons of theaters, art galleries and music venues, the Plateau may lay claim to the greatest concentration of artists in Canada. For the full experience, explore the streets on foot.

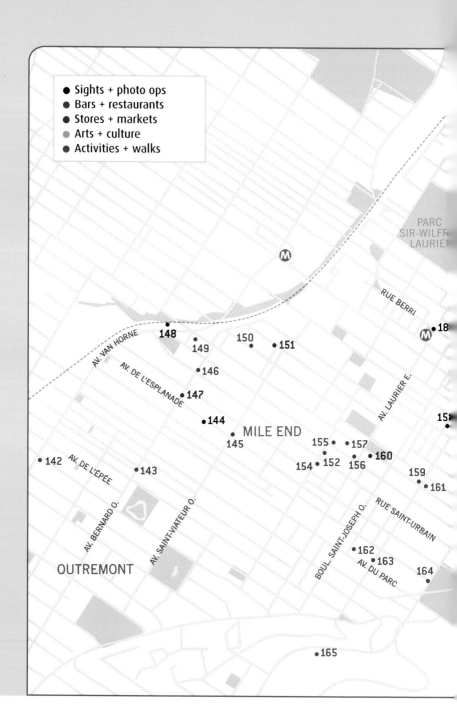

- Sights + photo ops
- Bars + restaurants
- Stores + markets
- Arts + culture
- Activities + walks

PARC
SIR-WILFF
LAURIEI

RUE BERRI

AV. VAN HORNE

148

149

150

•151

146

AV. DE L'ESPLANADE

•147

•144

MILE END

145

AV. LAURIER E.

15

155• •157

•160

142 AV. DE L'ÉPÉE

•143

154• 152 156

159

•161

AV. BERNARD O.

AV. SAINT-VIATEUR O.

OUTREMONT

BOUL. SAINT-JOSEPH O.

RUE SAINT-URBAIN

•162

•163

AV. DU PARC

164

•165

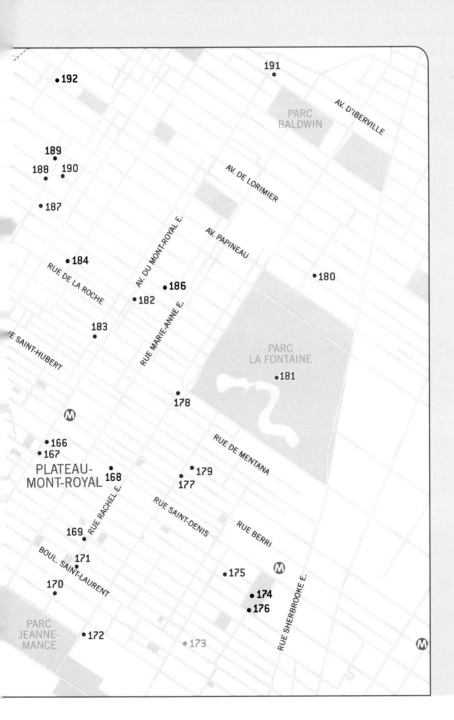

192

191

PARC
BALDWIN

AV. D'IBERVILLE

189
188   190

AV. DE LORIMIER

187

AV. DU MONT-ROYAL E.

184

AV. PAPINEAU

RUE DE LA ROCHE

186

180

182

RUE MARIE-ANNE E.

183

PARC
LA FONTAINE

RUE SAINT-HUBERT

181

178

RUE DE MENTANA

166
167

PLATEAU-
MONT-ROYAL   168

179

177

RUE RACHEL E.

RUE SAINT-DENIS

RUE BERRI

169

BOUL. SAINT-LAURENT

171

170

175

174

176

RUE SHERBROOKE E.

PARC
JEANNE-
MANCE

172

173

148 B

A Treasure on Van Horne

142

Red ceilings, Middle-Eastern patterns on the floor, hanging lanterns; when you enter **Damas**, you'll feel like you've voyaged across the ocean. The flavors that await you only confirm it. In fact, this could be one of the best restaurants in Montreal. The flavors of Syria are rich and enticing: sumac, pomegranate, pine nuts, lamb, yogurt, tahini and mint. The fattoush salad is tangy, sprinkled with pomegranate seeds and pita chips; the tasty Kabab bil Karaz is a lamb kabab with morello cherries; Maqlouba is a dish with saffron rice, eggplant and beef short ribs or lamb shoulder. Everything verges on perfection, and the meals are plentiful. Reservations recommended [1201 Avenue Van Horne].

The Top Smoked Meat

143

The competition for the title "best smoked meat in Montreal" is intense, and emotions run high. While all the delis use essentially the same preparation (brining and smoking), each place has its own spice recipe. And each Montrealer has his or her personal favorite, which they'll defend tooth and nail. I lean toward **Lester's Deli** for the flawless quality of its meat, but also for its homemade mustard, brown booths and friendly service—and because there's no lineup. The walls are lined with memorabilia, and the decor hasn't changed since 1951. Why mess with a winning recipe? In the summer you can enjoy your sandwich (I recommend "medium fat") out front; wash it down with a beer, served in a frosted glass [1057 Avenue Bernard].

Patsy Van Roost:
A Fairy's Magical Touch

144

It all began in 2012 during the holiday season. **Patsy Van Roost** wondered if it were still possible to bring magic to Christmas—a holiday she never liked. She had been living in Mile End for 23 years and, although she loved her neighborhood, she didn't know her neighbors and passed many of the same people each day without ever really talking to them. With no money to spend, the multidisciplinary artist had no choice but to come up with a project that would cost next to nothing, so she turned to what she already had: paper, envelopes and a sewing machine. She prefers thread to glue because, she explained, "Thread ties together, connects, unites, joins and repairs. This is my whole approach." And so she launched her project, *The Little Match Girl on Waverly*, which consisted of randomly delivering segments of the famous tale, one page at a time, to 25 different mailboxes, accompanied by a letter asking residents to hang them outside their house so that passersby could discover the touching story in the days leading up to Christmas. The residents of Rue Waverly were surprisingly enthusiastic, and one day, Patsy Van Roost ended up on the front page of the newspaper *Le Devoir*. It was here that she was first nicknamed the "Fairy of Mile End."

The artist decided to carry on in this way, to sow more magic as soon as she could. She targeted "commercial" holidays—the ones for which we buy a lot of things but no longer celebrate anything. On Valentine's Day, she asked 1,400 residents to share their "recipes" for cultivating love in the home, and she

144A

Vous êtes là où tout est encore possible.

received hundreds of responses! She then sewed 150 cloth pouches, which contained several copies of a recipe from each house printed on cardstock. She hung one pouch in front of each home that contributed. People passing by would read the words "*L'amour fleurit ici*" (Love flourishes here), and could then slip their hand in and draw out a recipe for love. And so, that Valentine's Day, the Fairy of Mile End created a cartography of love in her beloved neighborhood.

Then came Mother's Day, Father's Day, Remembrance Day... Patsy has been working exclusively as a "fairy" for five years now. Her projects might seem trivial at first glance, but they have actually changed the social fabric of the neighborhood in a major way, and have created a real sense of community. Over the past few years, she has spoken at conferences, conducted workshops in schools, and even taught in university. The house fairy naturally blossomed into an urban fairy, and is now spreading her magic well beyond Mile End.

I asked her what Montreal means to her. "For me, Montreal has been Mile End for 27 years," she replied. "It was here that I was born for the second time in my life. It was here that I became a woman, a mother and a fairy. Mile End is like a small village where you always see the same people, where you forge connections over the years, and watch children grow up. Mile End is a café like **Club Social** [180 Rue Saint-Viateur Ouest], where you meet your neighbors—the ones you know and the ones you'll get to know soon, it's **Café Olimpico** [124 Rue Saint-Viateur Ouest], where you collaborate on projects, and **Le Dépanneur Café** [206 Rue Bernard Ouest], where you go to cheer up on a rainy day. Mile End is also the **Jardin du Crépuscule** (Twilight Garden) by Glen LeMesurier [east of 101 Avenue Van Horne], and his sculptures that emerge here and there in front of the houses. It's also the most wonderful bookstore, **Drawn & Quarterly** [211 Rue Bernard Ouest], where I go when I feel lost, and the **Champ des Possibles** (A) (Field of Dreams), a park near the train tracks [Avenue Henri-Julien, near Rue du Laos]."

145A 146

Much More than a Club

145 There are two Mile End cafés that have earned the deepest love from locals. They say you have to choose: **Club Social** (A) or **Café Olimpico**. But why the competition? Maybe because these two Italian cafés are just a few meters from each other. Without taking anything away from Olimpico, I lean toward Club Social—I love being in the space. I'm also fond of the huge tree overhanging the terrace. It's a place where neighbors chat, and three generations and countless nationalities mix together, like some sociological experiment. Italian, French and English is exchanged with the utmost respect. Lattes are served in a glass, and cost three times less than they do in hip cafés. The name comes from the fact that it's actually a club: To drink alcohol there, you have to sign up for an annual membership. Anyone can enjoy coffee or food, however—no membership is required [180 Rue Saint-Viateur Ouest].

Divine Curry

146 I constantly feel the urge to return to **Thaïlande**, a restaurant in the heart of Mile End that's been open for ages. It has courteous service and dishes that are super flavorful, and the prices are modest. I always get the fresh and spicy mango salad, a pure delight for the taste buds; and the Kaeng Choochee, an excellent curry (chicken, shrimp, fish or tofu) with coconut milk and kaffir lime leaves, topped with fried basil leaves. Be sure to order the sticky rice, which is soaked for hours and steam-cooked in a conical bamboo basket. Use your fingers to make little balls, which you dip in choochee sauce—amazing [88 Rue Bernard Ouest].

Tamey Lau:
The Mile End Florist

147

Dragon Flowers is a florist unlike any other—and it is the extreme generosity and kindness of the owner that sets it apart. "Hello'morning," she says softly, as she greets people passing by her shop. She seems to have boundless energy, raising 14 children on her own, working all the while creating magnificent bouquets for all occasions, and always with a smile on her face.

For 25 years **Tamey Lau** has adorned her storefront, and the area around it, with hundreds of flowers and dozens of white birdcages. She also brings a lot of joy to her customers. "What are the flowers for?" She asks from time to time. "For your mother? I'll add a few more," and so she does, free of charge, as you might have guessed. The kind gestures, the gifts of flowers, the candy she sometimes hands out to children (with parents none the wiser), have all made her a beloved figure in her community.

One unfortunate evening in April 2013, a fire seriously damaged her shop. It was devastating for Tamey, the woman with a heart of gold. The Mile End community was saddened by the news, and an outpouring of empathy and support followed. Neighbors and clients quickly organized a fundraiser to show their love and to help her get back on her feet. In one day, they raised more than $15,000! And, to everyone's delight, the store reopened nine months later.

Since then, Tamey, one of the neighborhood's most endearing personalities, continues what she does best: working tirelessly to feed her "little monsters" while brightening up Mile End [159 Rue Bernard Ouest]

An Industrial Silhouette

148

An iconic symbol of Mile End's industrial past, the **St. Lawrence Warehousing Co. building** (A) [1 Avenue Van Horne], also known as the *Entrepôt Van Horne* (Van Horne warehouse), has an impressive huge metal water tower on its roof. Built in 1924, the seven-story, 172,000-square-foot (16,000-square-meter) building is still in use today. With its dramatic silhouette, unusual shape and imposing proportions, it's definitely one of the city's distinctive architectural landmarks. To take a great photo, walk to the top of the Rosemont-Van Horne overpass, which you can access via Rue Clark or the steps on Boulevard Saint-Laurent.

Underneath the overpass, at the intersection of Rue Clark and Rue de l'Arcade (east of **Parc Lhasa-De Sela**) is what some call **"no-name park."** (B) Built in 2016, it's a great example of a vacant lot being redeveloped and put to good use. The soil has been decontaminated and the asphalt replaced with grass. The pillars of the overpass have been turned into colorful murals, and park equipment has been added. The city did a thorough job turning a barren space into a vibrant area for residents to play and relax.

My Little Buttercup

149

At the border of Mile End and Rosemont is **Le Butterblume**, a charming café, restaurant and shop that has blossomed like a bright flower on this strip of Boulevard Saint-Laurent. The name is the German word for buttercup (the flower). With white walls and soft decor, the spot receives lovely natural light thanks to a large garage door, which stays open in the summer. The kitchen prepares snacks and light meals that are thoughtfully presented and full of flavor: bread, yogurt and homemade granola, toast and soup. On Friday, Saturday and Sunday, the team offers a creative brunch menu—it's one of the tastiest around. Stop by for a coffee, a snack, brunch or a drink (they have a nice wine selection) or even to buy fresh flowers [5836 Boulevard Saint-Laurent].

Rock and Roller Derby

150

There's no lack of action at the **Montréal Roller Derby** and **Montréal Roller Derby Masculin** (the female and male leagues, respectively) matches, which take place in Mile End at the Saint-Louis Arena [5633 Rue Saint-Dominique]. The contact sport takes place on an ovular track; players zoom around on roller skates with a simple objective: The "jammer" has to get past the opponent's "blockers" to score points, without falling or leaving the track. Fairly technical and physically demanding, roller derby is a combination of sport and spectacle. The atmosphere during a 60-minute match is loud and wild, but there's a family-friendly vibe. Beer and music add color to the affair. The first matches of the year are held in February and March, at Taz (see Reason #284). The regular season starts at the end of April and continues to August. You can buy tickets at the ticket counter the same day. Visit the website to see the schedule for the season [mtlrollerderby.com and mrdmontreal.com].

Jeans for Everyone

151

To find that pair of jeans you've been looking for forever, go directly to **Jeans Jeans Jeans** (A) [5575 Avenue Casgrain]. The store is located in a half-basement of an utterly nondescript building in the heart of what used to be the textile manufacturing district. There you'll be able to peruse a selection that appears to include every jeans brand on the market, including some of the world's best. One of the employees will help you to find the pair that's right for you—and it's an experience like no other. When you go into the change room, their expert salespeople will bring you dozens of pairs to try on. And they'll even hem your jeans for free while you pay at the cash. It's pretty much impossible to leave the store without a pair that fits you perfectly.

For a little pick-me-up after your shopping is done, try **Café Le Falco** [5605 Avenue de Gaspé]. The interior design is gorgeous, and the natural light is beautiful. They make siphon coffee, a method that's pretty impressive to witness; it produces a light-tasting, clear coffee with no residue. They also serve light Japanese dishes.

150

Bagels by the Dozen

152

There's no way anyone could write an entire book about Montreal without mentioning bagels. Hand-rolled and boiled in honey-sweetened water, they're quite distinct from New York bagels, which are larger, less sweet and less dense. After being boiled, they're coated with sesame seeds, and then transferred with a shiba (a 10-foot/three-meter maple plank) to a wood-burning oven to bake. The most popular spots are just 2,300 feet (700 meters) from each other: **Fairmount Bagel** [74 Avenue Fairmount Ouest], the first bagel shop to open in Montreal, in 1919, and **St-Viateur Bagel** (A) [263 Rue Saint-Viateur Ouest], founded in 1957. The difference? St-Viateur's bagels seem softer and slightly less sweet than those at Fairmount. But in truth, there is not a loser: They're both great. Make sure to visit them and try for yourself. I've never been able to make it home with a complete dozen—the aroma of warm bagels is absolutely irresistible. My family jokes that they must come in bags of eleven. Both shops are open 24 hours a day, seven days a week; cash only.

The Four Seasons

153

Aside from Moscow, no other metropolis in the world can claim to experience all **four seasons** so distinctly and spectacularly. The mercury sometimes tops 86°F (30°C) in the summer and can drop below -22°F (-30°C) in the winter. Through July heat waves and frigid Januaries, Montrealers live according to the rhythm of the weather, adapting as necessary. The cycle of the seasons is invigorating; it means constantly shifting one's leisure and activities. There's no denying that serious cold stretches can be tough and dreary. But anyone will tell you that they make the first days of spring that much better. If you visit Montreal in April or May, you may be lucky enough to experience the first day when spring really sets in. The warmth rouses Montrealers from their state of hibernation. The streets come alive, the terraces are packed and you'll see smiles everywhere—it's one of the most joyful days of the year.

152A

153

Micromanufacturing Tomato Sauce

154

Franco Gattuso decided to set up his little tomato sauce production, **Drogheria Fine** (A) [68 Avenue Fairmount Ouest], in a tight 300-square-foot (28-square-meter) space. To do so, he divided the room in two. The kitchen in the back is where *salsa della nonna* is prepared, and it's sold in the shop in front. Using his mother's recipe, Gattuso makes 75 gallons (300 liters) of tomato sauce each day. The Calabrese-style sauce is simple: tomatoes, basil, olive oil and sea salt—and it's perfect. In the summer, he opens the window on the street so passersby can buy gnocchi with tomato sauce for $5, which comes in a little Chinese-food-style takeout box.

Once you've devoured your gnocchi, why not get ice cream next door? Artisanal ice cream shop **Kem CoBa** (B) [60 Avenue Fairmount Ouest] made its reputation with twists of two kinds of soft ice cream. The flavors are astonishing: blueberry and honey; Madagascar vanilla and passion fruit; dulce de leche and mango; cherry and almond milk. The hard ice creams and sorbets are also delicious, such as the popular salted butter and the refreshing lime-mint sorbet. Open April to October.

One-way streets can make driving in Montreal a real headache. A good example is Rue Clark, which changes direction five times!

The Time-Traveled Sandwich

155

Opened in 1932, **Wilensky** is a family-run Jewish deli that takes its traditions quite seriously. The Wilensky's Special, a grilled sandwich, is just salami and bologna (it was invented during the Great Depression). Mustard is compulsory and the sandwich can never be cut in two—no matter how much you plead with the staff. A handmade sign makes it clear: "When ordering a Special, you should know a thing or two. It is always served with mustard; it is never cut in two." Another sign displays the changes in price over the years of the sandwich that made the restaurant famous: from $0.12 in 1932 to $4.09 (as I write these lines). Nothing else has changed in the restaurant since 1952. You won't find any brand name soft drinks: They make them like they used to, with syrup and carbonated water. Be sure to try the most popular flavor, cherry cola [34 Avenue Fairmount Ouest].

Heavenly Brew

156

Dieu du Ciel! microbrewery, which opened in 1998, was pretty much an instant success—it took off so quickly, in fact, that the little brewpub couldn't keep up with demand. Thus a manufacturing facility was created in Saint-Jérôme in 2007, increasing production capacity from 21,000 gallons to 345,000 gallons (80,000-1,300,000 liters). Dieu du Ciel's popularity should have come as a surprise to no one, given the quality of their bold beers, like Aphrodisiaque (a chocolate and vanilla stout) and Péché Mortel (a coffee stout), both ranked among the world's best beers by the famous website RateBeer.com in 2016. Despite the buzz, the pub has kept its relaxed atmosphere, and offers a great variety of beers brewed on-site, as well as light meals. The beer selection changes daily based on what's in stock. It's an essential stop for craft beer lovers [29 Avenue Laurier Ouest].

157A 159A

A Bread Bonanza

157

What I love most about **Boulangerie Guillaume** (A) [5134 Boulevard Saint-Laurent] is the variety of breads they offer. More than 80 products are made each day, often with ingredients rarely used in bakeries. I'll go to great lengths to get my hands on the potato cheddar bread (yes, you read correctly)—it's so soft it seems to have floated down from the heavens—and the little breads with blue cheese (if you know people who claim not to like blue cheese, offer them one and see whether they change their mind). There's also fig-hazelnut, white chocolate-mushroom, tamari sunflower seed—the selection is mind-blowing.

A few blocks down from there is the bakery **Hof Kelsten** [4524 Boulevard Saint-Laurent]. Jeffrey Finkelstein has had an amazing career: Per Se in New York, Toqué! in Montreal, El Bulli in Spain, and even Noma in Denmark, which won world's best restaurant title several times. Returning to Quebec after his years of training, Finkelstein hunkered down in his mother's kitchen, developed the ultimate baguette recipe and started distributing his bread in a few restaurants. He quickly became the baker for the top establishments in town, before he even had his own bakery. He finally decided to open a shop in 2013, and Hof Kelsten was born. Try the croissants, and sourdough, sunflower seed and caraway rye bread and traditional Jewish dishes, and the panettones during the holidays.

A Flowery Oasis

158

You'd think you were on a country lane, but it's very much a street; it has an official name and houses with proper addresses, including a magnificent ancestral home that's still inhabited today. The stretch of **Rue Demers** between Avenue Henri-Julien and Avenue l'Hôtel-de-Ville, north of Rue Villeneuve Est, isn't accessible by car. With its lovely layout and lush vegetation, it's one of the most charming streets in Montreal.

158

160 A · 160 B

Eat at the Counter

159

It's all about quality at **Comptoir Charcuteries et Vins** (A) [4807 Boulevard Saint-Laurent]. Share the house specialty, a small or large charcuterie platter, which features some of the chef's perfectly executed creations: dry sausage with fennel, pancetta, terrine, guanciale or the incredible duck prosciutto. The service is friendly, and all the dishes hit the mark: The food is seasonal cuisine and given the quality, the prices are very reasonable. The wine list would make Bacchus himself swoon. The Saturday or Sunday brunch (from 10 a.m. to 2 p.m.) is definitely worth trying as well [4807 Boulevard Saint-Laurent].

Another sure bet in the neighborhood is **La Salle à Manger**. Sit at the counter in this restaurant to enjoy whatever's being created with the ingredients on hand, or the classic dishes that customers love: carpaccio, veal tartare and squash soup (one of the best I've tried). I've been to Salle à Manger many times, and I've always had a wonderful evening, which is only heightened by some excellent wines [1302 Avenue du Mont-Royal Est].

Beautiful Objects on Saint-Laurent

160

There are a number of fantastic deco boutiques on Boulevard Saint-Laurent between Boulevard Saint-Joseph and Rue Bernard. Start your shopping journey at **VdeV** [5042 Boulevard Saint-Laurent], which has a superb selection of vintage and industrial furniture and accessories. Just north of it is **Jamais Assez** (A) [no. 5155], a shop devoted to the best in Quebec and international design for furniture and home decorations. Continue on to **Vestibule** (B) [no. 5157], a top destination for the art of living, with a vast selection of home accessories, dishes, clothing and sleek, timeless jewelry. A visit to **Piorra Maison** [no. 5377], a boutique and creative studio, is mandatory. It has everything for the home, in shabby chic style (decorative items, kitchenware, bedding, clothes) and several workshops for refurbishing furniture. Finish the day off at **Style Labo** [no. 5595], a laboratory for trends in vintage and industrial decoration.

When tipping at a restaurant or bar, the standard is to leave 15 percent of the total before taxes. To make your calculation easier, note that the two taxes that appear on your bill (QST and GST) have a combined rate of 15 percent. Add these two amounts to figure out the tip.

A Beverage at Buvette

162 A buvette is a wine bar that's a little more relaxed. That's what you get at **Buvette Chez Simone**, which opened in 2008. It's as contemporary as you can get, yet unpretentious—a feel-good type of place. With communal tables, lamps and a large bar, the design—by Zébulon Perron (see Reason #59)—was meant to bring people together for interesting conversations over a drink and a bite to eat—and maybe another drink or two. It's always full, yet never crowded, and offers a wonderful selection of affordable wines and a menu of small dishes that are well executed and uncomplicated [4869 Avenue du Parc].

The Restaurant with a Heart

161 **Robin des Bois** (French for "Robin Hood") is a unique restaurant that began donating all its profits to charitable organizations to fight social isolation and poverty 11 years ago. You can support them in their mission simply by sitting down and buying a meal; or you can donate your time and volunteer, assisting the permanent team by preparing meals or serving tables. To do so, create a profile online, then book your work shifts directly on the site. No previous experience is necessary; all you need is a desire to contribute. The chef has the crucial role of ensuring that the dishes are consistently excellent—and they are. Give Robin des Bois a try; it's great food for a good cause [4653 Boulevard Saint-Laurent].

Cakes like Grandma's

163

I love **Cocoa Locale** (A) [4807 Avenue du Parc], a charming little cake shop. Forget about industrially-manufactured cakes stuffed with additives, preservatives and too much sugar. Reema Singh, the young owner, makes cakes that taste just like those that grandma used to make, but with a modern take on flavors: chocolate and lavender, lemon and coconut, chai-chocolate, red velvet with beet juice, lemon and olive oil. Running the kitchen single-handedly, Singh can make up to 50 on the busiest days—and her business is sold out daily. To guarantee you get the cake you want, it's best to reserve it the night before or in the morning.

Cross the street to try some perfectly flaky savory Australian pies at **Ta Pies** [4520 Avenue du Parc]. Combining a takeout counter, a store and a small restaurant, the menu focuses on Australian and New Zealand comfort food, with a variety of pies (meat or vegetarian), sausage rolls and desserts you won't see often on this side of the planet.

In Memory of Mr. Hà

164

Hà is a restaurant that pays tribute to chef Hong Hà Nguyen (now deceased), who occupied the place with his own restaurant for more than 20 years. It's a vibrant spot, a treat for the eyes and the taste buds alike, with a menu of Vietnamese food with Thai, Malaysian and Laotian influences. The modern decor is a winner (check out the amazing lamps), as are the highly original dishes for sharing: chicken wings coated with soy sauce and lemongrass, and spiced and bursting with flavor; imperial rolls wrapped in lettuce leaves and mint; steam buns with braised pork (or crispy shrimp) with cuttlefish ink. Bloody Caesars are made with sake instead of vodka. The terrace, facing Parc Jeanne-Mance, is fabulous on a warm summer day [243 Avenue du Mont-Royal Ouest].

THE Reason to Love Montreal

165

Montrealers might not accept it, but their beloved "mountain" is in fact just a hill, one of the 10 Monteregian Hills in the south of the province. It has three peaks: Mount Royal Summit (764 feet/233 meters), Outremont Summit (692 feet/211 meters) and Westmount Summit (659 feet/201 meters). Deeply moved when he observed the immensity of the landscape in 1535, Jacques Cartier named the "mountain" as a tribute to Francis I, the king of France. **Mount Royal Park** (*Parc du Mont-Royal*) was created in 1876. It was designed by Frederick Law Olmsted, the American landscape architect responsible for designing New York City's Central Park. The **massive cross** (A) at the top is one of the most prominent symbols of Montreal. It's similar to the wooden cross that was erected by Paul de Chomedey de Maisonneuve in 1643 to thank God for sparing the city from a flood that would have devastated the colony in Montreal's early years. The cross that stands there today was installed in 1924. Mount Royal is where people go to walk, run or ride bikes,

165 A

to bask in the sun at **Beaver Lake** (*Lac aux Castors*) (B), or to enjoy the **Tam-Tams** (photo page 128) on Sundays in the summer, when thousands of hand-drum players, dancers, vendors and visitors gather around the George-Étienne Cartier Monument. In the winter, Mount Royal offers skating, hiking, snowshoeing, cross-country skiing and tobogganing. In the spring, mushroom pickers gather morels.

165 B

166A 167

Drinks Under the Ostriches

166

Named after a small bar in the Czech Republic, **Bily Kun** (A) [354 Avenue du Mont-Royal Est] is a chic tavern that opened in 1998. The decor is a stylish blend, recalling a French tavern (high ceilings, mosaic floor), but throwing in some taxidermy to surprise you. The stuffed ostrich heads that adorn the walls may be shocking upon your first visit, but you'll love them in no time. Enjoy a Czech beer or a shot of Becherovka, the herbal liqueur that's emblematic of the Czech Republic. The spirit is said to help digestion and calm the nerves.

Plan B [327 Avenue du Mont-Royal Est], a block away, is another great option. The beer, cocktail and spirits menu is varied enough to please everyone; the prices are reasonable and the staff is friendly. The real highlight, however, is the back terrace: Intimate and warm, it opens early in spring and closes late in the fall.

Rouge Gorge [1234 Avenue du Mont-Royal Est], the first wine bar to open on Avenue du Mont-Royal, wins customers over with its great decor and impressive menu. Serving mainly French wines, they also have some choice bottles from Europe and North America. There are plenty of new discoveries to be made, some of which are very affordable.

Buttery Brittany Delights

167

A kouign-amann is a pastry from Brittany that's insanely addictive: a decadent concoction of pastry dough, sugar and a staggering amount of salted butter. When baked, it has an utterly compelling salted caramel flavor. **Kouign Amann**, a pastry shop located in the Plateau, takes its name from the tender, flaky delicacy that is their specialty. They also make a very respectable croissant and tarte tatin [322 Avenue du Mont-Royal Est].

167

The Apotheosis of Chicken

169

The Portuguese Rotisserie **Romados** (A) [115 Rue Rachel Est] serves nothing short of the perfect chicken. Just look at the lineup that forms every evening—it's pretty clear there's a consensus. Perfectly grilled over charcoal, Romados' chicken is tender and juicy, with a peppery, smoky flavor. What really takes it over the top is the spicy homemade sauce (the recipe is a well-kept secret). The generous combo meals (quarter chicken, fries, salad) are unbeatable for quality and value. There are a few tables with stools, but it's better to take your food to go. Hot tip: Call ahead to place your order or for a delivery. For dessert, have a *pastéis de nata*, a Portuguese custard tart. You'll find what may be the best in town nearby at **Pâtisserie du Rosaire** [227 Rue Rachel Est].

Mushroom Obsession

168

A shop devoted solely to mushrooms: that was the dream of Pierre Noël. With **Mycoboutique**, he made this dream a reality. Noël is a seasoned and devoted mycologist, and his enthusiasm for fungus sometimes borders on obsession. He's great at helping amateurs delve into this fascinating universe. His store is an excellent source of dried and fresh mushrooms (morels, chanterelles, porcinis, milk caps, etc.), and it also offers courses and outings so people can learn more about the subject. They have dishes cooked on-site that showcase the gastronomic virtues of the food: velvety wild mushrooms, fougasse (French flat bread) with black trumpet mushrooms and the surprising porcini shortbreads. Magical! [4324 Rue Saint-Denis]

Irresistible Octopus Balls

170

You won't be able to resist falling in love with **Noren**, a Japanese micro-restaurant run by Élyse Garand and Hidenori Tsuda, a couple who spent seven years in Japan before returning to Quebec. It's "micro" because there are only 10 seats, and the menu has just three dishes: takoyaki (octopus balls), okonomiyaki (cabbage omelet with pork) and a weekly special. The food is as amazing as the options are limited. The takoyaki is made to order in molds heated on a plate, rotated with rods so they form little balls as they cook. They're served piping hot, with a texture that seems almost half-cooked. Dried fish flakes are sprinkled on top. They twist and dance from the heat—it's a strange living sculpture on your plate. I've never eaten anything like it. The specials of the week are always fabulous. Noren offers so much pleasure for such a low price. Note: Their schedule is a little unusual, and they don't take reservations [77 Rue Rachel Ouest].

A Candlelit Bar

171

A small Japanese figure adorns the door of this bar on Boulevard Saint-Laurent—that's it. No sign, not even an address. The mystery continues as you cross the threshold: a narrow hallway with a heavy curtain. I love the enigmatic aspect of **Bar Big In Japan**, which specializes in Japanese whiskeys: It feels like you're in a private bar or a speakeasy. The ambiance inside is intimate and subdued, with candles providing the only light. I prefer going soon after it opens or on weeknights, when it's less crowded, to really enjoy the hushed, romantic atmosphere [4175 Boulevard Saint-Laurent].

172

173B

173A

Mural Masterpieces

173 For several years different festivals and organizations have been working to transform Montreal into a sort of open-air museum. There are masterpieces to be seen on the walls of buildings throughout the city: sometimes abstract, often colorful and always vibrant and powerful. Regardless of whether they appeal to your personal taste, there's no denying that the murals bring a creative energy to the city, adding art to the urban landscape and promoting economic and social development. Art is taking over public space in Montreal, and the people love it.

In the space of just a few years, the **Mural Festival** (A) has become the biggest urban art event in North America. In June, Boulevard Saint-Laurent between Rue Sherbrooke and Avenue du Mont-Royal is literally transformed thanks to the talents of dozens of local and international artists. Since the festival began in 2013, it has helped create dozens of murals in the neighborhood; you can check them out as you walk around. They include *Barré* by Spanish artist Escif [3495 Rue Saint-Dominique, north wall]; *Mamie Chic* by Montreal collective A'Shop [corner of Boulevard Saint-Laurent and Avenue des Pins] and *Murale Pop Art* (B) by British artist D*face [3550 Rue Saint-Dominique, south wall].

Germaine is a mural on the south wall at 4625 Rue Saint-Dominique, by Montreal artist Rafael Sottolichio. Paying tribute to the work of playwright Michel Tremblay, it's part of the series *Hommage aux Bâtisseurs Culturels Montréalais* (Hommage to Montreal's Cultural Creators), created by MU—the arts organization—in 2010. Some of the characters are based on the writer's characters, like Germaine Lauzon, from the play *Les Belles-Soeurs* (also the source of the mural's title).

Decadent Sandwiches on the Terrace

172 The colossal sandwiches on homemade bread have made **Café Santropol** a favorite for Montrealers for 40 years now. The sandwiches topped with cream cheese are so huge, so packed, that you can barely get your mouth around them for a bite. Try the Killer Tomato, with sundried tomato cream cheese, fresh tomato, basil and garlic. A treat to savor on the most luxurious terrace in the neighborhood [3990 Rue Saint-Urbain].

174A 174B

Eclectic Architecture

174

The Plateau has an architectural richness that's undeniable. The buildings for which it's so well known were mostly built in the early 20th century. The neighborhood is all about eclecticism: There's a wonderful wide variety of facades, cornices, staircases, balconies and colors. I recommend taking a photo safari. Start with **Square Saint-Louis** (A), then head to **Avenue Laval**, between Rue Sherbrooke and Avenue Duluth: The wrought-iron staircases are charming and the superb Victorian houses are magical. Two of the homes have been classified as heritage buildings by the city:

174C

3470 and **3500 Avenue Laval**. On **Rue de Bullion**, between Roy and Napoléon, you'll see a long row of some 15 lovely historical houses in different colors, with mansard roofs.

A walk through the neighborhood wouldn't be complete without a look at the **Maison Coloniale** [4333 Avenue Coloniale], a modern home designed by acclaimed architect Jacques Rousseau. All windows and concrete, it looks a bit like a UFO that has landed on Earth—it's guaranteed to make an impression.

The triangular section of blocks where **Rue Gilford**, **Rue Villeneuve** and **Avenue Henri-Julien** connect is truly exceptional. And at **4660 to 4664 Rue de Grand-Pré** (B) are two semi-detached Second-Empire houses with stunning turrets. The homes were built before 1880. Be sure to take a look at the advertisement painted on the left wall, written in French and English and dating from the 20th century. On the right side is a **row of magnificent houses** (C) that are really special, with dormer or slate mansard roofs, richly detailed wooden verandas and small wrought iron balconies above the first floor. Unlike the other grid-like streets of the neighborhood, Rue Gilford runs diagonally, and the houses on the sharp corners are amazing [369 and 344 Rue Gilford].

More than Just an Alley

175

The best way to really get a feel for the lives of Montrealers is to stroll down the city's alleys. The quiet passageways are the ideal vantage points for observing interactions between neighbors, seeing animated games of ball hockey, hearing children laughing, admiring backyard gardens and peering into the little slices of paradise that Montrealers have created over the years.

Montreal's alleys first appeared as a result of a significant growth in population. With the increased housing, landlords were required to build service lanes to access the backyards. In the 1950s, these alleys had a bad reputation. Often poorly lit and dotted with dilapidated sheds, they tended to be dark and dirty places where you might encounter vermin and other shadowy characters. Things started to shift in the early 1980s, when Mayor Jean Drapeau introduced two revitalization programs that included demolishing old sheds and transforming alleys into small parks. Then, in the mid-1990s, **ruelles vertes** (green alleys) (A) appeared. Created by neighborhood volunteers in collaboration with a Montreal network, they're meant to reclaim the space for local residents and improve the quality of life in the area.

The first *ruelle verte* was created in the Plateau in 1997. In 2016, there were no fewer than 312 *ruelles vertes* in 11 neighborhoods: Some 39 miles (63 kilometers) have been "greened" to date—which equals 13 percent of the alleys in Montreal. The network's website lists all these alleys [eco-quartiers.org/ruelle_verte]. Discover them for yourself; some are truly beautiful, like the one connecting Avenue Christophe-Colomb and Rue de la Roche between Avenue Laurier and Boulevard Saint-Joseph, and the alley connecting Rue Dorion and Rue de Bordeaux between Rue Rachel and Rue Gauthier.

The only thing that tops a *ruelle verte* is a **ruelle champêtre** (B) (country alley), which has no asphalt whatsoever. The first such alley was built in 2006. You can find it between Rue Drolet and Avenue Henri-Julien, running from Square Saint-Louis to the Les Fusiliers Mont-Royal armory on Avenue des Pins. This peaceful haven is home to more than 100 varieties of plants (annuals and perennials) and shrubs, and even a few tropical plants (they're kept inside people's homes during the winter). It's a must-see.

175 B

A Cherished Poet

176

With his intense poetry, his youth and beauty and his tragic end, **Émile Nelligan** is a mythic figure in Quebec poetry. Before he was institutionalized for mental health problems at the age of 20, he lived on Avenue Laval; he died at the hospital in 1941, at the age of 61. A **commemorative plaque** can be seen at 3686 Avenue Laval. A monument honoring him was installed in the southwest section of **Square Saint-Louis**; the sculpture was created by Roseline Granet.

A Taste of Afghanistan

177

The Plateau has two quality Afghani restaurants; they're both bring-your-own-wine spots. I've been going to **Khyber Pass** (A) [506 Avenue Duluth Est] for 20 years, and I've never been disappointed. Inside, it has typical Afghani simple decor, and feels a bit like an apartment divided into three rooms. The little starters are big on flavor; the central dish is a generous helping of lamb or filet mignon accompanied by wonderfully fragrant rice. I recommend the table d'hôte (soup or salad, entrée, main course, dessert and tea or coffee)— you get to taste everything for under $30, a deal that's hard to beat. The terrace is lovely in the summer. **Fenêtre sur Kaboul** [901 Rue Rachel Est] opened more recently, so it's less well-known, but offers cuisine that's just as filling and flavorful, with more classic white-napkin decor.

175 A

Poutine, poutine

178

Were it only for **La Banquise** (A), the Plateau would be spoiled when it comes to poutine. In fact, many (myself included) think they have the best poutine in town. Open 24 hours a day, the restaurant is also known for its wide variety of Quebec's signature dish—they offer an awe-inspiring selection of 26 different poutines [994 Rue Rachel Est].

Bon, les Portugais font de la poutine! (So, the Portuguese make poutine!) is the jokey name of the poutine dish at **Ma Poule Mouillée**. This calorific creation has São Jorge cheese, chicken and grilled chorizo. The touch of spice from the chicken and chorizo give the poutine a real flavor boost. The rest of the menu at this little Portuguese restaurant is definitely worth trying as well [969 Rue Rachel Est].

For the ultimate greasy spoon experience, try the Pogo poutine at **Chez Claudette** [351 Avenue Laurier Est], a neighborhood institution that's open 24 hours a day from Thursday to Saturday. You won't find more comforting food anywhere. When you leave, check out the 7,500-square-foot (700-square-meter) mural across the street, entitled *Les Conteurs*. It pays tribute to the teachings of the National Theatre School, on which the mural was painted.

Chloé's Chocolates and Caramels

179

The flavors at **Chocolats de Chloé** are bewitching: fig and balsamic vinegar, cardamom, basil, aged rum and raisin, Sichuan pepper for the delicate chocolates. The chocolate candies (caramels) make you feel like a kid again, and the flavors are equally appealing: tortelines (pecan, caramel and chocolate), Monsieur Croquant (homemade sponge toffee and dark chocolate) and fresh homemade vanilla marshmallows wrapped in dark chocolate. The dessert that really gets me is creamy caramel with salted butter: I eat it with a spoon in a state of rapture. During the holidays, this caramel is so popular that supplies often run out before the end of the day [546 Avenue Duluth Est].

181A

The Plateau's Best-Kept Secret

180

If you don't live nearby, you probably don't know this little gem of an Asian restaurant that's set apart from the Plateau's busier streets. **Le Caractère Chinois** is the ideal little neighborhood restaurant: quiet, friendly, unpretentious and serving delicious food at affordable prices. To top it all off, it's a bring-your-own-wine restaurant. The menu isn't authentic Chinese, but rather Asiatic fusion, and it's really good. The duck rolls, dumplings with peanut sauce, sweet and sour soup, General Tao chicken and pad thai are all excellent, with perfectly balanced flavors. Your bill will be around $20, which makes it that much better [1870 Rue Gauthier].

Picnic in the Park

181

Named "Parc Logan" when it was opened in 1874, **Parc La Fontaine** (A) was rechristened in 1901 in honor of Quebec Premier Louis-Hippolyte La Fontaine. Spread across 86 acres (350,000 square meters) and featuring two big artificial ponds, it's a popular site for fun and relaxation. There's a children's playground, a dog run, baseball diamonds, soccer fields, and volleyball, tennis and boccie courts. In winter, the frozen pond is a beautiful place for skating (and it's free). At the north end of the park is **Debout!**, a bronze statue by Roger Langevin (1990). It's a tribute to Félix Leclerc, the father of Quebec songwriters.

Built on two former quarries, **Parc Sir-Wilfrid-Laurier** is three times smaller than its big brother La Fontaine, but it's just as pretty. There's a certain magic in the late-afternoon light at this park. The large public pool was recently renovated, and there's a wonderfully designed area for small children.

Diabolical Sauces

182 The Gorgon sauce at **Diabolissimo**, a shop specializing in fresh pasta and homemade sauces, is simply mind-blowing. The rich sauce with gorgonzola and hazelnut is sublime with long pasta; you'll be thinking about it for a long time after you try it. The pestos are also stunning. Try the super-flavorful curry pasta with their tomato pesto. I'm such a huge fan of their sauce with Italian sausage, red pepper, pistachio and fennel seed that I can barely resist licking the bottom of the plate. Diabolissimo is simply a paradise for epicureans who are short on time for cooking. It's also a specialty market, offering olive oil, vinegar, dried pasta from Italy, quality preserves, good coffee and excellent deli meats [1256 Avenue du Mont-Royal Est].

Five-Dollar Feasting

183 In an effort to attract new customers, **L'Entrepôt Mont-Royal** restaurant offers all its dishes for one low price, with no exceptions: $4.95 burgers, pasta, poutine, sandwiches, pierogies, tacos and salads are served in a decor reminiscent of a ski chalet. For the price, the varied menu (which has some vegetarian options) has impressive quality and quantity (they do offer extras for $1 to $2). As you can imagine, L'Entrepôt is extremely popular, particularly with students. If you can go early, you'll avoid the lineup. They don't take reservations [1019 Avenue du Mont-Royal Est].

Porcelain and Lace

184

Talented ceramists Maya Ersan and Jaimie Robson set up their studio-boutique in the Plateau in 2013. With delicate lines and soft colors, the porcelain objects from **Atelier Make** (A) [1241 Rue Gilford] are gorgeous. Bowls, cups, lanterns, serving trays, cream jugs: delicate decorative or table items that make great gifts. The shop is open on Saturday only, from 11 a.m. to 5 p.m.; you can also book an appointment to visit during the week.

The big gold button over the front door tells you you've reached a unique store. **Rix Rax** [801 Rue Gilford], at the corner of Rue Saint-Hubert, is a haberdashery that sells buttons, ribbons, thread, feathers, clasps, flowers, lace, belt buckles—basically any sewing and costume-making accessory. Their inventory is really something; the selection of buttons of all styles, shapes and textures—organized by color—will leave you speechless. Be sure to check out the magnificent 1882 cash register, which still works.

Return to the 1800s

185

Toward the end of the 19th century, the area north of Laurier Metro station was called Coteau-Saint-Louis. The town was mainly populated by quarry workers who extracted limestone from the large quarry that later became Parc Sir-Wilfrid-Laurier. The gray stones were used for a number of the prestigious downtown buildings, as well as many Plateau homes. Vestiges of that village architecture, now rare in Montreal, can still be seen at spots like **483 Rue Lagarde** (A) and **5208, 5257** (B) and **5280 Rue Berri**. These old homes stand in sharp contrast to the new condos popping up in the area. **Place du Coteau-Saint-Louis**, surrounding the north exit of Laurier Metro station, evokes the neighborhood's history, while its design decidedly faces the future.

Montreal Staircases

186

Whether they're straight, curved, spiral or circular, L-, S- or T-shaped, Montreal's **outdoor staircases** are one of the city's most distinctive architectural features—perhaps the feature that best represents the city. You'll never see so many wrought iron staircases in such a range of styles. They abound in many neighborhoods, like Rosemont, Villeray, Verdun, Hochelaga and especially the Plateau, where they're ubiquitous.

A bit of history: Exterior staircases first appeared in the second part of the 19th century, when row apartments started being built in working-class neighborhoods. The buildings were narrow but long—duplexes and triplexes. To ensure that these neighborhoods would have a bit of green space, municipal authorities required owners to leave a small yard in front of the buildings. This cut into the amount of space the apartments could have. To counterbalance that, staircases to upper floors where placed outside, saving precious indoor space. An added benefit was a lower heating bill, since owners wouldn't have to heat the shared staircase area.

Bewitching Pastries

187

Pastry chef Stéphanie Labelle, from **Rhubarbe**, creates nothing less than sweet little works of art. Her pastries have instant visual appeal, and the flavors are astonishing. Lemon tarte, panna cotta with tonka bean, blood orange and cardamom, grapefruit-pistachio layer cake—there are so many delicacies to savor on each visit (the creations change periodically). On Sunday, the pastry shop opens its doors for brunch. With its attention to detail and the quality of the food, Rhubarbe has become one of the top food destinations in town. Could it even be the best pastry shop in North America? I wouldn't be surprised [5091 Rue De Lanaudière].

A Cup of Tea in Iran

188

You may feel a little disoriented when you enter **Byblos Le Petit Café**. The aromas of saffron and cardamom wafting through the air conjure up the land of *One Thousand and One Nights*. I go there for their original breakfasts, served with Iranian tea. I love the omelet with feta, generously sprinkled with dill and accompanied by sweetbread. I also love the homemade jams: rose-petal-pistachio, pineapple-ginger, orange blossom, lime and nectarine [1499 Avenue Laurier Est].

Top Design

189

This is the kind of shop that blows me away on my first visit. Everything is beautiful at **BUK & NOLA**. You'll find rare and desirable decorations, all selected with great care. Cushions, posters (I want them all), small hand-painted furniture, wallpaper, table linen, candles and other chic and casual accessories that will add the winning touch to your home [1593 Avenue Laurier Est].

Welcome to Fred's Place

190

It's a tiny spot—miniscule, in fact—and you'll feel like you're in someone's apartment. In a way, that's accurate: Frédéric Houtin, the chef-owner of **Sain Bol**, carefully selected the spot and the decor. He cooks on a conventional kitchen stove, all with the aim of recreating a warm, cozy atmosphere of home. The focus is on healthy food, and you'll find plenty of organic, local and seasonal items. The menu features omelets, grilled cheese, salads, soups, gravlax and other light meals, prepared with different ingredients each day and according to customers' needs (allergies, intolerance, vegan, etc.). Open on weekdays (except Wednesday) for lunch, and weekends for brunch. If you want to go on Friday night, make a reservation. You're sure to love this tiny and truly delicious healthy restaurant [5095 Rue Fabre].

Craft Beer, Artful Food

closed

191

Quebec's craft beers are on display at **Le Sieur d'Iberville**, a microbrewery with 18 beers on tap and over 30 different kinds in bottles. This chic bar in the east Plateau is a great place for a drink. The food won't disappoint either—in fact, it's excellent. Not satisfied with being merely a great bar, Le Sieur is also an accomplished rotisserie. The chicken is brined, then roasted over a wood fire, then transferred to their smoker. The result is a juicy and tender chicken, with a campfire-cooked taste—a memorable meal, guaranteed. The burgers are hefty, piled with toppings, and the meat is ground to order. The restaurant is warm and welcoming, the bar is gigantic and the stools have footrests (hallelujah!). And of course, like any respectable bar, they show Canadiens hockey games. [2490 Avenue du Mont-Royal Est].

Ménick: The Sports Barber

192

The barbershop **Chez Ménick** has a cult following. Opened in 1959, the shop hasn't changed in decades. The walls are plastered with photos of the Montreal Canadiens and the Expos from yesteryear, and the floor is painted like a skating rink—you might think you've wandered into a sports museum. Sports is a very deep passion for Mr. **Ménick**, who decided to become a barber when he was

14 years old. He counts several hockey players among his friends, and spends a fair bit of time at arenas. "People started saying, 'He's the sports barber.' So I decided to call my shop 'The Sports Barbershop,' and it really brought people in." Some Quebecers will remember his talk show, *Ménick Reçoit*, which aired in the 1980s: It featured Ménick interviewing Quebec sports stars—and cutting their hair. That program is a big part of the current popularity of the barbershop and of its barber. Various film and sports stars have sat in Ménick's chair: Hulk Hogan, Chuck Norris, Jean Béliveau, Maurice Richard, Guy Lafleur, and Sidney Crosby, to name a few. If you want to experience it for yourself, just show up; no reservation is needed for a trim at this legendary barbershop [1960 Rue Masson].

Hochelaga-Maisonneuve

Once a Francophone and working-class neighborhood, Hochelaga-Maisonneuve (nicknamed Hochelag or HoMa), is socially very mixed, including students, the elderly, small families, and low-income and well-to-do households. The factories that moved away from the area left behind empty facilities, which were very quickly converted into accessible housing. It's not uncommon to meet residents who have lived here all their lives—some of them having moved a few times, but just a few blocks away. There is a small town feeling here, and the concepts of cooperation, mutual aid and solidarity are firmly rooted in the culture. This neighborhood has a lot to offer: Olympic Park, Maisonneuve Market, several cultural centers, dozens of parks and very beautiful historical buildings.

BOUL. SAINT-JOSEPH E.

RUE RACHEL E.

RUE D'IBERVILLE

RUE FRONTENAC

BOUL. SAINT-MICHEL

RUE SHERBROOKE E.

RUE HOGAN

RUE HOCHELAGA

• 193

195

RUE ONTARIO E.

HOCHELAGA-
MAISONNEUVE

RUE NICOLET

197

194

202
201 • • • 204
203 205

206

RUE DAVIDSON

198

AV. VALOIS

RUE SAINTE-CATHERINE E.

199

200

213

RUE NOTRE-DAME E.

213

BOUL. ROSEMONT

BOUL. DE L'ASSOMPTION

PARC MAISONNEUVE

BOUL. PIE-IX

RUE DICKSON

220

•221

•225

•223

•222

RUE VIAU

RUE DE ROUEN

207
•
•210
•209 • •208
•212

224
•
•226

RUE MORGAN

RUE LECLAIRE

216
•
•217

•218

•219

- Sights + photo ops
- Bars + restaurants
- Stores + markets
- Arts + culture
- Activities + walks

The Great Escape

193

Located between Wurtele, Florian, de Rouen and Ontario streets, **L'Échappée Belle** is the largest *ruelle verte* (green alley) (see Reason #175) in Montreal. Unveiled in August 2011, the alley is 1,191 feet (363 meters) long and has been beautified with 57 trees, 156 shrubs and 190 perennials. A very colorful hopscotch game has been painted in the middle, in the shape of a fish; the image has become a sort of emblem for the long urban alley where a little bit of nature has been able to take root.

Flavors of Asia

194

Sata Sushi has been satisfying the neighborhood's raw fish cravings for over 10 years. In this cozy little spot with dim lighting, wood takes center stage: The walls are hemlock and the counter is reclaimed barn wood. The sushi is creative, sophisticated and unbelievably fresh. The Neige is maki sushi with shrimp, avocado and coconut. The Sata, on rice paper, combines scallop, caviar, sweet potato and avocado—a revelation. And then there's the specialty: maki and nigiri "au gratin." Despite the name, you won't find any cheese inside; instead, a blowtorch is applied to salmon, white tuna, scallops and tofu, which sit on nori or a soybean leaf, until partially cooked. Fabulous [3349 Rue Ontario Est].

A Paradise of Graffiti

195

Le Sino (A) [2817 Rue Ontario Est] has a whole wall of spray paint cans spanning the color spectrum. They have every color imaginable, in hundreds of shades, arranged in glorious harmony. The shop is truly a Montreal graffiti hot spot. Aerosol cans, high-quality markers, protective gear, reference books—street artists will find everything they need under one roof. Montreal has a number of "legal" walls, places where graffiti artists can express their creativity and hone their technique without fear of being arrested; there were four on the island as of 2016. The biggest and most popular is the **Rouen Wall** (*Mur de Rouen*) [under the railway overpass at Rue de Rouen, between Rue Lespérance and Rue Moreau]—just a few blocks from Le Sino. These ephemeral works are constantly changing, so be sure to check them out.

Dr. Julien: The Community Doctor

196

You might be familiar with the African proverb "It takes a village to raise a child." Pediatrician Gilles Julien, better known as **Dr. Julien**, is certainly familiar with this philosophy. He developed the model of social pediatrics, an interdisciplinary approach that brings together the expertise of medicine, law and social work to support children at risk. It ensures that young people are treated not only with medical solutions, but also with social and legal solutions, so that children from precarious socio-economic backgrounds can develop their full potential.

In 1997, Dr. Julien founded his first social pediatric center in the Hochelaga-Maisonneuve borough. A second center was created five years later in Côte-des-Neiges. The atmosphere in these centers is friendly, comfortable and not intimidating. Children are not simply "treated." Their cases are also studied by a group of professionals who make a comprehensive diagnosis that takes into account physical, emotional, mental and societal factors, and suggest options to help the child and their family. In 2005, the *Fondation du Dr. Julien* was created to promote social pediatrics, to ensure the sustainability of the clinical model and to support it in practice.

In both centers (in addition to the *Garage à Musique*, a specialized center that promotes the self-actualization of young people through the teaching of music), Dr. Julien and his team provide care and support for more than 2,000 children and their families each year. Dr. Julien has been extremely active in his field over the years, always guided by an understanding that to solve a problem, you must go to its source. By attempting to heal through medicine alone, change is not effected, and there is no useful way forward. Enabling children to assume their role in society is a winning strategy because these children will one day become adults who will in turn contribute to the community. [fondationdrjulien.org]

The Vegan Antidote

197

Antidote is a café-restaurant-market whose mission is simple: to demystify veganism, to make it accessible (even cool), and to help people find 100-percent-vegan, organic and gluten-free products. They have cold-pressed juices, smoothies containing "superfoods," coffee, pastries, prepared vegan dishes and a small grocery section. Since it opened, Antidote has evolved into a charming neighborhood bistro. With their delicious and undeniably flavorful food, they prove that veganism doesn't mean deprivation. And if you think vegan food stops at quinoa and lentils, you're in for a surprise. Burgers with bacon and cheddar, pad thai, General Tao chicken, explosive Asian salads—all 100-percent vegan. It's good enough to convince even the most doubtful. You can even enjoy a real vegan wine with your meal [3459 Rue Ontario Est].

A Religious Gathering on Saturday

198

It's an amazing social phenomenon. **Wrestling** experienced a golden age in Quebec from the 1950s to the 1980s, largely due to its matches being televised by the national broadcaster. At the end of the 1950s, it attracted some 1,500,000 viewers per episode. Quebec wrestling doesn't appear on the small screen today, but it's still going strong in community centers and church basements. On Saturdays, the Inter Championship Wrestling organization holds matches at the **Église du Très-Saint-Rédempteur**. A crowd of 200 raucous fans gathers to cheer on the good guys and boo the villains (the distinction means the world in this theatrical realm). Characters with colorful names like Big Fat Seb, Bulldozer, Crazy Dan and Magic Mike battle each other in spectacles that are truly larger than life. Elbow drops and pile drivers are the main course, with a side dish of insults and foul language. Some things have changed, but wrestling will always be wrestling [side entrance of the church, at 1550 Rue Joliette].

The Vintage Spirit

199

Teak lovers should set a course for **Montréal Moderne** [3975 Rue Sainte-Catherine Est], which has the largest selection of Scandinavian furniture in the city. The store has developed a great reputation since it opened in 2001. You're sure to gasp at the sheer amount of mid-century furniture, especially pieces in the Danish Modern style, with timeless lines and quality craftsmanship.

A bit farther north, a few steps from the Joliette Metro station, is another paradise for vintage lovers. **Kitsch à l'Os... ou Pas** (A) [3439 Rue Hochelaga] is an enormous shop (2,150 square feet/200 square meters), filled with antique and retro furniture and accessories, from the early 20th century to the 1990s. The eight rooms, each with its own focus, are overloaded with cool finds: dishes, jewelry, small furniture pieces, paintings, decorative items and other treasures (all in good condition) from a bygone era. Take your time—the shop is bigger than it seems from outside.

Charming Studio-Boutiques

200

Looking for the coolest children's clothing and accessories in town? The owners of the studio-boutique **Electrik Kidz** (A) are young parents themselves (a couple). They initially decided to make some practical clothing for their little boy; next came the idea of creating a clothing line for under-five-year-olds that would be modern, urban and trendy—clothes that parents would love. Opened in 2010, the shop was an instant success. The designs counter male/female stereotypes, and the clothes are created with reduced impact on the environment. All in all, it's a great local company. Open from Monday to Friday [3921 Rue Sainte-Catherine Est].

A few steps away is **Bigarade**, a café, studio and boutique in a big, magnificently decorated space. What really catches your eye is the elegant and exceptionally high-quality products on display: fine linens and designer home accessories, made with fabrics in their on-site studio. They stand by the quality of their materials and manufacturing. The company guarantees its creations for life. The young entrepreneur behind Bigarade is Geneviève Lorange, a fabric designer who's deeply influenced by her grandmother's quilting. She recycles leftover batches of fabrics, recovers old tablecloths to give them a second life, and reproduces patterns from fine embroidery by digitizing them and printing them on natural fibers. Geneviève and her team leave a personal touch on each item by signing the label by hand [3889 Rue Sainte-Catherine Est].

201 202

Top Butchers

201 At **Boucherie Beau-Bien**, the customer is king. Behind the counter, you'll find a man that everyone calls "*Gros Dan*" (Big Dan). He's a former bodybuilder who took over the butcher shop in 2000 (it's been open for 90 years). Over the years, the local clientele has gradually become more conscious of what they put on their plates; today they'll spend a little more for locally sourced meat without antibiotics or hormones. They offer a number of marinated meats that are ready for the barbecue, and pre-cooked meats like pulled pork and ribs. If you can't find what you're looking for, the butchers will be very happy to prepare it for you. Before you leave, peruse the incredible array of hot sauces and marinades. It's such an amazing selection that I suggest a second nickname for Gros Dan: the King of Sauces [3748 Rue Ontario Est].

The Cornerstone of the New HoMa

202 The existence of **Place Simon-Valois**, at the corner of Rue Ontario and Avenue Valois, set off an amazing revitalization of the neighborhood, which in turn led to a massive real estate boom. The public square brought a new spirit to the area and attracted a number of businesses, like the fabulous **ArHoma** bakery (the pistachio croissants will change your life), sausage shop **William J. Walter** and the restaurant **Le Valois** (see Reason #203). Place Simon-Valois is located in the middle of **Promenade Luc-Larivée**, a linear park built where an old railway track once lay, and stretches from Rue Joliette to Avenue Jeanne-d'Arc (about 2,090 feet/ 637 meters). A great place to walk or cycle, the park offers terrific views of the Olympic Stadium Tower. If you go there, make a little detour to see an industrial building that's been transformed into a housing cooperative and reintegrated into the neighborhood. Known as **Station No. 1** (2111 Avenue d'Orléans), the building was Montreal's first hydroelectric relay station in its previous life. Inside the inner courtyard, you can see the old suspension crane with an imposing hook—a memento of the past.

203 A 204 A

Destination: Brunch

203

With its enormous terrace (it seats 120!) that looks out on Place Simon-Valois, **Le Valois** (A) [25 Place Simon-Valois] is supremely located. Open from 9 a.m. for breakfast, lunch, supper and weekend brunch, this restaurant is ambitious enough to offer a late-night menu as well, starting at 9:30 p.m.: An appetizer and main course costs $24. The menu is classic French cuisine adapted to seasonal ingredients: tartares, homemade *boudin noir* (blood sausage), flank steak, homemade fries and so on. They also lay claim to the most sophisticated brunch in the neighborhood. I recommend the egg croquette: a perfectly poached and runny egg, transformed into a croquette with panko breadcrumbs served on blinis with homemade smoked salmon. Heavenly.

Another brunch spot that is exceptionally located—just a few steps from Maisonneuve Market—is the bring-your-own-wine bistro, **Bagatelle** [4323 Rue Ontario Est]. Their breakfast menu is vast, with something for everyone: eggs, frittatas, French toast, open baguette sandwiches, croissants and more. The portions are generous.

Les Affamés [4137 Rue Sainte-Catherine Est] is a popular bistro and a brunch destination par excellence. Their inventive menu is sure to please lovers of that time-honored late-morning meal. Boudin, gravlax, elk flank steak and pulled pork are all great options, prepared breakfast-style, with eggs. The dishes fill you up and will satisfy the most demanding gourmands.

Earthenware Walls

204

Montreal painter and muralist **Laurent Gascon** has been paying tribute to the city's cultural icons by immortalizing them in unique ceramic mosaic murals since 2009. At the time I write these lines, he has created eight of them; you can see them as you walk on Rue Ontario Est, starting from Avenue Bourbonnière. The largest one—39 feet by 16 feet (10 meters by 5 meters), and consisting of over 4,500 pieces of earthenware—is an homage to singer and poet **Gilles Vigneault** (A). You'll find it on the east wall at 3845 Rue Ontario Est. Continuing west, you'll come face to face with **Plume Latraverse**, singer, author and composer (No. 2915), talented Italian poster artist **Vittorio Fiorucci** (2059 Rue Florian at the corner of Ontario), singer and songwriter **Pauline Julien** (No. 2743), **Robert Gravel**, founder of the LNI (see Reason #58) (No. 2371), **Marjo**, singer, songwriter and Quebec rock legend (No. 2222), **Raymond Lévesque**, a major Quebec singer (No. 1969) and **Paul Buissonneau**, actor and director (No. 1223). These artworks add life to Rue Ontario and honor the figures who have made a profound mark on Montreal over the years. A stroll from the first to the last mural will take you an hour.

205A 206A

Irish Pub, American Bar

205

Le Trèfle (A) [3971 Rue Ontario Est] is a great spot for a pint with friends. This Irish pub has a warm atmosphere, wooden decor and a copper bar. There are over 100 beers on menu; about half are from Quebec and the rest are from Belgium, Scotland, Denmark and the United States. The selection of Scotches and whiskies (over 60) is equally impressive. Sports-lovers will be happy to know that they show all the big hockey, soccer and football games. The kitchen is open until midnight and serves comfort food like French onion soup, grilled cheese with Quebec cheese and maple smoked bacon and homemade fish-and-chips. Oh, and they serve a decadent brunch from 10 a.m. on Saturday and Sunday.

One block farther west is another pub, inspired by American bars and serving platters of finger food and mugs of beer for $3. The menu at **Blind Pig** [3882 Rue Ontario Est] might not involve the full-on gluttony the name suggests, but it's still pretty indulgent: classic burgers and poutines, homemade Pogos, macaroni and cheese croquettes (kind of like Parmesan fondue), and po'boys (sandwiches with popcorn shrimp, jalapeno and spicy mayonnaise served on a baguette).

Nightlife in the Shadow of the Stadium

206

The neighborhood restaurant-bar **Monsieur Smith** (A) [4061 Rue Ontario Est] opened in 2012. With its two terraces (one in front and one in back), it quickly became a go-to spot for fun and somewhat wild nights. The back terrace is one of the few in the neighborhood that stays open until 3 a.m. They have cocktails with fun names, often inspired by the neighborhood, like the Homa God, the Long Ontario Iced Tea and the Mojito Olympique. The cocktails also come in a pitcher, for sharing. If you need sustenance with your liquor, they serve typical bar food like burgers and homemade sausages.

A combined microbrewery and bar, **L'Espace Public** [3632 Rue Ontario Est] aims to be a gathering place and a second living room, where you'll always feel at home. Mission accomplished. The homemade beers, especially the surprising sour beers, are well worth going out of your way for; one is named "*Donne Un Bec À Matante!*" ("Give your auntie a kiss!").

208A

Casual Café

207 There are always customers at **Hoche Café**—always. They have the best coffee in the neighborhood, and it's populated with students who come here to work, locals picking up a coffee on the way to work and friends meeting up for a light meal. The mismatched furniture gives the café a relaxed atmosphere, and children are welcome. I really like their lattes in all their forms (café, chai and matcha) and the fresh-squeezed juices. For lunch, try a main salad or a decadent grilled cheese. At the counter is an appreciable selection of homemade baked goods (muffins, brownies, biscuits), including several gluten-free and organic options. Be sure to try the peanut butter cookies [4299 Rue Ontario Est].

A Loveable Neighborhood Market

208 **Maisonneuve Market** (A) may be smaller than its siblings, the Atwater and Jean-Talon markets, but it still has a great selection. There are about a dozen stalls with fresh produce, baked goods, cheese, meat, fish, flowers and specialty items. For fruits and vegetables, the quality-price ratio is the best in town. From April to May, I'm a devoted regular at **Capitaine Crabe**, which sells snow crab directly from Rimouski. The kiosk is set up at the back of the market and is only open during this delectable crustacean's all-too-short season [4445 Rue Ontario Est].

207

208A

The Paradise of Beer

209

For the couple who own **Le Bièrologue**, the mission of the business is clear and simple: to showcase 100-percent-Quebecois products. Driven by an exceptional passion for beers from regional microbreweries and for other local products, they opened Le Bièrologue in 2012, aiming to make these products more accessible. They've certainly succeeded: Since the store opened, they've had over 800 beers, ciders, sausages, cheeses and other local products on their shelves. The beer selection is amazing, ranging from great classics to bolder, lesser-known choices. Don't hesitate to ask them questions; they know their products very well [4301 Rue Ontario Est].

209

Traces of the Past: The Old Market Pavilion

210

When the Hochelaga municipality was annexed to the city of Montreal in 1883, a handful of French-Canadian property owners who lived in the eastern part of the neighborhood wanted to remain autonomous. Thus, they decided to found the city of Maisonneuve, which would be a model industrial city. The creators of this "Francophone Westmount" included the businessman Oscar Dufresne, his brother, Marius, an engineer and architect, and Alphonse Desjardins, founder of a successful credit union. A very ambitious urban development plan was part of this megaproject. Unfortunately, the economic crisis caused by World War I undermined their grand plans, and the visionaries sank $18 million dollars into debt. Maisonneuve was forced to join with Montreal in 1918. Of the five grandiose buildings that were imagined, four saw the light of day, and they're still standing: **Maisonneuve Market**, the **Hôtel de Ville** (Maisonneuve city hall) (see Reason #211), the **Maisonneuve public bath** (see Reason #212) and **Caserne No. 1** (Station No. 1) (see Reason #213). They're superb architectural works that really stand out in this historically disadvantaged neighborhood. The beaux-arts-style market building—the masterpiece of the neighborhood—opened its doors in 1914. It once specialized in the sale of livestock and was one of the biggest produce markets in Quebec. The square facing the pavilion, at the corner of Rue Ontario Est and Avenue Morgan, is **Place Genevilliers-Laliberté**. In the middle stands *La Fermière* (1915), a hexagonal fountain monument depicting a 17th-century gardener (an homage to Louise Mauger who, along with her husband, were the first farmers in Ville-Marie, the original French settlement in Montreal). It's one of the major works by Quebec sculptor Alfred Laliberté (1878-1953) [4375 Rue Ontario Est].

211

212A 212B

The Monumental Library

211 An immense and very attractive building, the former **Maisonneuve city hall** is another one of the four massive buildings that sprang from the imaginations of the model city's designers. Today the building houses the **Bibliothèque Maisonneuve** (Maisonneuve Library). It is also beaux-arts design, with a Corinthian-style colonnade, a triangular pediment and huge bronze doors. Inside, the original architecture has been preserved.

Note the floor mosaic depicting the coat of arms of the city of Maisonneuve, the 1912 inauguration plaque, the marble staircase, the stained glass windows and the magnificent multicolored skylight [4120 Rue Ontario Est].

A Majestic Bath

212 The **Maisonneuve public bath and gymnasium** (A) (today called the **Bain Morgan**) is another one of the four opulent buildings in the former city of Maisonneuve. Opened in 1916, the building's beaux-arts architectural touches (spans, monumental staircases, columns and a triangular pediment) evoke the heroic spirit of its creators. In front, you can see *Les Petits Baigneurs* (B) (The Little Swimmers), a piece by Quebec sculptor Alfred Laliberté. This public bath is generally considered to be the most beautiful in North America. At the time, most workers' apartments lacked bathrooms, and the baths were built to remedy hygiene problems: The heated public baths gave residents (men, above all) a way to wash themselves. Women were admitted only on Tuesdays [1875 Avenue Morgan].

213

An Unusual Station

213

Opened in 1915, Maisonneuve's **Station No. 1**, today known as **Caserne Letourneux**, is a building with remarkable and uncommon architecture. Marius Dufresne, the architect, really carried out an exercise in style here, taking inspiration from Frank Lloyd Wright's Unity Temple in Chicago. The symmetrical composition of the limestone building highlights the central tower, which was used to hang fire hoses for drying. When Maisonneuve was annexed to Montreal, the station's number was changed to 44, and firemen occupied it until 1961. Since 2016, the station and the park next to it have served as the training center for Montreal's professional soccer club, the Impact [4300 Rue Notre-Dame Est].

Carle and Gilles: Loving Montreal

214

In my research for this book, I discovered **Mes Quartiers** and **C'est toi ma Ville**, two well documented personal blogs that have valuable information on some dozen neighborhoods, walking tours, lists of must-sees, murals, free outings, maps and photographs... I was curious about the authors and why they were so devoted to sharing information about Montreal, so I decided to contact them.

It turns out they are a youthful couple in their forties who both work full time (Gilles Beaudry is a hospital worker, and Carle Bernier-Genest is a consultant for a nonprofit organization) and together spend another 40 hours a week writing their blogs, without any sponsors or additional income. Their blogs are aimed at Montrealers who want to discover more about their own city, explore new neighborhoods, or learn about ideas from other cities around the world that could be applied here. However, the blogs are also a great resource for tourists who want to get off the beaten track. "Montreal is the illuminated fountain in Jarry Park, the young people picnicking on the Lachine Canal in Saint-Henri, the engaging shops on Avenue Monkland and the green alleyways in Rosemont-La-Petite-Patrie," Gilles told me. Carle then went on to explain the origins of their shared passion: "We met in 2009. To get to know each other, we decided to go for a walk in a neighborhood about which we knew very little, and we found ourselves in NDG. Our relationship was built on a stroll through the city."

Gilles and Carle live in Hochelaga-Maisonneuve, a neighborhood they chose for its vibrancy and energy. Gilles described some of his neighborhood's main attractions: "I like the bell tower at the **Nativité-de-la-Sainte-Vierge Church** (1855 Rue Dézéry)—it's the tallest one still in use in Montreal, and it towers in the Hochelaga sky like a Venetian campanile. I like **Alfred Laliberté's *La Fermière* fountain**, which spurts in all directions in front of Maisonneuve Market—worthy of the public squares in Europe." Carle added to the list, "We love the **Luc-Larivée pedestrian walkway** that crosses the neighborhood diagonally. There are more and more green alleyways, amazing murals and small sidewalk libraries, and **Rue de la Poésie** on Rue La Fontaine, just south of Rue Ontario Est, where people hang poems on trees."

And as for the rest of the city? "I like the footbridges that cross the Lachine Canal, with their impressive view of the industrial past and modern skyscrapers. The small residential streets around Parc Molson that people have transformed into open-air gardens. Parc René-Lévesque, where a long expanse of green reaches out into Lac Saint-Louis. And all the ponds in the many pastoral Outremont parks," Gilles explained. Murals and graffiti fascinate Carle. "There is so much excitement around street art in Montreal. Works by really talented artists, like Garbage Beauty, ReyMidax, Enzo & Nio, Lilyluciole and MissMe. The city already has more than 500 murals by renowned artists like A'Shop, Monk.E, Bryan Beyung, Stare and Rafael Sottolichio." [mesquartiers.wordpress.com and cbernier. wordpress.com]

100 Bell Towers

215 Montreal has been called "the city of a hundred bell towers." Mark Twain even quipped it was "a city where you couldn't throw a brick without breaking a church window." It's easy to imagine that he was on Rue Adam, which has five churches in a section of less than two miles (three kilometers). One of them, the **Église du Très-Saint-Nom-de-Jésus** (built in 1906), is the size of a cathedral. A jewel of the city's religious heritage, it's stunningly decorated: The interior is gilded throughout, with frescoes, huge arches and a spectacular organ, made by legendary Quebec organ-makers Casavant Frères [4215 Rue Adam].

Classic Bistros

216 **Chez Bouffe Café Bistro** (A) [4316 Rue Sainte-Catherine Est] is a neighborhood bistro of the best kind, with vintage decor (I love the turquoise chairs), a nice ambiance, delicious food and very reasonable prices. Located at the edge of Parc Morgan (the small terrace looks out on the park) and across from the Théâtre Denise-Pelletier, the restaurant posts new dishes on its blackboard each week, alongside its menu of timeless classics like burgers, tartares and succulent fish-and-chips (the chef is British).

Among the bring-your-own-wine restaurants in Hochelaga-Maisonneuve, one classic spot has proven it's the real deal. With wide windows and bare tables, **État-Major** specializes in meat—the suckling pig and veal filet are particularly excellent. If you can afford it, splurge on the foie gras as an appetizer; the dish is worthy of the best restaurants anywhere. And make sure to leave room for the salted caramel donuts [4005 Rue Ontario Est].

In Montreal, several churches have been converted into condos, unthinkable in many parts of the world.

The Nicest Park for Kids

217

Completely renovated in 2015, **Parc Morgan** has reclaimed its title as the heart of the neighborhood, and has helped revitalize the Rue Sainte-Catherine area in the process. The view from the park's chalet is rewarding: you can see the fountain, majestic Avenue Morgan—it ends at the old Maisonneuve Market pavilion—and the Olympic Stadium Tower that overlooks it all (see photo on pages 188-189). The fountain, which is illuminated at night, is the focal point of this new public square. The main attraction is definitely the play areas for kids of all ages, along with the huge and wonderfully designed water park. There's also a zone for outdoor exercises and pétanque courts [4370 Rue Sainte-Catherine Est]

Viauville's Gray Stone Houses

218

There's a sharp demarcation on Rue La Fontaine, Rue Adam and Rue Sainte-Catherine. East of Rue Sicard, the facades switch suddenly from brick to stone. This is the border of **Viauville**, a neighborhood created in 1892 based on urban planning by Charles-Théodore Viau, the businessman responsible for the Viau cookie company (maker of the Whippet, a chocolate-coated marshmallow treat that's legendary in Quebec). Toying with the idea of converting this area into a model city, Viau insisted that land buyers use stone when building the facades of their new homes. Viauville was never granted city status, but the gray stone facades testify to that moment in history. Take a walk and admire the middle-class houses that have retained their distinctiveness, like those at 4700, 4730, 4744, 4797 and 4930 Rue Adam.

219

The Heritage Shop

219 Marché **4751** is as far as you can get from a sterile, impersonal box store. It's a business that truly has a loving bond with the city, and the owners, Alyssane McKale and Hicham Faridi, are heartwarmingly sweet. A combined grocery store and neighborhood café, Marché 4751 sells organic and local products, fresh bread, cheese, coffee, fruits and vegetables, soaps, craft beers and a few tasty dishes cooked on-site: tagine, chili, empanadas, mini-pizzas and more, all reasonably priced. In 2012, the business received special mention from the city for its efforts to protect the local architectural heritage, and especially for its work in restoring 1930s stained glass windows and a dome, uncovered during renovation work, above the shop's entrance [4751 Rue Sainte-Catherine Est].

Life in a Château

220 Built between 1915 and 1918, **Château Dufresne** was a residence for the Dufresne brothers (see Reason #210). The building's opulence was a reflection of their wealth and their success in the business world; it's surely the most luxurious two-story in Montreal. Inspired by Petit Trianon, a small château at Versailles, France, these two semi-detached homes originally had almost 40 rooms. Oscar and his wife lived in the house to the east, while Marius and his wife inhabited the house to the west. The extravagance reaches its peak with the lavish interior ornamentation and the presence of commodities that were innovative for their time: central heating and vacuum, dumbwaiters, an elevator and garages that can hold up to five vehicles. Today, the château has been transformed into the **Dufresne-Nincheri Museum**. It's the only Montreal residence from the 1910s that has maintained its original furniture and decor, and is open to the public [2929 Avenue Jeanne d'Arc].

A City and its Stadium

221

Most Montrealers will tell you they have a love-hate relationship with the **Olympic Stadium** (A). It's true that its construction cost three times more than was expected—a debt that Montrealers continued to shoulder for 30 years after the Olympic Games. Still, this underloved structure is an icon, and an inseparable part of the city. With a capacity of 65,000, it's the largest stadium in Canada; its 541-foot-high (165-meter) mast is the tallest inclined tower in the world. The tower's 45-degree angle is really spectacular. By comparison, the Tower of Pisa has only a five-degree lean. What's more, the 18-story tower is actually inhabitable; a credit union plans to set up 1,000 employees there in 2018. From the top, you can admire the landscape for 50 miles (80 kilometers) around. Whether you love it or not, the stadium is one of the city's major landmarks, and it has hosted many of the city's most important events over the years. Over 70,000 people attended its unveiling at the opening of the 1976 Olympic Games. It was the home of the Montreal Expos baseball team from 1977 to 2004, and hosted six Grey Cup games (Canada's national football championship) and a number of finals matches for Montreal's soccer club, the Impact. Then there were legendary concerts: Pink Floyd, U2, Madonna and the Rolling Stones. Pope John Paul II even made an appearance, meeting 60,000 young people there in 1984. Today the plaza is more dynamic than ever before, thanks to innovative activities like the **Premiers Vendredis** (First Fridays), which brings in food trucks (from May to October, the first Monday of each month); **Les Jardineries**, a temporary zone (June to October) with an inspiring design, a true urban oasis where you can have a drink and a bite to eat; and the **Village Mammouth** (December to March), where you can slide, skate and enjoy the winter [4141 Avenue Pierre-De Coubertin].

221A

222A

Heaven on Earth

222

I think this is the place in Montreal that I've visited the most. When my boys were young, the **Biodôme** (A) [4777 Avenue Pierre-De Coubertin] was always the best choice when the weather was too bad to go outside. This "living museum" reproduces five of the Americas' ecosystems: a humid tropical rainforest, a Laurentian maple forest, the Gulf of St. Lawrence, the Labrador coast and the sub-Antarctic Islands. The feeling of entering a tropical forest in the middle of January, surrounded by parrots and golden lion tamarins (a small orange monkey from Brazil), while outside the thermometer has dropped shockingly low, is pure pleasure. You visit with lynx, otters, starfish, puffins and penguins. A mix of a zoo, an aquarium and a botanical garden, the Biodôme is also a research center. It really is the perfect activity to do with kids of any age.

Older children will be thrilled by a visit to the **Planetarium** [4801 Avenue Pierre-De Coubertin], the biggest such center in Canada. The two large silver domes that comprise the building were completed in 2013—the architecture is truly unique. The museum has high-tech equipment that lets you touch the stars (or at least feel like you can). Together, the Biodôme, the Insectarium and the Botanical Garden make up the Olympic district's **Espace pour la Vie** museum complex, the largest natural science complex in Canada.

Eastern Time

223

In front of the Planetarium is a **sundial** made by Dutch sculptor Herman J. van der Heide. Designed according to traditional construction techniques, it's fully functional: an aluminum dial (called a "gnomon" or "stylus") on a graduated plate indicates Eastern Standard Time. But it also has an unusual feature: The piece is inclined 15 degrees from the normal position on a sundial, which would have the stylus pointed to the celestial pole. That doesn't mean that the time indicated on the dial is wrong: The lines were designed to compensate perfectly for the difference of inclination from the equatorial sundial. The sundial was a gift from the Dutch city of Rotterdam in 1967, for the 325th anniversary of the founding of Montreal.

The Fast Track

224

For a good dose of adrenaline, **Action 500** is your spot: It's the largest indoor karting track in Canada, and the largest laser tag and paintball center in North America. What makes the center really special is that it's open 24 hours a day, seven days a week. Feel like zipping around the track at 4 a.m.? No problem. It's ideal for parents whose kids are early-risers. The environment is safe, and the karts have good tire grip, which means that kids as young as four years old can double up in a kart with their mom or dad [5592 Rue Hochelaga].

Soccer Fever

225 In 2012, the Montreal **Impact** officially became the 19th club to join Major League Soccer (MLS). For the occasion, **Saputo Stadium** (built in 2008) was expanded to a capacity of almost 21,000, with a design specifically tailored to soccer. Visibility is excellent and the atmosphere is incredible—thanks largely to loyal supporters. The family area is well conceived, with a lively terrace and special activities for children. It's easy to score tickets to regular season games, and the prices aren't bad. During elimination matches, the team moves to the Olympic Stadium. It's not uncommon to see over 60,000 spectators getting worked up into a frenzy as they cheer on their heroes.

Since the team was founded in 1992, the Impact has really helped soccer take off throughout the province; hundreds of small leagues have formed. Now soccer has actually surpassed hockey as the most popular sport in Quebec in terms of active players.

Proudly Brewed at Oshlag

226 The first establishment in Quebec that's both a microbrewery and a microdistillery, **Oshlag** emerged as an offshoot of the beer-making revolution that has overtaken the province; the company wanted to push the craft spirits movement forward. The brewery part only produces seasonal beers, and has no regular products—a bold strategy. Each new arrival is released in limited quantities and for a limited time. Creatively inspired, their beers really stand out in the market (blue corn, chardonnay, pinot noir, juniper, etc.). Their first spirit arrived in stores in December 2016, and it too is leaps and bounds ahead of the products typically seen on shelves: a hopped vodka, greenish-yellow in color, that's best enjoyed straight to appreciate the flavors and the touch of bitterness. Oshlag products are beautifully designed and make great gifts. To find their beers, go to Le Bièrologue (see Reason #209), and stop at the liquor commission (SAQ) for their hopped vodka [2350 Rue Dickson].

222A

Rosemont, Petite-Patrie, Little Italy, Mile-Ex

A vast area extending east of Mile-Ex and Little Italy to Boulevard Lacordaire, the Rosemont—La Petite-Patrie borough is a paradise for small families and a bastion of green and sustainable development. In the past two years, more than 2,000 tons of asphalt has been removed, and the borough is home to 55 parks! Rosemont has more than twice the number (in length) of green alleyways found in the Plateau. These neighborhoods are truly designed to be lived in, and have great places to eat and drink, too! Welcome to my neck of the woods!

MILE-EX

PETITE ITALIE

RUE WAVERLY
RUE CLARK
RUE JEANNE-MANCE
BOUL. SAINT-LAURENT
RUE SAINT-DENIS
RUE SAINT-HUBERT
AV. CHRISTOPHE-COLOMB
AV. DU PARC
AV. PAPINEAU
AV. DE LORIMIER

RUE JEAN-TALON E.
RUE BÉLANGER
RUE SAINT-ZOTIQUE E.
RUE BEAUBIEN E.
RUE RACHEL E.

PARC LA FONTAINE

261
260
262
263
264
258
259
257
256
265
254
255
252
253
251
241
242
243
244
239
240
238
249
245
237
236
234
233
246
247
248
250
232

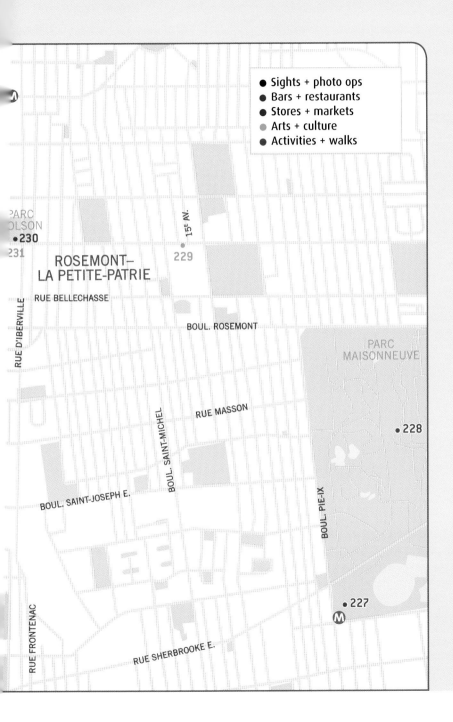

- Sights + photo ops
- Bars + restaurants
- Stores + markets
- Arts + culture
- Activities + walks

PARC
OLSON
●230
231

ROSEMONT–
LA PETITE-PATRIE

15ᴱ AV.

229

RUE BELLECHASSE

BOUL. ROSEMONT

PARC
MAISONNEUVE

RUE D'IBERVILLE

RUE MASSON

●228

BOUL. SAINT-MICHEL

BOUL. SAINT-JOSEPH E.

BOUL. PIE-IX

●227
Ⓜ

RUE FRONTENAC

RUE SHERBROOKE E.

227A

A Global Garden

227

With its impressive plant collections and thematic gardens, Montreal's **Botanical Garden** (A) (*Jardin Botanique*) [4101 Rue Sherbrooke Est] is one of the best botanical gardens anywhere. It has 10 exhibition greenhouses and 20 themed gardens, and an incredible 22,000 plant species and cultivars over its 185 acres (75 hectares); it's a true living museum, with plants from all over the world. My favorite parts are the authentic Chinese Garden, built entirely by Chinese artisans according to the traditions of their craft; the Japanese Garden, with its meticulously maintained bonsai trees; the tropical rainforest greenhouse and the orchid and aroids greenhouse—both great places to take refuge on a cold winter day. There are popular events that return to the Garden each year, like **Butterflies Go Free** (late-February to April), **Gardens of Light** (a lantern festival—September and October), the **Great Pumpkin Ball** (October) and happy hour at the Garden's restaurant (Fridays and Saturdays in the summer).

The Botanical Garden is also where you'll find the **Insectarium** [4581 Rue Sherbrooke Est]. Visitors get the chance to discover the fascinating world of insects and arthropods, beautiful butterflies and creepy spiders. The Botanical Garden and the Insectarium are open year-round. Take your time; you can easily spend a whole day there.

228

Cross-Country Skiing

228

The Rosemont neighborhood has eight miles (13 kilometers) of urban ski trails, second only to Mount Royal Park with its 13 miles (22 kilometers). The slopes in Rosemont's **Parc Maisonneuve** aren't steep, so they're perfect for beginners. The best approach is to cross over into the Botanical Garden. The paths between the park and the Garden are connected, and you can continue on into the arboretum. Signs are posted around the park, with information on the different plant species. There are lots bird feeders, so you're bound to see some feathered friends as well. You can find another ski trail along Rue des Carrières and the train tracks, between Rue d'Iberville and Rue Clark. Rather than nature, it's the industrial graffiti-dotted cityscape that gives this trail a unique feel.

Books for All

229

Rosemont is also the neighborhood with the most **self-serve mini-libraries** in Montreal. The project was started as a citizen's initiative to help promote reading and to make books more accessible throughout the city. The idea is simple: Take a book, free of charge (there's no obligation to bring it back), and leave another one in its place. The boxes (they resemble a newspaper box) are uniquely decorated, each according to its owner's creative spirit. After a resident launched the program in 2012, a Rosemont community development group lent its support and created a map for locating the boxes. In 2016, there were 16 in the east-Rosemont area [cdcrosemont.org/bibliotheques].

230A

A Pretty Skating Pond

230

Parc Molson (A) is one of the prettiest parks in Montreal and a great place for families to go skating in the winter. The skating area encircles the gazebo and branches out in trails that stretch throughout the park. What better way to spend an evening than skating on jewel-like ice pathways under huge trees? In the west section, which is bisected by Rue d'Iberville, you can see *Temps d'Arrêt*, a 16-foot (five-meter) sculpture by artist Jean-Pierre Morin. The sculpture embodies the spirit of the park: a place for play and relaxation, where you can forget the city's hustle and bustle for a while. On Rue Beaubien Est, which runs along the south side of the park, you'll find a number of cafés and restaurants where you can warm up with a hot chocolate or have a post-skating meal: **De Froment et de Sève** (2355 Beaubien Est), **Détour Bistro** (2480 Beaubien Est), **La Grand-Mère Poule** (2500 Beaubien Est), **Les Beaux-Frères sur Beaubien** (2534 Beaubien Est) and **Café Mucho Gusto** (2536 Beaubien Est). Hot tip: You can get your skates sharpened at the store **Vélo Intemporel** (2548 Beaubien Est).

229

The Last Neighborhood Movie Theater

231

It's a true classic that's still going strong—even though it's competing against giants. **Cinéma Beaubien**, which opened in 1937, is the last neighborhood movie theater that's still operating in Montreal. For a time, it seemed that the story wouldn't have a happy ending: Cineplex Odeon, which owned Cinéma Beaubien, announced that the theater would close in 2001. But local residents mobilized to prevent the closing, and a social economy enterprise was created to take over operation of the theater. It mainly runs Quebec films and the top foreign films (in French or with French subtitles—time to brush up on your French!). It has a wonderful retro look and small, comfortable screening rooms—it's a rare gem of a theater [2396 Rue Beaubien Est].

232

231

Beer and Brouhaha

232

Broue Pub Brouhaha offers a great selection of beers (some of which they make), and has an interesting program of events as well. Special mention should go to Lundis Douteux (Dubious Mondays), a weekly event that showcases the worst of the worst in bad film and video. But it's the food that really keeps people coming back, especially the Poutiflette: poutine with fries cooked in duck fat, bacon, onions and caramelized leeks, with a creamy sauce, cheese curds and even a slice of wonderful Pied-De-Vent cheese from the Magdalen Islands. (I suggest reading that last sentence twice—it could be too indulgent to grasp the first time around) [5860 Avenue de Lorimier].

Brunch, Brunch, Brunch

233

Eating at **Régine Café** (A) [1840 Rue Beaubien Est] is like visiting that aunt who insists on stuffing you with food well past your limit. The decor is baroque; velvet and purple are given center stage. The bountiful breakfasts definitely verge on decadence: bone-in ham, baked beans, homemade brioche, delicious cretons, freshly squeezed juices and hot chocolate made with 70-percent dark chocolate. Yes, Régine is undeniably the brunch queen. The restaurant is packed on the weekend; try to go on a weekday, or before 10 a.m. on the weekend, if possible. They also have high chairs and kids' meals.

Santa Barbara [6696 Rue de Saint-Vallier] is a vegetarian-leaning restaurant with a California touch. It's carved out a niche in the area's brunch scene with originally named dishes like the Mathématicienne, the Soldat d'Artillerie (Artillery Soldier) or the Architecte—it's a nod to Saint Barbara, the patron saint of a number of professions. The restaurant abounds with fresh ingredients: kale, avocado, organic yogurt, eggs and seasonal fruits—it all adds up to great meals.

Fixe Café Bistro [5985 Rue Saint-Hubert] offers brunch with a Spanish influence, with a menu that varies according to what's in season. With original combinations like spinach pancakes with lime cream, poached eggs and smoked mackerel and a Spanish omelet with a cherry tomato and olive salad, they make a very distinguished brunch—not to mention a sublime coffee.

An Old-Fashioned Butcher

234

Professional butcher Marc Bourg opened **Le Marchand du Bourg** in 2010. It isn't your standard butcher shop: The only meat sold there is beef. The original decor pays homage to butcher shops of the past. But what's even more striking is the lack of a refrigerated display. The meat at Le Marchand isn't pre-cut or pre-packaged; rather, Bourg cuts every rib, striploin, tenderloin and flank to order, according to the customer's desired thickness. Le Marchand sources only from the best cattle breeders in Canada. The house specialty is a remarkable 60-day dry-aged prime rib. The aging process is strictly controlled, resulting in meat that's amazingly tender, with a taste of hazelnut. In fact, the butcher is courageous enough to offer beef that's been aged even longer: 120 days, 180 days, 365 days and even two years. The beef aged that long is only available by special order, and it's a very high end product indeed (the price tag confirms it). The 60-day-aged beef is a little more accessible, and it's available year-round, along with your standard steaks. A luxury, for when you want a slice of something extraordinary [1661 Rue Beaubien Est].

Huguette Couture: A True Montrealer

235 To truly experience Montreal you need to do more than walk around, you need to meet the people who live here. The people of Montreal are genuine, happy and helpful—and it won't take long to find out that they like meeting people, and they love to chat. And while complaining is a common pastime, you can be sure that deep down they are proud of their city.

Although we had never met before, Huguette Couture insisted on inviting me to her house so that we could speak face to face: "It's more pleasant than on the phone," she said. It's true. She spent two hours telling me about Montreal, her childhood, the trams, the alleyways. Now 86 years old, she could easily pass for someone 20 years younger. She has lived most of her life in Rosemont, on Avenue des Érables, and has nothing but praise for the city where she was born. "Montreal offers us freedom; we have everything here. When driving back home from the South Shore (*Rive-Sud*), I see all the bridges, and all the lights... It feels like the city belongs to me. From an airplane you can get a better view of Mount Royal and the river. All of it belongs to us! We're so lucky!"

She remembers the tennis matches with friends in the street. As a young adult, she would walk to Parc La Fontaine. "There were bands on certain evenings. But what we loved the most was a gondola ride on the lake." Her first apartment, small and on the ground floor, cost $45 a month. That was in 1951. She and her husband liked to go out on the town. They would go to a big restaurant at least once a month. They went to Chez Butch Bouchard, the steakhouse owned by Émile Bouchard, the former captain of the Montreal Canadiens, at the corner of Rue Saint-André and Boulevard de Maisonneuve Est, and Chez Queux, a mainstay in Old Montreal that only recently closed its doors. "Those were the good old days, when everyone smoked!" she reminisced, although she herself quit smoking for good in 1996.

They bought their first car 10 years after they were married. Before that, they went everywhere by bus or tram. "The tram seats were made of wicker. The winters were no joke: The trolley would often derail because of the ice, and the men would get out and push." A major fan of the Montreal Expos, she would go to as many as 15 games per season. "I always needed a box of Cracker Jack during the game!" Madame Couture had a good career. For 25 years, she worked as a telephone operator, bookkeeper and office manager at Durivage, a baked goods factory on Rue Dandurand.

A true Montrealer at heart, she proudly affirmed: "Everything in Montreal is beautiful to me. I've always lived on the island and I'll never leave."

236

The Bacon Bar

236

A "bacon-centric" bar—admit it, the concept is intriguing. **Brutus** doesn't go for moderation: Decadence is the name of the game. The Bloody Caesar (renamed the Bloody Brutus) is served with a rose made of bacon. The poutine? That's right: topped with bacon. In fact, if you so desire, it will even be served in a bowl made of—wait for it—bacon. The bar is done up in black and gold (sort of a "Gothic-glam" look) and has big cushioned booths. You'll also find the biggest selection of bourbons in Quebec [1290 Rue Beaubien Est].

Fabulous Flavors of Petite-Patrie

237

Les Empoteuses (A) [1106 Rue Beaubien Est] serves breakfast, brunch and light lunch. The menu varies from week to week according to what's available at the markets. Dishes include French toast with blueberries and lavender cream, eggs Benedict (the hollandaise sauce is shockingly perfect) and morning poutines, a clever combination of potato, braised ham, egg, hollandaise sauce, and (the essential) cheese curds. They also make and sell little jars of original preserves (ginger-pear, rosemary-lemon-blueberry, peach-basil), candied onions, pepper jellies, fruit ketchup and pickled vegetables. To top it all off, the staff is as friendly as can be—it's the kind of place you want to return to often.

Ariane Maurice prepares heavenly pies in a lovely spot with the name **Pâtisserie Bicyclette**. Her pies are big—they serve eight—and topped with fresh, quality ingredients. The ginger-bourbon pecan pie on shortcrust is the most popular item; and I have weakness for the wildflower honey and pear mousse on buckwheat graham crust, or chai-infused dark chocolate cream. The crusts are really remarkable—as are the famous cannelés [1256 Rue Saint-Zotique Est].

237 A

My Oasis

238

Ever since **Isle de Garde** (A) [1039 Rue Beaubien Est] opened its doors in 2014, it's been my neighborhood bar—my place of refuge. It's a warm and welcoming place where you know the beer will be great and the food delicious. Isle de Garde has one of the most interesting beer menus in town. There are 24 drinks on tap: a kombucha, a cider and a rotating selection of 22 craft beers from Quebec (some of which are brewed by the bar). All the beers are served at the correct temperature and in the proper glass and format. In the summer, the terrace on Rue Beaubien is fantastic. The kitchen offers macaroni and cheese, a charcuterie platter, tartare and a burger (made with aged beef from **Le Marchand du Bourg**; see Reason #234).

Right next door, at **Automne Boulangerie** [6500 Avenue Christophe-Colomb], you'll find the best baguette in the area. Julien Roy, one of the two young owners, won best apprentice baker in France's prestigious Mondial du Pain in 2013. Do not resist the alluring cheese baguette.

The Perfect Neighborhood Café

239

Residents of Petite-Patrie are lucky to have **Caffè Mille Gusti**; it's a real gem. Every day of the week, Joe Scalia, the owner, is there to welcome customers with a *bella* or *bello*, taking the time to chat with each of them. He remembers every conversation, and he'll kindly ask you how your move went or how your kids are doing. Scalia loves kids; they're always welcome in his establishment. If you order a sandwich, ask him to add "mille gusti," a tasty spicy pesto made with pickled vegetables and peppers, made by Joe himself [1038 Rue Saint-Zotique Est].

Montreal Olives

240

The story of Francis Senécal, owner of **Héritage Kalamata**, is a fascinating one. Introduced to olive-growing in Greece during a trip to a friend's homeland, Senécal discovered a deep love for the country, its people and its food. He was so inspired that he decided to begin cultivating unused land belonging to his friend, and to become an olive and olive oil producer. Since then, he and his wife have returned to Greece each year after Christmas to harvest the fruit of their olive groves. They sell their produce at their Petite-Patrie boutique and workshop and in various places in Quebec. Their olive oil is herbal and fruity with a peppery finish. I can't get enough of their olives stuffed with curried sautéed cashews, lemon olives, or "La Bomba," an olive stuffed with a delectable mix of eggplant, artichoke, carrot, mushroom and hot pepper. A guaranteed smash hit at cocktail hour [1129 Rue Bélanger].

Great Food on Bélanger Street

241

La Récolte is a restaurant that brought something new to the part of Rue Bélanger that could easily be called "Little Mexico." With mismatched cutlery, colorful decor and a thorough lack of pretention, the place has been mainly known for its fantastic brunches on Saturday and Sunday. Customers pleaded for more, so the restaurant now serves gourmet dinners from Wednesday to Saturday. Presentation is a priority, and the dishes, made exclusively with local Quebec products, are consistently excellent. The menu changes with the seasons. When asparagus is in season, it makes an appearance on the menu; when squash is ready, the gourd is put to delightfully inventive uses. You can taste the love that chefs have for local products. This is quality food, without question [764 Rue Bélanger].

Little Mexico

242

When you want to make mouthwatering Mexican meals, the bakery-butcher-market-restaurant **Sabor Latino** is your best friend. The aisles are packed with hundreds of Latin-American products, including fruits and vegetables like guavas, chayotes and tomatillos. You can almost always find ripe avocados to whip up that last-minute guacamole. I usually pick up some *queso fresco*, fresh cheese that's great on tacos (ask to try the different varieties at the counter). They also sell the freshest corn tacos on the island, nachos and cilantro for an incredibly low price. When I'm not up to cooking at home, I go to the restaurant section and order guacamole and marinated shredded beef for tacos. And I never leave Sabor Latino without a churro or two, cooked on-site and still warm [436 Rue Bélanger].

An Address in a Song

243

You may or may not have heard of the rock group Beau Dommage, but on their first album, from 1974, they mention a specific Montreal address: 6760 Rue de Saint-Vallier. Since then, the address has taken on a mythic status in the city. In 2015, the alleyway at the spot was officially named **Ruelle Beau-Dommage** (A) in honor of the band. At the south end, you can see a mural depicting the cover of that famous album. A member of the group, Robert Léger, lived at the address in 1972. At the time, he paid $65 in rent for a seven-room place; today, the average price for a similar lodging in Petite-Patrie is around $1,215. It's a clear indication of the neighborhood's ever-growing popularity [Rue Saint-Zotique Est, between Saint-Vallier and Saint-Denis].

Some other murals in the neighborhood are worth mentioning as well. There's the highly photogenic **Montréal Love** (B) by Nicolas Fortin (Rue de Bellechasse at the corner of Avenue Christophe-Colomb); two major pieces by American artist El Mac, **L'Esprit d'Été** (C) (Boulevard Rosemont, between Avenue Christophe-Colomb and Rue de la Roche) and **La Mère Créatrice** (D) (Rue de Bellechasse, at the corner of Rue Saint-Hubert); and **Más–Penser à Prendre le Temps** (E) by French artist Mateo (Rue de Fleurimont at the corner of Avenue Papineau).

243 B

243 A

243 C

243 D

Travel Back in Time

244

The Rosemont neighborhood has an institution that hasn't changed in 60 years: **Le Roi du Smoked Meat**. The 1950s-style red booths and huge jars of pickles and peppers add a deeply nostalgic touch. Time truly seems to have stopped in this restaurant, which opened in 1954. And there's more good news: The smoked meat holds up to anything you'll find at a deli in the Plateau. The long-term staff (some have been there for over 50 years) have definitely seen their share of late-night shenanigans over the years. It's open till 5:30 a.m. from Thursday to Sunday, closing at 2:30 from Monday to Wednesday, making it a magnet for late-night revelers who need to soak up the booze after the bars close. Their smoked meat poutine is a top hangover cure [6705 Rue Saint-Hubert].

Miss Dumpling

245

If you pass by the window of a tiny restaurant in Saint-Hubert Plaza on any given day, you're bound to see two women patiently preparing hundreds of dumplings by hand. Everything is out in the open at **La Maison de Mademoiselle Dumpling**: The women work their fingers with delicacy and precision. You can't get dumplings that are any fresher. There are about eight tables inside, and a few Chinese products for sale on the shelves. The menu is short: six appetizers, a few kinds of dumplings, two desserts and tea. But really, you come here for the dumplings: pork, beef, chicken, seafood or vegetarian, boiled or fried—everything is perfect. You can also take a bag of frozen dumplings to go [6381 Rue Saint-Hubert].

246A

In restaurants, bills are divided by the number of patrons.

The Beautiful Rebel

246

Belle et Rebelle (A) [6321 Rue Saint-Hubert] was one of the first boutiques to specialize in women's clothing designed in Montreal. It's now 10 years running and has brought customers the work of over a hundred Quebec creators, both established and up-and-coming. The list of names includes Mélissa Nepton, Matt & Nat, Ève Gravel, Le Bonnetier and Jennifer Glasgow. All the clothing, jewelry, accessories and decorations are chosen with care. On the last Saturday of each month, shopping means helping: The store donates 20 percent of its day's sales to Maison Passages, an organization that helps women in difficulty. The boutique's little sister, **Petite Rebelle** [6583A Rue Saint-Hubert], offers design from here and beyond, aiming toward a slightly more casual look.

Yummy Umami

247

There's no doubt about it: Charles-Antoine Crête of **Montréal Plaza** is one of Montreal's most talented chefs. After working as Normand Laprise's right-hand man at Toqué!, Crête decided to open his own restaurant. It's elegant and modern, decorated with playful souvenirs of childhood and items typically found at a grandmother's house: cherub lamps, a Smurfs collection, a grandfather clock, a stuffed bear head. The menu is short and to the point—fish tartare + crispy, cannelloni baloney (yes, real baloney), fried Brussels sprouts—no frills, no wasted words. On your plate, however, the abovementioned dish turns out to be more than you'd expect: The Brussels sprouts are topped with homemade mayo and Parmesan. It's umami delight. The service is spot-on—attentive yet friendly and casual—and the food is first-rate. Other delights include whelk gratiné, char confit, venison tartare and Jerusalem artichoke. The restaurant is as bold as its food is tasty [6230 Rue Saint-Hubert].

247

248A 249A 251

Family First

248

I must have passed by **Casa do Alentejo** (A) a thousand times before I really noticed it. The facade may be a little dingy, but behind it is a wonderful Portuguese restaurant with a family atmosphere and typical decor. They serve succulent charcoal-fire grilled chicken and impressive fries, and the price point is excellent. A great spot to go with the family [5938 Rue Saint-Hubert].

Cà Phê Con Leche [5912 Rue Saint-Hubert] has a strangely bilingual name, and there's a touching story behind it. The combination of Vietnamese (*cà phê* means "coffee") and Spanish (*con leche* means "with milk") is a symbol of the love story between Kim, from Vietnam, and Yasmin, from Venezuela. The couple joined forces to open a café-restaurant that reflects their dual history. The two-part menu has family meals and drinks from their two countries of origin—a pleasing mixture of pho and arepas. You're sure to get a warm welcome and to feel like you're right at home. If the weather is nice, be sure to try the terrace in the back.

Heavenly Coffee

249

I'm passionate about the coffee at **Pista** (A) [500 Rue Beaubien Est], a beautiful little spot a few steps from Beaubien Metro station. It all started with Maxime Richard, whose previous endeavor saw him serving coffee from a cycle that grinds the beans using the leg-power of the cyclist. After two years of selling his coffee around town (mainly at festivals), the young barista decided to give his coffee setup a permanent roof. Thus, this chic café was born, with a color scheme of white, pale green and a touch of gold. Try the beautifully balanced coffee and the avocado toast, topped with a perfectly poached egg.

Moustache [35 Rue Beaubien Est] is another nice café, located farther west. Take the opportunity to pet Jay, the mascot, a big and adorably nonchalant Bernese mountain dog. With a large communal table, it's a great place to work for a few hours, and you can fuel up with vitamin-packed smoothies like the Mango Lassi (mango, coconut milk, honey) or the Tout Vert (green apple, kale, fennel, parsley, lemon, ginger). In summertime, the cold-brew coffee is a definite winner.

250

A Library for Clowning Around

250 Just a stone's throw from the Rosemont Metro station is the **Bibliothèque Marc-Favreau**. It's named after the actor responsible for the famous Quebec clown character, Sol. The library has incredible light, and it's an environmentally friendly building (protecting the environment was a passion of Favreau's). With wood walls, ceilings and floors, it's clearly a family-oriented facility. There's a colorful room with a heated floor for kids four and under; a technology room for teens, with plenty of computers and multimedia software; and a reading room for adults, with lots of windows and a fireplace (it's the only room where silence is required). Right behind the library is **Parc Luc-Durand**, which is wonderfully designed for kids. It's dedicated to the actor who played Gobelet, the clown who paired with Sol to make such a mark on Quebec's television culture [500 Boulevard Rosemont].

Rosemont Vietnamese

251 **Y Lan** is an unpretencious Vietnamese family restaurant that serves traditional Southeast Asian cuisine. The dishes are terrific: flavorful and unbelievably affordable. That combination—and the fact that it's a bring-your-own-wine spot—is what keeps me going back to Y Lan. The La Vong fish, a typical Hanoi dish, is excellent: cubes of white fish lightly breaded and sprinkled with cumin, with lots of fresh dill. To eat it, you roll it up in a lettuce leaf with vermicelli and fresh herbs, then dip it in shrimp sauce. Exotic and exquisite [6425 Rue Saint-Denis].

Discover a Wine Cave

252 **Cul-Sec Cave & Cantine** has a concept that's very refreshing: It's a small bistro, but also a neighborhood "wine cave," offering extraordinary privately imported wines. Many wines are natural, most are organic, and all are great bottles from top wineries. You can discover real treasures (with the precious guidance of the sommelier) for a good price. They have a refined menu as well (you have to order food to buy wine). You can enjoy food and drink at a table or take them to go. The menu offers cheese and charcuterie platters, beet salad, foie gras mousse, oysters and lemon-cabbage risotto. But, as the decor suggests, the wine is the top draw here. *Salut* [29 Rue Beaubien Est].

252

Davide and Luciano

253

Il Bazzali (A) [285 Rue Beaubien Est], a restaurant that seats about 20, serves up Northern Italian cuisine. It also offers the lovely tenor singing voice of Davide Bazzali, one of the chef-owners. Bazzali is a talented opera singer and treats customers to Italian classics while he cooks. I know what you're thinking, but it isn't irritating—quite the opposite. The music adds wonderfully to the charm of this little neighborhood bring-your-own-wine restaurant. I recommend the five-course table d'hôte, which is reasonably priced ($35 or $55) and varies each week based on the available ingredients. Reservations recommended.

When you walk through the door at **Luciano** [1212 Rue Saint-Zotique Est], you feel instantly welcomed by the Italian *famiglia*. Luciano, the undisputed master of fresh pasta, mans the stove, and Ange Forcherio takes care of food and wine service. (Tell him what you like and your budget, and he'll help you find a wine that won't disappoint.) The food is simple and memorable, and the menu smart and concise: Luciano will delight you with his *spaghetti cacio e pepe* (spaghetti with pecorino and black pepper) and the *tagliatelle porcini* with mushrooms, caramelized onions, white wine and veal sauce.

A Decadent Stroll Through Little Italy

254

Take a trip that will make your taste buds rejoice (although your waistline might protest a little). Start at the south end of Little Italy, at the pastry shop **La Cornetteria** (A) [6528 Boulevard Saint-Laurent]. Devour a ricotta-filled *cornetto*; it'll give you strength for the journey ahead. You should also be informed that the chocolate *torta caprese* (a gluten-free flourless cake made from almonds) is fabulous. Next, head to **Milano Fruiterie** [6862 Boulevard Saint-Laurent], a neighborhood institution since 1954. They have thousands of types of pasta imported from Italy (well, it seems like thousands), the most affordable Parmesan in town, olives that bring people in from all over the city and unbelievable mozzarella di Bufala balls. You might need a coffee fix afterward: Enjoy a full-bodied espresso or a latte at **Caffè San Simeon** [39 Rue Dante], the best Italian café in town (and the prices are great, too). Finally, a visit to **Alati-Caserta** is a must [277 Rue Dante]. Pick up a few cannolis, or a lemon granita in the summer; it's perfectly sweet and sour. Savor your treats in **Parc Dante**, across the street, while you watch locals playing bocce.

Indulge in a Vice

255

The bar **Vices & Versa** has the nicest terrace in Little Italy: an enclosed backyard with a lovely view of Parc Soeur-Madeleine-Gagnon right next door. With the wooden fence and the park's greenery, and the big tree that provides shade overhead, it's just about perfect. Opened in 2004, Vices & Versa was one of the first bars to specialize in Quebec craft beers, and it also has a menu that highlights local products (artisanal sausages and charcuterie, Quebec lamb and cheese) at very fair prices [6631 Boulevard Saint-Laurent].

The Best Pizza in Montreal. Period.

256

Fabrizio Covone left Montreal for Naples when he was just 22. His goal was to find the secret to great Neapolitan pizza. Two years later, he returned to Montreal, and he brought the secret with him; he also brought a 7,700-pound (3,500-kilogram) oven. Able to reach temperatures of 900°F (482°C), the oven allows the crust to achieve a magnificently light, crunchy texture. Then there's the tomato sauce, which is perfectly balanced. I recommend the Margherita, a simple no-frills pizza (tomato sauce, mozzarella and basil). With courteous and efficient service, a huge Italian wine menu and consistently delicious food, **Bottega** has climbed to the highest echelon in my list of favorite restaurants. Definitely the best pizza in Montreal [65 Rue Saint-Zotique Est].

257

An American-Style Picnic

257

This small restaurant (it seats only about 30) located kitty-corner from Parc de la Petite-Italie has a brilliant concept. When the weather is nice, customers at **Dinette Triple Crown** can bring their food to the park after ordering at the counter. You're provided with napkins, utensils and condiments in a picnic basket (you return them when you're finished). The food is hearty, tasty Southern-American: fried chicken, macaroni and cheese, smoked brisket, pulled pork sandwich, sweet potato fries and so on. Everything is homemade: the bacon, the marinades, the sauces, the bread, the cocktail syrups and the desserts. Go here for great Southern cooking, and if you like, the ultimate picnic [6704 Rue Clark].

Pots and Guns

258

It may be the only business in Canada that sells both kitchen supplies and...hunting rifles. **Quincaillerie Dante**, a family business run by the Vendittelli family since 1956, has evolved slowly over the years. It started as a general store specializing in Italian-made building tools. The gun counter was added in the 1960s. Elena Faita-Vendittelli, the daughter of the shop's founding couple, has become more and more involved in the business. Her passion for kitchenware is contagious: She's progressively added high-quality kitchen items to the hardware section. If you share her passion, you'll be excited by the colorful casserole dishes, artisanal cutting boards and chef's knives. Don't forget to satisfy your curiosity with a look at the rifles and scopes [6851 Rue Saint-Dominique].

Bulk Up

259

With over 3,000 products from the four corners of the globe, Épices **Anatol** sets the standard for Montreal bulk stores. The variety is remarkable: spices, herbs and dried fruits, nuts, seeds, legumes, pasta, cereals, candy, coffee and tea. There are 100 different kinds of nuts alone: plain, salted, toasted, mixed, seasoned. You can find many packets of spices and fine herbs for just a dollar. Madagascar vanilla beans are three times less expensive than anywhere else. Another nice thing about shopping here is that it reduces waste: You can buy exactly the amount you really need. Looking for peony root, ras-el-hanout (a spice blend), wild pansy or Persian saffron? Anatol definitely has your back [6822 Boulevard Saint-Laurent].

260

Urban Honey

261 Opened in 2012, **Alvéole** is an inspiring company that opened in 2012. Its mission is to take the concept of "local honey" to a whole new level, and to support the crucial role of bees in the city's ecosystem at the same time. Alvéole produces its own honey and helps schools, businesses and local residents install hives on their roof or balcony or in their backyard. They also give guidance on operating and caring for bee colonies and extracting honey. There are now 350 hives throughout Montreal and the surrounding areas, and the beekeeping community produces three tons of honey a year. At the Alvéole shop, in the heart of Mile-Ex, you can find the essential beekeeping tools, and you can also buy jars of honey from different neighborhoods (usually available from September to December). The urban honey tasting boxes, with honey from Montreal, Quebec City and Toronto, are the coolest thing ever. The Montreal box contains honeys from the neighborhoods of Villeray, NDG, Westmount, Saint-Henri and the Plateau. The differences in color and taste are astonishing, because each neighborhood has its own vegetation, which has a direct effect on the honey the bees produce [7154 Rue Saint-Urbain].

Mexican Street Food

260 **Le Roi du Taco** (*El Rey del Taco*) combines a Mexican greasy spoon and a small grocery store—it's the perfect destination for a pre- or post-market snack. They serve traditional Mexican breakfasts starting at 10 a.m., and a lunch and dinner menu that's quick and tasty, a thousand times better than any fast food around. You'll be welcomed with colorful nacho chips and homemade salsas, which you can boost with an order of guacamole with cilantro. Pozole, a traditional soup with corn and pork, will warm you up in no time. Try the very tender and perfectly spiced lamb tacos, served on super-fresh corn tortillas [232 Rue Jean-Talon Est].

261

My Market

262

Another essential stop in Montreal is **Jean-Talon Market** (A) (Marché Jean-Talon). Established in 1933 on a former lacrosse (originally a First Nations sport) field, the market has a great location: It's just south of Rue Jean-Talon, which has long been a busy road, and it's close to Boulevard Saint-Laurent— the Main. Today, no matter the season, you can visit this major gathering place for local producers, to buy fresh, seasonal fruits and vegetables and products that are hard to find in the supermarkets: fresh peas, Romanesco broccoli, comb honey, wild blueberries, zucchini flowers, Armenian cucumbers and garlic blossoms. On top of all the stands and kiosks, there are dozens of specialty shops throughout the area.

One of the shops open year-round is **Les Jardins Sauvages** kiosk. You can admire the marvels collected by nature explorer François Brouillard—dozens of wild plants and mushrooms, like fiddleheads and morels in the spring, glasswort, sea parsley and chanterelles in summer and fall. In the winter, they offer cooked dishes with ingredients gathered from the forests of Quebec (soups, sauces and meats) [south specialties aisle].

Artisanal ice cream shop **Havre-aux-Glaces** (B) should definitely be on your itinerary. The range of ice cream and sorbet flavors is fantastic, as delicious as they are inventive: raspberry, lemon, maple caramel brûlé, pink grapefruit, mango, matcha, apricot milk and orange blossom. Try as many as you want—none will disappoint [south specialties aisle].

Épices de Cru is a spice-hunters dream: Ethné and Philippe de Vienne aim to help you take any dish up a notch, with their exceptional spice mixtures. Be sure to try the Route de la Soie (Silk Road), a blend of three major cuisines (Persian, Chinese and Indian); it's incredible on duck breast. Another highlight is the satay blend, which raises any chicken dish to the "wow" level [south specialties aisle].

Le Marché des Saveurs du Québec brings together more than 7,000 artisanal Quebec agricultural foodstuffs. Cloudberry preserves, cattail heart marinades, ox-eye

262 A

262A

daisy capers, oils, vinegars, teas, more than 225 varieties of cheese and the largest selection of artisanal alcoholic drinks around: You'll make some awesome discoveries [280 Place du Marché-du-Nord].

Sausage-maker **William J. Walter** dominates its field with a vast selection and exceptional products. I don't think I've ever eaten a sausage that matches the deliciousness of the William Suisse, a smoked sausage with pork, beef, veal and chunks of melted Swiss cheese; or the Glutenberg Red beer sausage, slightly spicy and with the perfect texture [244 Place du Marché-du-Nord].

Boucherie du Marché is a butchery that's always packed, because of its unbeatable marinated meat. The veal flank steak is amazing [224 Place du Marché-du-Nord].

The breads at **Joe la Croûte** fly off the shelves at an incredible speed. It's pretty common for the shelves to be totally bare at the end of the day—it's a sure sign of the impeccable quality of the loaves. They make a different batch every day [7024 Avenue Casgrain].

Finally, it's absurd to leave the market without trying a maple pecan pie at **La Fournée des Sucreries de l'Érable**, the best pie in the world, with a subtle caramel flavor and a generous helping of nuts [near the main entrance].

262B

262 A

Revived Neighborhood

263

A unique neighborhood squeezed between Mile End and Parc Extension, **Mile-Ex** was long occupied by different textile and food processing businesses. Its location close to Jean-Talon Market makes it a sector with enormous potential, and revitalization is now underway. The first new-generation establishment to take root in the neighborhood was **Dépanneur Le Pick-Up** [7032 Rue Waverly], a small corner store that's also much more. They serve super-high-quality sandwiches; it's crucial that you try the "vegetarian pulled pork".

The restaurant that started the ball rolling was **Mile-Ex** (A) [6631 Rue Jeanne-Mance]. Opened in 2012, it offers gourmet street food, with a focus on seafood. They have a decadent burger, and tasty ribs rub shoulders with squid rolls, grilled octopus, cold marinated salmon, crab cakes and sautéed whelks with leeks. The place is cozy but festive. They don't take reservations.

A few years later, **Manitoba** [271 Rue Saint-Zotique Ouest] appeared, a rustic-chic restaurant in a magnificent space, where foraged food takes the spotlight.

263 A

Über-Cool

264

The spot that best represents the spirit of Mile-Ex is definitely **Alexandraplatz** (A). A seasonal bar that opens up when it's warm, it took over part of an industrial building, and you enter through a garage door. With picnic tables on the terrace, it's a strange yet welcoming oasis in the middle of an industrial wasteland, completely off the beaten track and pretty much unbeatable as a place to have a few drinks on a lovely summer evening. The **Marché de Nuit** is held there five times each summer, in collaboration with the Association des Restaurateurs de rues du Québec (a street food association). Local artisans, DJs and food trucks set up outside the bar from 2 p.m. to 11 p.m.—it's basically an old-fashioned block party. Do whatever it takes not to miss it. The bar is open from April to October [6731 Avenue de l'Esplanade].

264 A

For Vinyl-Lovers

265

You won't stumble upon **180 g** by accident. Located on a dead-end street in an industrial area, the café-music store is a favorite for music lovers. The name refers to the weight of a modern-day vinyl record, the reissues and deluxe versions that are somewhat heavier than their ancestors. The friendly place serves coffee from the independent roaster **Saint-Henri**. Sip a cup while you listen to interesting records, new or used, with some very helpful suggestions from the owners. The selection is great and varied, from hip-hop to super-indie to Californian or German electronic music. Make a note of the address before you go, because it's not so easy to spot [6546 Rue Waverly].

Many shops, restaurants and cafés, especially smaller ones, close for the construction holidays (the last two weeks of July). The same goes for the first two weeks in January—a well deserved rest after the holidays. During these times, it is best to contact businesses before you head out.

265

Parc Extension, Villeray, Saint-Michel, Ahuntsic

The very multicultural district north of Rue Jean-Talon is composed of four distinct neighborhoods. It is home to students and young couples with children who benefit from being close to the Metro system, a wide range of services, cuisine from all around the world and affordable housing.

PARC-NATURE DE
L'ÎLE-DE-LA-VISITATION

•285

LAVAL

•286

RUE FLE

PARC DE
LA MERCI

291

BOUL. GOUIN O.

290

AHUNTSIC

RUE SAINT-HUBERT

AV. CHARLAND

BOUL. HENRI-BOURASSA O.

•288
289

RUE SAUVÉ O.

BOUL. SAINT-LAURENT

RUE SAINT-DENIS

RUE CHABANEL O.

BOUL. DE L'ACADIE

277

27

•287

•2

RUE JARRY O.

PARC
JARRY

● Sights + photo ops
● Bars + restaurants
● Stores + markets
● Arts + culture
● Activities + walks

PARC-EXTENSION

266
267

RUE JEAN-TALON

BOUL. LACORDAIRE

• 283

• 282

RUE VIAU

SAINT-MICHEL
• 281

• 280

RUE D'IBERVILLE

VILLERAY

AV. PAPINEAU

RUE VILLERAY

Ⓜ
• 279

BOUL. PIE-IX

BOUL. SAINT-MICHEL

BOUL. ROSEMONT

15ᵉ AV.

• 278
Ⓜ

RUE DE CASTELNAU E.

274
73•
• 272
271•
270•
269•
Ⓜ
• 268
Ⓜ

AV. CHRISTOPHE-COLOMB

Ⓜ
RUE SAINT-DENIS

RUE BELLECHASSE

RUE D'IBERVILLE

RUE MASSON

Ⓜ

• 284

266A

The Culinary Magic of India

266 Parc Extension is famous for its legion of Indian restaurants: **Malhi** [880 Rue Jarry Ouest], **India Beau Village** [640 Rue Jarry Ouest], **Punjab Palace** [920 Rue Jean-Talon Ouest], **Maison Indian Curry** [996 Rue Jean-Talon Ouest] and more. If you're a local, you have to declare a favorite; it's like being part of a tribe. My own preferred choice is **Bombay Mahal** (A) because the meals are never dull, but tangy [1001 Rue Jean-Talon Ouest]. The butter chicken is the most popular item, but the vegetarian options are also worth exploring. The baingan bharta, a purée of smoked eggplant, onions, tomatoes and spices and topped with cilantro, and the mutter paneer, a mix of peas and chunks of fresh cheese, are both very worthwhile—as is the naan bread. At lunchtime, the vegetarian thali plate is only $6—in this day and age, getting such a delicious meal for that price seems like a small miracle.

The Eyebrow Factory

267 When you enter **Beauté Dee's**, you feel like you've been catapulted into a beauty salon in the heart of Bombay. The salon offers threading, an ancient Indian hair removal technique that's extremely precise, pretty much painless and perfect for the face. Dee's Beauty is a true factory for eyebrow epilation. Hundreds of women visit the salon every day (the treatment is always quick), sitting one after another in the chairs of the salon's many threading experts. The result is perfect eyebrows for a ridiculous price ($5) in just a few minutes. No appointment necessary; just show up [1014 Rue Jean-Talon Ouest].

Delicious Alep

268

A few steps from Jean-Talon Market you'll find **Alep** and its smaller sibling, **Le Petit Alep** (A). They're my favorite restaurants in the neighborhood: an exotic Syrian and Armenian menu, dishes grilled to perfection and tapenades that are bursting with flavor: happiness kilometers away from the war. I often find myself daydreaming about the boneless marinated lamb, which is braised for hours and served with almonds, pine nuts and sublime rice—it's divine. And then there's the kabab terbialy, a skewer of filet mignon covered in a garlic tomato sauce—it may be the most flavorful dish I've ever tasted. You're probably starting to get the picture: I have pretty strong feelings for Alep. The atmosphere is casual, the prices are reasonable and the wine cellar may be the city's best-kept secret. My friends and I love it so much, we've created a new verb: *Want to Alep?* [191 Rue Jean-Talon Est]

A Cortado on De Castelnau

269

Café Larue & Fils (A) enjoys a prime location facing Sainte-Cécile church and its square at the corner of Rue De Castelnau Est and Avenue Henri-Julien. The view adds a lovely touch of solemnity to your coffee-drinking experience, inside or from the outdoor terrace. The brightly lit café makes a bold *cortado*, a little coffee drink made with one-third espresso and two-thirds steamed milk. Café Larue & Fils is effectively the central hub of **Place De Castelnau**, a public square on the street of the same name, between Avenue de Gaspé and Rue Drolet. The square is set up for the public from June to September: The sidewalks are decorated with urban furniture and painted in geometric whites and blues, transforming the stretch into a vibrant area to relax or hang out with friends [244 Rue De Castelnau Est and 405 Rue Jarry Est].

268 A 269 A

Artisanal Ice Cream

270

Artisanal ice cream shop **Les Givrés** charms you right off the bat with its unique flavors like campfire (toasted marshmallow and caramel), bagel (cream cheese and sweet bagel toast) and spicy butternut squash (squash and allspice). All the ingredients are made on the premises; the caramel, the pistachio butter, the praline, the brownies, the marshmallows and even the cones are homemade. The rule here is natural and artisanal, with no colorings, artificial flavors or preservatives. Spoil yourself and try their ice cream sandwich, made with buttery cookies and filled with chocolate or caramel sauce—wonderfully decadent. Open seasonally [334 Rue De Castelnau Est and 2730 Rue Masson].

Armenian Delights

271

At **Chez Apo**, the lahmadjounes (Armenian pizza with very thin crust similar to pita bread) are so fresh they may well still be warm from the oven when you buy them. Topped with an aromatic blend of ground beef, onions, garlic, parsley and the perfect dash of peppers, it's hard to resist eating them on the way home—but the experience is best if you hold off. They reheat quickly (about a minute at 400°F/200°C); then top them with lettuce, onions, herbs, fresh tomatoes and a splash of lemon juice to enhance the flavor. Roll them up into wraps and enjoy. You can also top them with whatever else you have on hand: tzatziki, parsley, mint, olive oil, cucumber. Delicious every time. It's a feast for an astonishingly low price [420 Rue Faillon Est].

272 273A

Tabouleh, Shish Kebab and Baba Ghanoush

272 **Daou**, which opened 40 years ago, was the favorite spot of René Angélil, husband and manager of Céline Dion. In fact, he loved it so much that he got the restaurant to cater the celebrity couple's renewal of their marriage vows in Las Vegas. The decor may be a little somber, but at Daou you can discover intensely fresh and flavorful traditional cuisine from Lebanon. Tabouleh, grape leaves, fattoush, baba ghanoush and hummus make marvelous accompaniments for mouthwatering marinated and grilled meat dishes. The shish kebab, made with cubes of filet mignon, is fabulous. For dessert, try the baklava or the mouhalabia, a rice pudding with Lebanese flavors [519 Rue Faillon Est].

The Darling of Montreal Fashion

273 The two young entrepreneurs behind the women's clothing and accessories label **Cokluch** (A) [410A Rue Villeray] decided to open their studio-storefront in the Villeray neighborhood. Taking inspiration from street fashion, Cokluch offers comfortable clothing with a rebellious touch, all made in Montreal. The brand started in 2007, and its popularity quickly spread. Today it has some 40 points of sale across Canada. In 2016, the duo launched a clothing collection for kids aged six months to four years, called **Cokluch Mini**.

When you leave the shop, head west for a taste of Italy at the friendly **Café Vito** [151 Rue Villeray]. In the summertime, the wooden benches outside are soaked in sunlight—the perfect destination for a strong dose of vitamin D.

A Spanish Pioneer

274

Another one of Villeray's most essential stops is the tapas bar **Tapeo**. It was one of the pioneers of the neighborhood's renewal when it opened in 2004—the tapas trend has really taken off since then—and of Spanish cooking in Montreal. The chef, Marie-Fleur Saint-Pierre, offers a true culinary journey with her tapas menu for sharing. Everything is so delicious that it's hard to choose. Marinated swordfish carpaccio, veal flank, cod fritters, sherry beef shoulder, grilled octopus, sautéed mushrooms and heavenly vine tomatoes, lightly topped with oil and accompanied by goat cheese... You have no idea how hungry I am while writing this. Reservations recommended [511 Rue Villeray].

Picnic on Wheels

275

The entrepreneurs behind the café **Oui Mais Non**—who also own La Graine Brûlée (see Reason #42)— are marketing geniuses. In addition of being the owners of the most original café in Villeray, they offer a "picnic cart". Customers can wheel it to **Jarry Park** (just two blocks west) for a wonderful picnic with the café's delicious food (vegetarian or not, according to your preferences). All the necessary dishware is provided, along with themed decorations (pennants, soap bubbles and even a piñata. The cart itself serves as a table. For groups of eight or more, you should make a reservation 48 hours in advance [72 Rue Jarry Est].

Principled Meats

276A

276

The artisanal butcher shop **Pascal le Boucher** (A) [8113 Rue Saint-Denis] specializes in environmentally responsible meats. Pascal Hudon is part of the new generation of ethical butchers who are concerned about the well-being of animals and the traceability of their sources. It's important that Hudon's meat suppliers share his values and respect for animals. The animals must have access to pasture and a healthy diet, without hormones or antibiotics, and they must not be fattened up merely to meet the needs of a profit-based industry. Hudon makes it a point of honor to use the entire carcass. This philosophy brings its share of challenges. For instance, when he buys a whole steer, he'll have only two flanks in stock. That means he has to educate his clientele, to some extent; most customers are unfamiliar with his approach to business. Along with his offering of cuts, Hudon sells homemade sausages and prepared dishes, including his famous Bolognese sauce, made with beef neck and shank. Also, be sure to try the phenomenal PLB meatloaf sandwich on a kaiser bun.

Around the corner, you'll find **LOCO** [422 Rue Jarry Est], the first zero-waste grocery store in town. The goal here is long-term progress and increased awareness (LOCO still has some suppliers that don't meet all the business's hoped-for standards; but still, the idea is there). They sell nuts, flour, dried fruits, pasta, rice, legumes, coffee, tea, fresh fruits and vegetables, etc. Many of the products are sold in bulk; you can use designated jars or bring your own containers. All in all, it's an inspiring business model.

277 | 278

Minimalist and Without Fail

277

Trilogie is an unexpected treasure in this area, just a few yards from the Metropolitan (Highway 40). The restaurant has minimalist all-white decor and mismatched chairs, wooden stools and birdcages, and serves an impeccable lunch made by an all-female team. The crushed cucumber salad appetizer is simply exquisite: The heat of the Szechuan peppers, the sweet and sour black vinegar and the freshness of the cucumber combine to startle the taste buds—it's totally addictive. The dumplings (a daily special, vegetarian and umami—with pork, shrimp and cabbage) are served with a choice of homemade sauces: peanut, vinegar or soy. Order a chrysanthemum tea, and the service will leave a smile on your face. Open from 11 a.m. to 3 p.m., Monday to Friday only [8521 Boulevard Saint-Laurent].

Cakes that Approach Perfection

278

I've been a regular customer at **San Pietro** Italian bakery and pastry shop for over a decade. The authentic family business opened in 1979, with Pietro and Carmela Calderone at the helm. Today, their son runs the bakery, their older daughter takes care of operations, their youngest is in charge of cakes and their granddaughters serve customers. San Pietro has the best cold pizza in Montreal, from the sublime tomato to the white pizza with olive oil and rosemary. Their cakes are covered in a light cream instead of being slathered with too-sweet icing—they're not of this Earth. Try the Black Forest, or get a cake made to order, any way you like it. Choose a decoration style from their vast catalog, or bring a photo of the cake of your dreams. I can confirm that they're up for any challenge: I once requested a heavy-metal-themed cake, with the Iron Maiden logo. Enough said [1950 Rue Jean-Talon Est].

Don't be surprised to see a ton of moving trucks if you visit Montreal on July 1. With most leases ending on June 30, July 1 is the city's unofficial moving day.

A Ray of Sunshine

279 Blue booths, yellow walls and colorful Mexican decor: **Le Petit Coin du Mexique** exudes good feeling. The restaurant is run by the Juarez family, with the matriarch Guadalupe at the oven. Start your meal with the pure and simple tortilla soup: a perfectly balanced base of tomatoes, garlic and onions garnished with strips of fried tortillas, sour cream and *queso añejo* (old cheese). Or go for the *sopes*, small homemade corn-flour tarts topped with *frijoles*, a black bean purée. One of the star dishes is without question the tacos *al pastor*: pork meat marinated and roasted on a spit vertically, like a kebab, then chopped finely. It's served on little corn tortillas and garnished with pineapple and cilantro. It's sour-sweet, lightly spicy and completely delicious [2474 Rue Jean-Talon Est].

A Realm of Random Treasures

280 Welcome to thrifting heaven; a treasure-hunter's paradise; a labyrinth for lovers of bric-a-brac: the one and only **Marché aux Puces Saint-Michel**. This flea market mecca with its jumble of overloaded booths is the perfect place to search for that singular retro or kitsch item you've been looking for. You'll probably find it, and at a reasonable price, too—especially if you know how to bargain a little. Antiques, books, LPs, hockey cards, posters from another time, furniture, jewelry, lamps, old suitcases and a billion other items, many highly unusual, some utterly useless, offered by friendly, funny sellers. It's the only market in the region to have stayed true to its original role as a kind of giant garage sale. For those who love great finds, the market is not to be missed. Friday to Sunday, from 9 a.m. to 5 p.m. [7707 Avenue Shelley].

Let the Kids Skate

281

A flagship project of the Montreal Canadiens Children's Foundation, the **Bleu Blanc Bouge** (A) program builds refrigerated outdoor rinks that meet the regulations of the National Hockey League. The name is based on the Montreal Canadiens' nickname "Les Bleu, Blanc, Rouge" (The Blue, White, Red). "Bouge" means *move* or *be active*. The foundation has already donated six rinks in Montreal and three other elsewhere in Quebec (a tenth is planned for Trois-Rivières in the fall of 2018). The first was built in the Saint-Michel neighborhood, at Parc François-Perrault, in 2009. The refrigeration system makes it possible to maintain quality ice in all types of weather, prolonging the skating season. The goal is to motivate young people to play outside, stay active and develop a healthy lifestyle. In the summer, the areas are transformed into basketball courts and ball hockey and in-line skating terrains.

Also in Parc François-Perrault is the playful art piece *Le Mélomane* (B) by Jean-François Cooke and Pierre Sasseville, suitably positioned in front of Joseph-François-Perrault high school, which is known for its classical music arts program. The piece is a funny representation of the magical power of music: It depicts an ostrich plunging its head into the speaker of a gramophone [7525 Rue François-Perrault].

281B 281A

The Ultimate Lasagna

283

Maison du Ravioli makes close to a ton of fresh pasta every day. The business opened in 1975 and was the first producer of fresh pasta on the island of Montreal. Today it supplies 280 restaurants and is open to the public, with an impressive variety: spaghetti, rigatoni, tagliatelle, farfalle, cheese or meat tortellini and more. The squash ravioli is fabulous: cook them *al dente* and then mix with a bit of butter and sage. But the lasagna really steals the show. Offered in servings of four or eight, they're stuffed with sublime little veal balls, delicately rolled by hand by Italian grandmas. Heavenly [2479 Avenue Charland].

An Italian Sandwich Par Excellence

282

Confession: I'm obsessed with the subs at **Café Milano**. My weekend runs tend to be thin pretexts to make a detour toward Saint-Léonard. My favorite is the steak-capicollo with lettuce, roasted onions, pickled eggplant and hot peppers. And while I'm there, I have to buy the archetypal Italian dessert, a cannoli. An Italian sparkling water goes great with everything. *Mamma mia*—it's as close as you can get to heaven. Open 24 hours a day; cash only [5188 Rue Jarry Est].

A Skate Park Beloved by Kids and Parents Alike

284

Le TAZ (A) [8931 Avenue Papineau] is one of the largest indoor sports centers in Canada. It's the ultimate destination for sports on wheels: skateboards, BMX, in-line skates and scooters. It's also a godsend for parents who are happy to see their kids get some exercise in a safe and monitored indoor skate park, rather than waste their days away on YouTube. The place is gigantic (85,000 square feet/7,900 square meters), and it accommodates everyone: from kids to adolescents to adults, from beginners to experts and those in between. You can rent equipment on-site, and take a course if you aren't ready to start out on your own. Parents will also appreciate the rest area with sofas and free Wi-Fi.

284B

When you go there, take a few minutes to check out **Comme un Jeu d'Enfant** (Easy as child's play) (B), a mural by internationally renowned Parisian artist Seth (Julien Malland). Located at the intersection of Rue Jarry and Avenue Papineau, at the edge of the Saint-Michel neighborhood, the huge piece represents the meeting of cultures: It shows two children of different backgrounds connecting and merging into each other.

284A

285

The Oldest Church in Montreal

286 A true heritage treasure, **Église de la Visitation** is the oldest church in Montreal and one of the oldest in Quebec. Built between 1749 and 1751, it's the only church from the French Regime that still exists in the province. Its facade combines baroque and neo-classical styles; the austerity contrasts with the richness and delicacy of its interior, which features one of the most remarkable ensembles of woodcarving in Quebec. Completed between 1764 and 1836, the decoration inside is the work of three generations of craftspersons. The sculpted keystone is particularly stunning [1847 Boulevard Gouin Est].

An Old Village in the Park

285 **Parc-Nature de l'Île-de-la-Visitation** is one of the city's smaller nature parks, and one of the most interesting. Along with being a site for recreation and activities, the park is also a historic district. Located in the former village of Sault-au-Récollet, it's home to ruins of old mills, relics from the city's industrial past. It's also where you'll find the Maison du Pressoir (Apple Press), an 1813 building that was used for cider manufacturing, and the Maison du Meunier (windmill), which was built in 1727 and now houses a charming bistro. In spring and summer alike, the park is a great destination for for cycling with fabulous views of the Rivière des Prairies, and for snowshoeing, cross-country skiing and sledding in winter. Bird-watchers will try to spot Baltimore orioles, great blue herons, peregrine falcons and black-crowned night herons. You can rent ski equipment, toboggans and binoculars at the park [2425 Boulevard Gouin Est].

286

Mohamed Hage: The Urban Farmer

287 Why not take unused spaces in big cities and use them to feed people? Why not grow food where people live, rather than hundreds of miles away? When Mohamed Hage asked himself these questions in the mid-2000s, he came up with the idea for what would become **Les Fermes Lufa**, the Montreal company that now delivers baskets of vegetables, picked fresh each day in winter and summer, to more than 5,000 people. Mr. Hage is a true visionary: Born in a village near Beirut, he is a young entrepreneur in his thirties who took advantage of advanced horticultural techniques and his knowledge of urban agriculture to build a commercial rooftop greenhouse in 2010—the first of its kind in the world.

Using Google Earth, he searched for large rooftops in Montreal, and ended up choosing a huge industrial building in the Ahuntsic neighborhood to build his greenhouse. "We use spaces that are completely unused, and everyone wins. The building benefits from the insulation provided by the greenhouse, and saves a lot in heating and cooling costs, while the greenhouse benefits from the heat emanating from the building. We take an island of heat and transform it into an island of freshness. And at the same time we provide Montrealers with fresh produce every day."

Lufa now produces 1,000 to 1,500 pounds (450 to 700 kilograms) of vegetables per day during the summer, and about half that amount during the winter. Pretty impressive for a farm that doesn't require any arable land! Mohamed Hage wants to take his vision even further, "If we used the roofs of 19 medium-sized shopping malls in Montreal, we could make the city self-sufficient in vegetables."

His entire operation is carried out sustainably. The greenhouses don't use synthetic pesticides, herbicides or fungicide; they collect rainwater for irrigation, which is also reused; they take advantage of solar energy; use organic means to control pests; and reduce the amount of transportation required to the bare minimum.

I have been ordering the Lufa baskets for several years, and I'm always blown away by the freshness of my salads in the middle of January! I'm still amazed that the cucumbers, tomatoes, peppers and fresh herbs come from a greenhouse just two miles (three kilometers) from my home—not imported from somewhere in the United States, 1,500 miles (2,500 kilometers) away. I also appreciate the fact that many local businesses, such as poultry producers, bakers and cheese makers, partner up with Lufa to take advantage of its large distribution network.

What does the future hold for Lufa? Its business model is attracting a lot of interest from abroad, and will likely be franchised soon. Lufa hopes to develop in the near future in other North American cities, such as Boston, Toronto and Chicago. Mr. Hage, I wish you the very best! Your vision and your business are truly inspiring. [1400 Rue Antonio-Barbeau]

288A

Gourmet Goods on Fleury Street

288

Le St-Urbain (A) [96 Rue Fleury Ouest] is much more than a neighborhood bistro; it's a restaurant that's worth traveling many miles for. The constantly evolving menu is adapted to seasonal products. Try the scallops or the razor shell clams as an appetizer, if they're available. The meat is always perfectly prepared. For dessert, you have to try the warm donuts with fleur de sel caramel. They should probably be illegal.

The inscription on the exterior sets the tone: "*Les bons crus font les bonnes cuites*" (Good wines make good drunkenness). You're guaranteed to eat well at **Les Cavistes** [196 Rue Fleury Ouest]; but the real draw here is the exceptional wine menu, which consists entirely of private imports. The attentive service and impeccable food (the fish is always a standout) make this restaurant a great neighborhood bistro.

The Most Loved Bakery in Ahuntsic

289

One of the most decadent brunches in town can be found at **La Bête à Pain**, a jewel of a bakery that combines a pastry shop, caterer and restaurant. On Saturdays and Sundays, it serves fixed-price five-course brunches ($22); the menu changes from week to week. La Bête shows real attention to detail: artisanal butter, delicious jams, excellent home-smoked salmon, and of course, succulent breads. All their offerings go great with a glass of private import cava or white wine. No reservations required. Stop by for a light snack on weekdays or grab takeout, like duck leg confit or veal and ricotta meatballs. The scrumptious breads, like the *savoyarde*, with potato, crème fraîche, Gruyère and prosciutto, are irresistible. La Bête à Pain can tend to be a victim of its own success; the shelves are frequently empty at the end of the day [114 Rue Fleury Ouest].

289

290

A Lebanon Palace

290

At **Palais des Chaussons et Pizzas**, you'll find a selection of Lebanese dishes that are cooked on-site and ready to eat, along with some 40 varieties of mouthwatering morsels that are perfect for receptions or improvised dinners. The large counters showcase meat kibbehs, zaatar, cheese rolls and Armenian pizzas of all kinds, vine leaves, hummus, baba ghanoush, tabouleh and fatouche salad. Don't leave the premises without trying one of their desserts, like the katayef achta, small pancakes filled with orange blossom cream, served in a cone and topped with pistachios and syrup. Tasty, pretty, light and delicate [77 Boulevard Henri-Bourassa Ouest].

Stroll Along the Rivière des Prairies

291

A calm and scenic riverside walk awaits you near Henri-Bourassa Metro station. Head northwest to take **Rue Somerville**; there you'll see gorgeous modern houses contrasting with historical homes, with huge verandas and bay windows, like the one at no 70. When you reach the end of the street, enter the verdant **Parc Nicolas-Viel**. Continue on to **Boulevard Gouin Ouest** (this street is actually the longest street on the island of Montreal, running alongside the Des Prairies River for about 30 miles/50 kilometers). Other century-old houses, like the magnificent residence at nᵒ 215 (A), are breathtaking. Next follow Avenue Norwood, and find the passageway by nᵒ 11845; from there, you'll reach **Parc de la Merci**. If you want to feel like you're far from the rest of the world, cross the railway bridge via the walkway to reach the tiny **Île Perry** island. Then continue your promenade along Rivière des Prairies until you reach **Parc des Bateliers**. This stretch of greenery seems to have been designed specifically for seeing beautiful sunsets and watching ducks.

Before you leave, visit the **Croix de Chemin**, a stone cross that dates from 1874, at the corner of Gouin and Avenue de Bois-de-Boulogne; it stands out visibly from the other wood crosses. On foot, the whole trip there and back (not including lounging in the park) takes just under two hours.

291A

Off the Beaten Path and Day Trips

Montrealers can sometimes seem unaware of it: Surrounded by water and dotted with majestic riverside parks, their city has amazing opportunities to connect with nature. Here are some day trips that offer a totally different experience in the Montreal area and give you a chance to discover the charms of other nearby parts of *la Belle Province*.

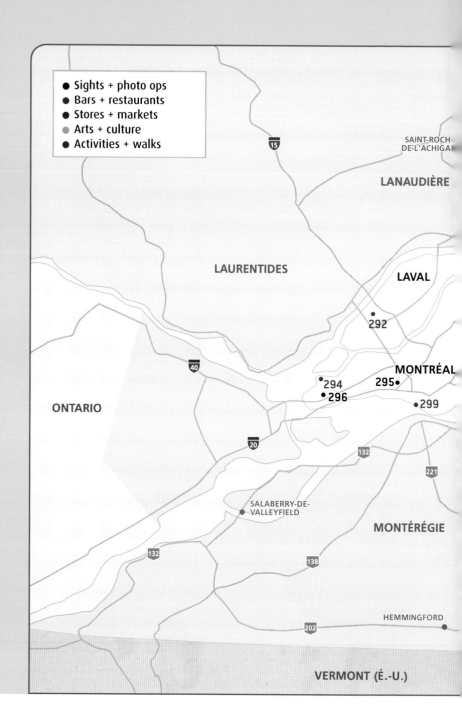

- ● Sights + photo ops
- ● Bars + restaurants
- ● Stores + markets
- ● Arts + culture
- ● Activities + walks

SAINT-ROCH-
DE-L'ACHIGA...

LANAUDIÈRE

LAURENTIDES

LAVAL

● 292

ONTARIO

MONTRÉAL

● 294
● 296

295 ●

● 299

SALABERRY-DE-
VALLEYFIELD

MONTÉRÉGIE

HEMMINGFORD

VERMONT (É.-U.)

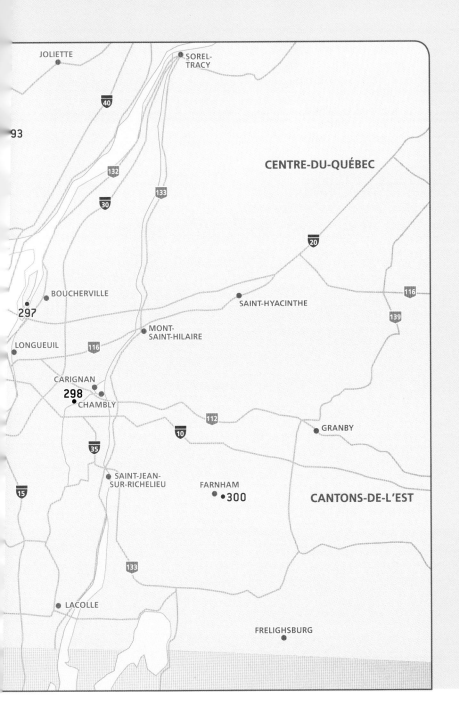

JOLIETTE

SOREL-
TRACY

40

93

132

133

CENTRE-DU-QUÉBEC

30

20

116

BOUCHERVILLE

SAINT-HYACINTHE

297

139

LONGUEUIL

116

MONT-
SAINT-HILAIRE

CARIGNAN

298

CHAMBLY

112

10

GRANBY

35

15

SAINT-JEAN-
SUR-RICHELIEU

FARNHAM

•300

CANTONS-DE-L'EST

133

LACOLLE

FRELIGHSBURG

Pick Your Own

292

There are three farms for where you can pick your own fruits and vegetables on Avenue des Perron in Laval, just 20 minutes from downtown Montreal. Their proximity makes them ideal destinations for a last-minute family activity. A half-day is enough to get there and back, with your arms full. At **Ferme Vaillancourt** [3155] you can enjoy the simple pleasure of picking your own strawberries, raspberries, tomatoes and eggplants. For apples, go to **Verger Gibouleau** [n° 3675]. You drive into the orchard on a tractor—an experience that kids find absolutely thrilling. At **Ferme Turcot** [n° 7209], you can pick eggplants, strawberries, raspberries, sweet and hot peppers, Spanish onions and tomatoes. If you're a blueberry fiend like me, head to **Ferme Marineau**, (A) farther west in Laval [4356 Boulevard Dagenais Ouest].

Forest to the Plate

293

In the heart of the forest at Saint-Roch-de-l'Achigan, overlooking the rapids of Rivière Saint-Esprit, is the most mind-blowing establishment in the region: **À la Table des Jardins Sauvages**. Owned by Nancy Hinton and François Brouillard, the bring-your-own-wine restaurant is open on Saturday evening, and on some Fridays and Sundays for groups or special events. Brouillard is a master picker who specializes in edible plants and wild mushrooms. He's a leader in the local and seasonal food movement. For 30 years, he's helped people discover the incredible wealth of Quebec's forests, finding miraculous edibles that truly enrich our culinary experience. In the no-frills rustic chalet, chef Hinton (she and Brouillard are life and business partners) creates an extraordinary culinary adventure with ingredients like hedgehog (or sweet tooth) mushrooms, sea parsley, glasswort, sandwort, ox-eye daisy capers, bee balm, roseroot shoots, Labrador tea and wild game, all expertly put to use in inventive dishes. The five-course fixed price menu is changed each month to best showcase the products available; it can be found on their website, so customers can bring wines that pair well with the food. You can also discover their products year-round at their Jean-Talon Market kiosk (see Reason #262). Give yourself about an hour to get to the restaurant from downtown. Cash only, and reservations are required [17 Chemin Martin, Saint-Roch-de-l'Achigan].

The Biggest Park in Montreal

294

No need to flee the city to enjoy nature, no matter the season. Over one square mile (2.6 square kilometers) in size, **Parc-Nature du Cap-Saint-Jacques** is the largest park in Montreal. The peninsula offers various views of Rivière des Prairies and Lac des Deux Montagnes. It also has a natural beach, which is super popular during summer heat waves, and an outdoor center that's open year-round. It's great for cross-country skiing (18 miles/30 kilometers of trails), snowshoeing (3 miles/5 kilometers of trails) and walking (4 miles/7 kilometers of trails). The park also offers a wealth of opportunity for sledding, cycling, para-skiing and winter bird-watching. You can also visit an ecological farm and see cows, sheep, donkeys and rabbits. From March to mid-April, a maple grove with some 1,800 taps tempts guests with a feast of pancakes with maple syrup, homemade soup and snow taffy. Binoculars, cross-country skis, snowshoes and sleds are available to rent. The park is a 30-minute drive from downtown [20099 Boulevard Gouin Ouest].

295 | 296

A Few Steps Away from Massive Planes

295

Parc Jacques-de-Lesseps, right beside Pierre Elliott Trudeau International Airport in Dorval, is a spot for aircraft enthusiasts to get a close-up look at the planes as they land and take off: It was specially designed to offer a terrific view of the runways. The first park of its kind in the country, it's named after a French pioneer of aviation and the first pilot to fly over Montreal, in 1910. There are bleachers and hills where you can get a better view, and signs that help you identify planes. For an unforgettable experience, go there around 7 p.m. in the summertime, when large airplanes pass in front of the setting sun. It's all free. About a 30-minute drive from downtown [corner of Avenue Jenkins and Avenue Halpern, Dorval].

The Animal Refuge

296

The **Ecomuseum Zoo** is the only outdoor zoo on the island of Montreal. It's open year-round (it closes only on Christmas day!) for visitors to get a close look at animals native to Quebec. What I like most about the place is that it takes in "refugees": orphans that were injured or born in captivity—animals that are unable to survive in their natural habitat. The Ecomuseum Zoo gives them a permanent home and protection from predators. I was blown away by the howling of the wolves, the mysterious beauty of the arctic foxes and the bizarre head movements of the barn owls. You can see otters, lynx, eagles, white-tailed deer, woodland caribou, flying squirrels, coyotes, possums and plenty of turtles and ducks. It's worth visiting in summer and winter alike—different seasons offer totally different experiences. Give yourself about two hours for the visit; it's about 20 minutes from downtown [21125 Chemin Sainte-Marie, Sainte-Anne-de-Bellevue].

Camping just Six Miles from Downtown

297

Parc National des Îles-de-Boucherville is barely 20 minutes from downtown Montreal. Nonetheless, it's a place where the air is clean, the noise of the city is forgotten and you can enjoy a nice lunch among foxes and white-tailed deer. The park consists of a string of five islands in the St. Lawrence River. It offers an abundance of activities throughout the year: hiking, cycling, canoeing, kayaking, standup paddle surfing, cross-country skiing, snowshoeing and fishing. The campground at Île Grosbois (May through October) has no facilities. You can rent fully equipped Huttopia tents (also called "ready-to-camps"). As you sit on an Adirondack chair in front of a campfire, you'll feel like the city is a million miles away (although from the islands, you can see the silhouettes of the skyscrapers downtown). Tranquility, and a well-deserved break assured [55 Île Sainte-Marguerite, Boucherville].

298

297

A Chimpanzee Sanctuary

298

Gloria Grow and Richard Allan chose Carignan as the site to create the **Fauna Foundation**, a nonprofit organization that comes to the aid of primates that have been mistreated in zoos and medical research labs. Currently the sanctuary has 14 chimpanzees and five monkeys; they're fed and cared for, and they're free to roam through a number of areas.

The two founders invested all their savings into building the refuge, and the organization now relies on donations. Note: It *isn't* open to the public. However, you can attend symposiums and information seminars that are held on fixed dates. The goal is to inform people about the organization, the chimpanzee species and concepts of social responsibility. You have to book ahead to attend. It's 16 miles (25 kilometers) from downtown [faunafoundation.org]

299 B

An Open-Air Art Gallery

299

Parc René-Lévesque (A) [398 Chemin du Canal], in the Lachine neighborhood, is a long peninsula that covers half a square mile. Located alongside the St. Lawrence River, the park is popular with cyclists, cross-country skiers, in-line skaters and walkers, who love the 2 1/2 miles (four kilometers) of paths. It's also a great place for contemporary art: You'll find 22 sculptures from artists from Quebec and beyond along the paths. The standout is *Hommage à René Lévesque* (B), by Robert Roussil. The nine concrete columns, of varying height, crowned with a ring of undulating flames, commemorates the political career of René Lévesque and his nine years at the head of the provincial government. The columns are designed to be lit up like torches, so dusk is a particularly good time to see them. At the western end of the park you can watch the sun set over Lac Saint-Louis. Bikes are also available for rental. Take the opportunity to visit the **LeBer-LeMoyne**

House [1 Chemin du Musée], the oldest fur-trading post in Canada and the oldest building in Montreal; it was built between 1669 and 1671. Just 20 minutes from downtown.

299 A

Nectars of the Gods

300

On the wine route in the Eastern Townships (Cantons-de-l'Est), there are two vineyards that stand out for their exceptional products and their warm, welcoming environment. I discovered **Les Pervenches** (A) [150 Chemin Boulais, Farnham] for the first time when I dined at Toqué! (see Reason #30). I was astonished to find that despite, the climate, a Quebec vineyard could produce such a high quality wine, one that ends up on the menu of the best restaurant in town. A few years later, a chardonnay at Nora Gray (see Reason #90) confirmed it for me. I firmly believe this is the best vineyard in Quebec. The tiny seven-acre estate promotes the principles of organic and biodynamic agriculture, and only sells its wines at the winery and in a few major restaurants. When you visit, you can walk through the vineyards and see the different varieties of grape using a self-guided audio tour. Their production is limited, so call ahead to make sure they have wine in stock before making the trip.

At the foot of Mount Pinnacle in Frelighsburg you'll find **Clos Saragnat** [100 Chemin Richford], (photo page 244), an 86-acre (35-hectare) estate that gets optimal sunshine. Christian Barthomeuf, one of the owners, actually invented ice cider, in 1989. When you visit the vineyard and orchard, which are certified organic, you end up learning a lot about permaculture and ecosystems. Sixty-minute guided tours, with three tastings, are offered from June to October. They're fascinating; I could listen to Barthomeuf talk for hours. Farnham is an hour's drive from Montreal, and Frelighsburg is an hour and a quarter.

300A

The Best of Montreal According to...

There are as many treasures in Montreal as there are Montrealers. Any local has his or her favorite spots, ranging from hidden gems or famous institutions, places they love to share with friends and family. They're the spots that give the city its very essence, its uniqueness and charm. Here are 75 extra reasons (plus a few more) to love Montreal from 12 individuals who love the city with all their heart.

MARIE-JOËLLE PARENT

GUY A. LEPAGE

ARIANE MOFFATT

JEAN-RENÉ DUFORT

REBECCA MAKONNEN

JEAN-PHILIPPE WAUTHIER

MITSOU

SUGAR SAMMY

HERBY MOREAU

CŒUR DE PIRATE

DENIS GAGNON

ANNE-MARIE WITHENSHAW

Marie-Joëlle Parent loves...

A Tropical Paradise in the Heart of the City

301

Time stops when you walk into the **Westmount Conservatory**, a Victorian-style white greenhouse built in 1927. It's the perfect spot to snap out of the winter blues. Sit on one of the benches with a good book and let yourself be lulled by the peaceful sound of the cherub fountain. Don't forget to take a photo—it'll be a surefire Instagram hit [4574 Rue Sherbrooke Ouest].

Espresso and Books

302

I always feel at home at **Café 8 Oz.** The atmosphere is set by colorful chairs, grandmother dishware from thrift shops and a wall of used books. Their coffee comes from Tandem, the famous small roaster, and their pastries are delivered by the king of Montreal sweets, Patrice Demers (see Reason #96) [5851 Rue Saint-Hubert].

301

My Childhood Restaurant

303

When I was a kid, my parents took me to **Pizzeria Napoletana** in Little Italy almost every week. We always ordered the same thing: Vesuviana pizza (mozzarella, tomato sauce, olives and capers) and the *tortellini alla Panna* (cream and Parmesan). The delicious experience ends with a Tartufo ice cream dessert. The place is packed with nostalgia for me. Bonus: It's bring-your-own-wine [189 Rue Dante].

A Trip to Tokyo

304

When I'm craving authentic ramen, **Yokato Yokabai** is where I need to be. The small restaurant with somber decor serves excellent miso and tonkotsu; the latter is a rich broth made from pork bones and cooked for 12 hours. The soups are made to order with the ingredients you select. The staff yells "Welcome!!" (in Japanese) at you when you walk in the door [4185 Rue Drolet].

Tea on The Main

305

Entering **Cardinal Tea Room** is like stepping into another time. Above the restaurant Sparrow, you'll be amazed to discover a two-floor tea salon with a mezzanine and a huge chandelier. The decor is thoroughly 1920s. The English tea and scones are served in porcelain dishware with flowers [5326 Boulevard Saint-Laurent].

The Store Where You'll Find Everything

306

To find an original gift or unusual items for the home, **Magasin Général Lambert Gratton** (*magasin général* = general store) is the perfect place. Lambert Gratton, the owner, has a surprising selection of vintage objects and made-in-Quebec gourmet products. It's the kind of store that I fully endorse [4051 Rue de Bullion].

AND MORE...

- **Buvette Chez Simone** [4869 Avenue du Parc; see Reason #162].
- Rue Laurier Est, between Rue de Brébeuf and Avenue Papineau [**Parc Sir-Wilfrid-Laurier; Le Fromentier** (No. 1375); **Byblos Le Petit Café** (No. 1499 ; see Reason #188); **Tri Express**–which is also a choice for Guy A. Lepage (No. 1650)].
- The gnocchi at **Drogheria Fine** [68 Avenue Fairmount Ouest; see Reason #154].

Guy A. Lepage loves...

Le Moineau Masqué

307

I have a very expensive coffee machine that breaks down every three weeks. Every time it happens, I curse, and then I put on my clothes (I go naked in my house) and head to **Le Moineau Masqué** café. They serve 49th Parallel coffee, which is delicious, the staff is very friendly, there is a courtyard with tables in the summer, and the day my expensive coffeemaker comes back fixed, I'm secretly disappointed [912 Rue Marie-Anne Est].

The Readers' Bookstore

308

There are big bookstores full of cushions, as pretty as they are useless, and then there are bookstores full of books and knowledgeable booksellers. **Le Port de Tête** is one of these. If you want to try something unusual or venture into new reading material, ask the booksellers to make a suggestion. They really know their stuff [262 Avenue du Mont-Royal Est].

The Sushi Bistro

309

Tri was a renowned Montreal sushi chef (Kaizen, Treehouse) who decided to open his own sushi restaurant, **Tri Express**. You can eat in, where it's always full and crowded, or you can order a feast for takeout. Truly delicious [1650 Avenue Laurier Est].

Smokehouse Supreme

310

Without a doubt my favorite smokehouse. Formerly located on a street that changed directions, making it more difficult to access, and the collateral victim of a fire, **Le Boucanier** has a new location, to everyone's delight. Fish and daily specials are prepared by the Atkins brothers. It's fine cuisine for people on the go. A must [1217 Avenue du Mont-Royal Est].

The Playful Pub

311

I don't like board games, but my friend and actor Normand D'Amour does—and he takes them very seriously. He opened two bars where people can play games and take a break from "real issues." **Randolph** has just about every board game you could think of. Oh yeah, and there's beer, too [2041 Rue Saint-Denis; 6505 Rue des Écores].

The Puppy Spa

312

A dog grooming outfit in the Gay Village called **Doggy Style**—you can't make this stuff up. My beloved 8-pound poodle always leaves there adorably coiffed and feeling more cheerful. Check it out if you're traveling with a pet [1638 Rue Amherst].

AND MORE...

- **Damas**, the best restaurant in Montreal [1201 Van Horne Avenue; see Reason #142].
- Brioche and macarons at **Rhubarbe** [5091 Rue De Lanaudière; see Reason #187].
- **Quincaillerie Dante**: As chef Anthony Bourdain put it, the only place in North America where you can "kill a rabbit, cook a rabbit, and eat a rabbit under the same roof." [6851 Rue Saint-Dominique; see Reason #258]
- The best butcher in town, **Le Marchand du Bourg** [1661 Rue Beaubien Est; see Reason #234].

312

Ariane Moffatt loves...

Inspiring Avant-Garde Music

313 During the most recent edition of the Red Bull Music Academy, at a night devoted solely to synthesizers, I totally fell in love with **Eastern Bloc**, a center for avant-garde digital art. I know that any time I go there I'll leave somewhat transformed [7240 Rue Clark].

A Paradise After Dark

314 A combined art gallery, production studio and creative space, **Never Apart** is a jewel, both for its design and its spirit. It's proudly queer and actively engaged, with a focus on beauty—the place just has tons of character. They hold public and private events [7049 Rue Saint-Urbain].

The Perfect Pre-Show Pizza

315 The imaginative minds behind **Moleskine** aren't new to the restaurant game; that's clear from the moment you arrive. If you manage to resist the enticing pizza on the main floor, you'll find more extensive (and scrumptious) offerings upstairs. It's a great place to stop with the family before leaving for a day in the country [3412 Avenue du Parc].

Badass Tacos

316 There's a badass gang of gals behind **Fortune**, a little spot that makes, in my opinion, the best tacos in town. They use fresh and mostly local ingredients to create the perfect mix of flavors. A friend showed me the restaurant, and I've been returning every chance I get [6448 Boulevard Saint-Laurent].

The White House on de l'Esplanade

317 I'm a little reluctant to share this magical spot with the world. **Casa Bianca** is a boutique hotel located in front of Parc Jeanne-Mance (it's as though the cross on Mount Royal is blessing its existence). This hotel is totally unique. I stayed there once after seeing a Christmas concert by the legendary Wainwright-McGarrigle musical family. The evening is like a wonderful dream in my memory [4351 Avenue de l'Esplanade].

The Little Brother

318 When your local watering hole is named **Larrys**, you know it's a golden age for Montreal restaurants. This spot is the little brother of Lawrence, the beloved restaurant next door—but Larrys more than holds its own. Show up in the middle of the afternoon for a glass of white wine and small dishes that are created according to the inspiration of the day. You'll feel right at home [9 Avenue Fairmount Est].

Game, Set, Match

319

The Rogers Cup, the annual tennis championship that's masterfully run by Eugène Lapierre and his team, is a smash hit every year. **Uniprix Stadium** and all its tennis facilities are ideal for watching matches or for hitting some balls around yourself. Bonus points for the clay courts on the roof of the building [285 Rue Gary-Carter].

The Marché des Possibles

320

An open-air summer event for the community with a family-friendly vibe, the **Marché des Possibles** is a creative, fun place to gather. There's kids' yoga, DIY workshops, concerts, live entertainment, food trucks and a relaxed atmosphere. I love the improvised feel and the way things are always changing [corner of Rue Saint-Dominique and Rue Bernard Est].

The No-Name Bar (Yes, That's the Name!)

321

It's a great place to go for one last drink before heading home (on foot, of course). The **No-Name Bar** has an intense focus on aesthetics; spending time there leads to grand conversations about changing the world. The mixologists won't crack a smile—they leave that to the eclectic and somewhat enigmatic clientele [5295 Avenue du Parc].

AND MORE...

- The restaurant **Noren** [77 Rue Rachel Ouest], a tiny Japanese restaurant, is run by a super-endearing Quebecois-Japanese couple (see Reason #170).

Jean-René Dufort loves...

I have to admit, I have a love-hate relationship with Montreal. I'm not the kind of Montrealer who will defend his city to the death. In truth, the city has a number of flaws that I find deeply exasperating. It's not the most beautiful city; its architecture is fading, and it doesn't seem to know whether it's coming or going. I like to talk behind its back when I'm traveling; when I'm feeling nasty, I sometimes compare it to Kabul. The best description of Montreal I've ever heard came from a British friend who lives in Copenhagen. After visiting the metropolis, he told me, "Montreal is like the actor Bill Murray: a guy who is a bit disheveled, wears Bermuda shorts and sandals and an old T-shirt; he's a bit of a hippie, very chill, super friendly, someone you'd like to have a beer with, but not someone you'd ask to help with the prep work when you're painting your apartment."

Nonetheless, here are some spots I like in my city—because there really are a few out there.

The Ivory Tower

322

The **Université de Montréal tower**, which students affectionately describe as a phallus, houses the science library. You'll find floor after floor of books, and desks covered in graffiti and science jokes. You can spend the whole day there without seeing anybody. It's an incredible spot, exclusively for those in the know [2900 Chemin de la Tour].

The Multi-Ethnic Park

323

Parc Jarry is incredible. In the summer, you can play tennis or soccer or watch a cricket match, a soccer game or pick-up ball hockey. An afternoon in this park is like a trip around the world without leaving the city. This is true multiculturalism [Boulevard Saint-Laurent, between Rue Jarry Ouest and Rue Gary-Carter].

The Most "Montreal" Spot of All

324

Place Roy is a tiny square with cobblestones in the Plateau, and surprisingly, it's the spot that I find to be the most "Montreal" (and the most "Plateau" as well). It has somewhat bizarre sculptures by Michel Goulet. I love the fact that it's hard to figure out whether it's on a street or an alley. When it snows, it's simply magnificent. When I become mayor, I'm going to make it a pedestrian-only zone [Rue Roy Est, between Saint-Christophe and Saint-André streets].

324

322

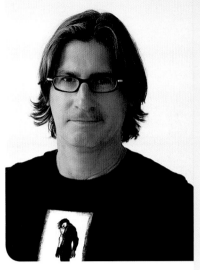

A Ribbon of Blue and Green

325 Montreal is an island—but it doesn't know it; its water is mostly hidden from view. But you can really appreciate the proximity of the mighty St. Lawrence River from its banks in Lachine. The parks along the river (**Parc René-Lévesque** [see Reason #299], **Parc des Saules** and **Parc Saint-Louis**, **Fort-Rolland** and **The Fur Trade at Lachine National Historic Site**) are sure to make you fall in love with the city.

AND MORE...

- The restaurant **Grumman**. Feast on tacos in a garage, with a nice glass of wine, on artisanal tables—you can't get more Montreal than that [630 Rue de Courcelle; see Reason #104]
- The **Mies van der Rohe gas station**, abandoned on Nuns' Island (*Île des Sœurs*) and recently restored. For architecture lovers [201 Rue Berlioz; see Mitsou's Reason #342].
- A giant on the landscape of Old Montreal, long abandoned, **Silo No. 5** is an essential sight. It's amazing, and should really be considered a centerpiece of the city [Rue Mill; see Reason #2].
- **The alleys behind Boulevard Saint-Laurent**, for the fantastic graffiti and murals—truly astonishing.
- The **Olympic Stadium**, a singular postcard image of Montreal and an architectural marvel [4141 Avenue Pierre-de-Coubertin; see Reason #221]
- **NDG** (Notre-Dame-de-Grâce), the most Montreal neighborhood of all. A mix of English and French, it has the perfect blend of two cultures that really defines the character of the city.

Rebecca Makonnen loves...

The Enduring Chapel

326

As a child, I would go to see the crèches from around the world at **Saint Joseph's Oratory**. Then I would make my way to the **Votive Chapel**. Brother André's tomb, the lanterns, the colors, the smell of wax... It is a setting that invites contemplation. To this day, I stop by when I'm in the neighborhood. Turn off Facebook and take the time to breathe [3800 Chemin Queen Mary].

The Best Café

327

Even though I have a top-notch coffeemaker, I've been going to **Café Olimpico** once or twice a week for 10 years. Neither flashy nor pretentious, the place attracts an eclectic array of Mile Enders, and poets come here to reimagine the world. Barista Forde is on a first-name basis with customers, and always remembers their orders. Sublime coffee, great terrace [124 Rue Saint-Viateur Ouest; 419 Rue Saint-Vincent].

Gin and Tonic at La Licorne

328

La Licorne is my favorite theater, and I like almost all their productions. Their programming is bold, young, wildly creative and contemporary. Recently renovated, it is now especially beautiful. Bonus: You can order a drink and bring it into the auditorium [4559 Avenue Papineau].

Drinking to Music

329

Since 1942, music has been the main feature at **Verre Bouteille**, a bar/show venue laid out like a long hallway. Sometimes, if you're lucky, musicians come to "break in" songs before an upcoming tour. They usually drop by after a show or a recording, and the atmosphere is always inclusive. It's a great night out [2112 Avenue du Mont-Royal Est].

326

Historical Houses on Gouin Boulevard East

330

Cycling eastward from Parc-Nature de l'Île-de-la-Visitation is a pleasure, especially if you take the time to admire the historical residences on Boulevard Gouin Est. The Brignon-dit-Lapierre House (A) (No. 4251), Alphonse Pigeon House (No. 4898) and Andegrave House (No. 5460) are remarkable. You can stop to read the plaques that provide a history of some of the houses, or simply take some time to admire them.

Leonard Cohen Lives on Here

331

Elegance, panache, humility, tongue-in-cheek humor. All of these describe the best ambassador the city has ever had, the man who put Montreal on the map more than anyone else. Cohen lived at 28 Rue Vallières, between Rue Saint-Dominique and Boulevard Saint-Laurent, facing Parc du Portugal, where he is remembered. And forever in our hearts.

AND MORE...

· Pistachio and caramel ice cream at **Havre-aux-Glaces** at the Atwater Market. [138 Avenue Atwater; see Reasons #100 and 262]
· A small salad, fried potatoes and a kir at **L'Express**, at two o'clock in the morning, when you're a bit hungry, and still have some energy [3927 Rue Saint-Denis; see Denis Gagnon's Reason #363].
· **Outremont**, the neighborhood where I spent an idyllic childhood.
· **Mile-Ex** where mechanics shops and hipster bars cohabit (see Reason #263).

Jean-Philippe Wauthier loves...

Guilt-Free Junk Food

332 **Chez Tousignant** serves an excellent burger with very good fries, a great poutine and everything else you'd expect along those lines. The aroma of grilled food, retro decor—when you leave, you'll really feel like you've treated yourself [6956 Rue Drolet].

Third Wave Coffee

335 **In Gamba** is one of the first third wave coffee shops that opened in the Plateau. The founder is no longer in charge, but the new owners have kept the tradition going, and they continue to serve the best coffee around. As a bonus, the terrace is always a great place to take in the Montreal summer [5263 Avenue du Parc].

Mouthwatering Mexican

333 The best Mexican restaurant in town is without a doubt **La Tamalera** [226 Avenue Fairmount Ouest]. It's a tiny, unassuming place—you might not even notice it. But it's your destination if you want to try a great *barbacoa* with guacamole as an appetizer, and—for the sake of deliciousness—a *panuchos yucatecos*. Afterward, head to **In Gamba** (see Reason #335) for a coffee.

An Evening at Bistro Chez Roger

336 The **Bistro Chez Roger** is a gathering place for regulars and new arrivals to the Rosemont neighborhood. Canadian TV personality Christiane Charette helped spread the word by recording *Charette en Direct* there for several years. Since the fall of 2016, it is the home of *La Soirée est (Encore) Jeune*, a radio program. It's an institution [2316 Rue Beaubien Est]

The Park at the Foot of the Mountain

334 **Parc Jeanne-Mance** is the best spot in Mile End to get your fill of greenery. Grass, trees, a soccer field, tons of space to run around—it's a portal into nature in the middle of the city [Avenue du Mont-Royal Ouest, between Avenue du Parc and Avenue de l'Esplanade].

The Little Home of Great Food

337 **Petite Maison** is chef Danny St-Pierre's base in Montreal. After carving a place in the hearts of residents of Sherbrooke, he decided to do the same for Plateau residents. Simple cuisine that's utterly delicious. His little home is our home [5589 Avenue du Parc].

Gaspé Comes to Town

338

Some people from Gaspé have created something of an outpost in Mile End, serving up great coffee and good food. Welcome to **Pagaille Café**, the neighborhood bistro par excellence. France is the perfect hostess; bonus points awarded for the pebbles that were brought from the shores of Gaspé to decorate the café's windows [101 Rue Villeneuve Ouest].

The Legendary Theater

339

The **Monument-National** is a historic building in the Quartier des Spectacles neighborhood, and it's been witness to the city's cultural awakening over the years. The mythical room is really worth seeing, even when it's empty. Every Thursday, the café next door becomes a set for the recording of the TV program *Deux Hommes en Or*. Does the building really deserve to be called a "monument"? Absolutely [1182 Boulevard Saint-Laurent].

AND MORE...

- The café **Le Butterblume** is a pretty island in an industrial area that has sprung to life [5836 Boulevard Saint-Laurent; see Reason #149].
- **Agrikol** is an exotic novelty, but it's one that will be around for a long time. It serves Creole food that's impossible not to love. A slice of Port-au-Prince in Montreal—it's just about perfect [1844 Rue Amherst; see Reason #41].

Mitsou loves...

Shared Fridges

340 Fifteen to 25 percent of the food purchased by households ends up in the garbage. To counter waste and promote cooperation and sharing, some Montrealers have set up fridges in their alleys, for people to drop off, or take, cooked meals, fresh produce, bread and so on. The year 2016 also saw the creation of **Frigo des Ratons** and **Frigo des Écureuils Gourmands** in the Rosemont neighborhood. The **Fridge de la Petite-Patrie**, in the chalet in Parc Montcalm on Avenue Papineau, also takes donations. Initiatives like these may come and go, but they show that Montrealers are engaged with the place where they live. As for a shared fridge in my own neighborhood—I can only dream.

Fluke and A'Shop

341 A pioneer of street art in Canada, **Fluke** has revamped the walls of Montreal personally. In 2010, he founded **A'Shop**, a combined studio and artists' collective that is responsible for a number of spectacular murals that have given the city a human touch. I attended a workshop that introduced me to the fabulous work of these significant artists whose creations can be found on walls and rooftops around Montreal, on buildings owned by powerful companies, on trailer-trucks—and even on bodies. A gray and gloomy city is a thing of the past [3081 Rue Ontario Est].

Towers of Style

342 Montreal is home to *five* buildings designed by Mies van der Rohe. The famous German architect is responsible for prestigious **Westmount Square** [between Rue Sainte-Catherine and Boulevard de Maisonneuve, and Avenue Wood and Avenue Greene]. He was also involved with the urban planning for Nuns' Island (*Île des Sœurs*) and designed **three high-rise apartment buildings** [201 Rue Corot; 100 and 200 Rue de Gaspé] and the first **gas station** [201 Rue Berlioz] built there. The glass and concrete buildings are elegant and refined—in a word, sublime. It's another reason to (re)discover this island at the city's gates.

Roman Specialties, in a Prison

343 An underground restaurant? In a former prison? With a charming grandmother running the oven? It's a bizarrely enticing premise. Even more enticing is the grilled swordfish or the mushroom pasta I love to order there. International artists tend to make a point of visiting **Da Emma** in Old Montreal. There's a small table in the kitchen where the boss's husband sits. Emma herself sits our children down at the table when we bring them. Warm and family friendly [777 Rue de la Commune Ouest].

AND MORE...

- The **Lachine Canal** and its surroundings, which harken back to Montreal at the beginning of the 20th century.
- **Want Apothecary**: contemporary fashion and beauty products with 19th-century atmosphere [4960 Rue Sherbrooke Ouest].
- **Hôtel William Gray** is a spot to meet up with friends, to hang out or do some work—it's perfect in every way [421 Rue Saint-Vincent; see Reason #352].
- **Espace Pepin** and **Maison Pepin** have urban fashion and decor—very cool [350 and 378 Rue Saint-Paul Ouest; see Reason #25].
- **Les Fermes Lufa**, for the pleasure of eating a Montreal-grown lettuce *in the middle of winter!* [1400 Rue Antonio-Barbeau; see Reason #287].

341

Sugar Sammy loves...

Côte-des-Neiges Meat...

344 Côte-des-Neiges, the neighborhood where I grew up, is the perfect embodiment of multiculturalism and bilingualism. My career would have been very different if I hadn't grown up in that urban village. I often get serious cravings for the grilled Portuguese chicken at **Da Silva** [5334 Chemin Queen Mary], a cool and affordable restaurant. **Farhat** (A) [3513 Avenue Swail] has delicious sandwiches with charcoal-fire grilled meat—you'll have a hard time not eating two at a time. If you feel the need, you can go ask for forgiveness at Saint Joseph's Oratory afterward.

...And NDG Seafood

345 Avenue de Monkland is like a western version of Mile End's vibrant Rue Bernard Ouest. You'll find Anglophones and Francophones alike at **Croissant Monkland** [No. 5549], the **Monkland Taverne** [No. 5555], **Ye Olde Orchard Pub** [No. 5563] and **Gia Ba** [No. 5766]. **Lucille's Oysters Dive** is my favorite seafood restaurant; it has a great atmosphere and an incredible chef. Their Bloody Caesar is an appetizer and a drink, all in one! [No. 5669]

Get Weightless at La Ronde

346 Each year, my brother, my sister and I used to wait with feverish impatience to go to **La Ronde**. We looked forward to meeting other children who shared our fundamental priorities: winning the biggest stuffed animals and going on the biggest rides. My favorite has to be **Monstre**. The most dizzying: **Bateau Pirate**. The combination of joy and terror is unlike anything else [Île Sainte-Hélène].

Laughing in English

347 At Place des Arts galas or the audition showcase at ComedyWorks, there's something for everyone to love at the **Just For Laughs** festival. I had the opportunity to see the best comedians in the world and performed with some of the biggest names in the business: Louis C.K., Dave Chappelle, Bill Burr and George Lopez. Respect!

Harvard in Canada

348 I truly enjoyed the years I spent at **McGill University**. The school attracts the best professors, and students from around the world. The campus is magnificent; it's reminiscent of the great American universities. One of the best spots is **Avenue McGill College** on winter evenings—it offers a picturesque winter scene [845 Rue Sherbrooke Ouest].

344A

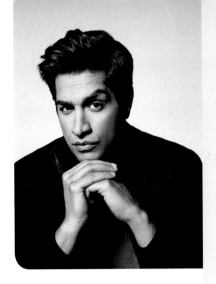

Jazz at Métropolis

349

I love the Jazz Festival; as an adolescent, I spent many an evening there with my friends. My favorite spot for concerts is **Métropolis**[1]. In 2011, I saw Prince's famous midnight concert there: It lasted four hours and had seven encores. Another one of my favorite concerts was Jamiroquai (I had front-row seats). So many memories! [59 Rue Sainte-Catherine Est]

Three Montreal Clothing Brands

350

When I'm in Paris, I try to wear clothes that I bought in Montreal; it's a way to make sure my wardrobe is exclusive. I love the leather jackets at **m0851**, a company that started in Mile End and now has over 20 stores around the world. I also love the clothing at **Frank + Oak**, whose collections are designed and produced in a Mile End workshop. Their apparel ranges from casual to fancy, but it's always cool. You can have a "private shopping" experience on the third floor at 1420 Rue Stanley, where you can also sip a coffee from Café Névé and get a haircut. For shoes, I like the family-owned Montreal company **Browns Shoes** [m0851, Frank + Oak, Browns Shoes: various outlets in Montreal].

Montreal Canadiens For Life

351

It's become a real obsession. I could be in any sports bar, at a hotel in Paris or at the airport: I have to watch Montreal Canadiens games, or at the very least find out what's happening moment by moment. The mere act of wearing a Canadiens cap outside the country leads to new friendships based on the shared love of hockey and our very special team. Go! Habs! Go! [Bell Centre: 1909 Avenue des Canadiens-de-Montréal].

AND MORE...

- **Mount Royal** (see Reason #165) is a city treasure. The chalet lookout (Belvédère Kondiaronk) is where I first came up with the idea for my bilingual show.
- The **Osheaga** festival (see Reason #369). I like to go every year.
- The **Metro** is the perfect way to get around if you're heading out to see a hockey game or checking out the big festivals.

1. Metropolis' name changed to M. Telus in 2017.

Herby Moreau loves...

Old Montreal is definitely the number one reason to love Montreal. The little cafés and restaurants on Rue Saint-Paul, Place d'Armes in front of Notre-Dame Basilica, the bike path in the Old Port—it's one of the nicest neighborhoods in North America. Every time I leave, I look forward to returning. I've spotted Brad Pitt drive by on a Vespa, Bono walking toward Olive & Gourmando, Mickey Rourke riding a BIXI at three in the morning, Jake Gyllenhaal waiting in line for a coffee. Each time, he said the same thing: *What a great city!* My son was born in the neighborhood, and contrary to popular opinion, it's perfect for the whole family. We like to visit the Montreal Science Centre and stroll around Chinatown. And yes, grocery stores are just five minutes away. We get the boxes delivered and walk back on foot—how nice is that?

Great Views

352 I've had the good fortune to be invited to **357C** [357 Rue de la Commune Ouest]. The gorgeous building houses a private club started by Daniel Langlois, creator of Softimage. Not just anyone can wander through its doors. The rooftop terrace offers the best view you can get of Old Montreal, the Old Port and the river. There's another fantastic view on the terrace of **William Gray**, a luxury boutique hotel [421 Rue Saint-Vincent].

Memory Lane

353 Trees, sculptures, a fountain and a walking path; in the summertime, the scenic **Cours Le Royer** becomes a veritable festival of wedding photography (with plenty of tourists as unpaid extras). When I was younger, I told myself that someday I'd live on this narrow lane; I even imagined teaching my son how to ride a bike there. Junior is 11 years old now, and sure enough, that's where he learned. It's a spot that's filled with emotion for me [Rue Le Royer Ouest, between Rue Saint-Dizier and Rue Saint-Sulpice].

Cultural Center 2.0

354 From the ashes of two abandoned properties, Phoebe Greenberg created the **Centre Phi**, a multidisciplinary space devoted to the evolution of new media. Exhibition rooms, recording and editing studios, theaters and cinemas: It has everything a creator needs. It's a gem. Director Denis Villeneuve documented the demolition of the buildings in his short film *Next Floor* [407 Rue Saint-Pierre].

Portuguese Park

355 If you walk too quickly you might not even notice the park at the corner of Boulevard Saint-Laurent and Rue Marie-Anne. If you slow down, you'll find Portuguese, Italians, Africans and old-time Quebecers mixing and mingling in Parc du Portugal. The office of the **Nuits d'Afrique Festival** (second week of July) is right nearby. Across the street, **Bagel Etc** [4320 Boulevard Saint-Laurent; see Anne-Marie Withenshaw's Reason #371] offers breakfasts that are beloved by night owls. The house that belonged to **Leonard Cohen** looks out on the park.

King Karl

356

I'm someone who likes to be out and about, and I find Montreal especially beautiful at night. It's after dark when you'll meet characters like Karl Mèche, who has been one of the leading promoters of Montreal nightlife for 25 years. Want proof? When the Rolling Stones came to town, he got a call: "Hi Karl, it's Mick Jagger." Recently, Karl decided to start a concierge service for people who want to have a night on the town and are seeking the best hot spots. Awesome.

The Hidden Bar

357

Hidden behind the restaurant Foiegwa, with no sign to point it out, **Atwater Cocktail Club** doesn't make things easy for newcomers. But once you're inside this speakeasy, you'll be very glad you came. The owners created a cocktail bar to unwind and let the hours flow by. You may well be there until three in the morning, when they're shutting their doors. [512 Avenue Atwater].

AND MORE...

- **Zébulon Perron** designs spaces that add spirit to the city, environments that are great for catching up with friends for a few hours (see Reason #59).
- For its dizzyingly high ceilings and its gilding, **Crew Collective & Café**, a former bank that was converted into a great place for a brew [360 Rue Saint-Jacques; see Reason #23].
- The pad thai at **Hà**. The place has a lovely history, friendly owners and a magnificent terrace. A warm and welcoming restaurant [243 Avenue du Mont-Royal Ouest; see Reason #164].
- **Hubert Marsolais**, passionate restaurateur and aesthete, has an irresistible hold on Montrealers. **Le Club Chasse et Pêche** [423 Rue Saint-Claude; see Reason #15]; **Le Filet** [219 Avenue du Mont-Royal Ouest]; and **Le Serpent** [257 Rue Prince]: three different ambiences, each a success in its own right.

357

Cœur de pirate loves...

Vintage Clothing

358 Shopping in thrift stores means discovering textures, colors, and patterns from the past in the present. **Annex Vintage** [56 Rue Saint-Viateur Ouest] offers items from the 1990s and from independent designers. They have a nice selection of patches, which I often buy. **Citizen Vintage** (A) [5330 Boulevard Saint-Laurent] also has a great selection of clothing that is both stylish AND sustainable.

358A

Sitting on the Steps at Place des Arts

359 The best spot for watching shows and festivals is **the steps at Esplanade Place des Arts**. Set back from the street, it's also the ideal place to take a time out, away from the hustle and bustle yet still in the center of the action, so you don't have to miss anything. The steps are the epicenter of the Quartier des Spectacles, and where everything happens. Find yourself a spot, and let the show begin! [beside 175 Rue Sainte-Catherine Ouest]

Hot Yoga

360 Less intense than bikram, the type of yoga practiced at **Moksha Yoga** is a great antidote to the cold days of winter. Be prepared to sweat! This type of yoga is done in heated rooms, and classes are between 60 and 90 minutes. Health, peace and environmental awareness are all important values here. Ommmmm... [3863 Boulevard Saint-Laurent; 4260 Avenue Girouard].

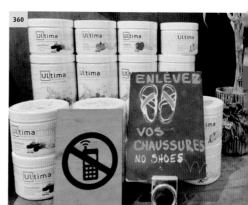

360

Local Streetwear

361 Quality streetwear clothing and accessories, the city's biggest selection of Vans, and collections and designers that can't be found anywhere else: **Off The Hook** is probably the only store that has everything I need. The owners emphasize Montreal and Canadian brands, beautifully showcased here [1021 Rue Sainte-Catherine Ouest; 421 Rue Saint-Vincent].

The Small Steps in the Museum

362 I enjoy taking **the stairs inside the Montreal Museum of Fine Arts** that lead from the main foyer to the upper and lower levels. The stairs have an unusual depth and height, which makes the experience a little destabilizing; you need to pay attention to keep pace. It's a sure way to bring you into the here and now, and to be conscious of your surroundings. Children find them amusing, and sometimes parents do, too. I'm certainly a fan! [1380 Rue Sherbrooke Ouest]

AND MORE...

- In both summer and winter, **Mount Royal** has the impressive distinction of being a favorite of all Montrealers (see Reason #165).
- **Café Olimpico** is a classic, and still the best café in Montreal (see Reason #144) [124 Rue Saint-Viateur Ouest; 419 Rue Saint-Vincent].
- Try **Alexandraplatz**, a bar tucked away in a former garage, for an early evening drink in the summer (see Reason #264) [6731 Avenue de l'Esplanade].
- **Café Parvis** and **Furco** are former downtown fur shops revamped as restaurant-bars for locals to enjoy [433 Rue Mayor; 425 Rue Mayor].
- **Montreal Biodôme** (see Reason #59) is an oasis in the middle of the city, and a perfect playground for children.

Denis Gagnon loves...

Setting the Standard for 30 Years

363 It's a real classic: an institution that has stayed true to its vision for three decades. **L'Express** offers classic dishes and a menu that will never go out of style: bone marrow with coarse salt, stew and so much more. I love to go there for breakfast on Saturday or Sunday morning; it costs no more than any local deli. The atmosphere is friendly and the service is exceptional. It's my favorite restaurant; may its doors stay open forever [3927 Rue Saint-Denis].

A Post Office, Reimagined

364 Once a simple post office, the **1700 La Poste** building now evokes a neo-classical temple. Under the direction of patron Isabelle de Mévius, it's become a major center of arts and culture. The impressive space is open to the public, showcasing the work of artists that are under-represented in other Montreal galleries. The building itself is a jewel, and it's very worthy of the smaller gems within [1700 Rue Notre-Dame Ouest].

Locks from the Past

365 The Lachine Canal has red-brick industrial buildings, bike paths, walking paths and a strip of greenery; it's definitely one of Griffintown's main attractions. With the Pont des Seigneurs (*pont* = bridge) above them, the **Saint-Gabriel Lock** (one of five locks on the canal) is an especially interesting spot. Pleasure boats stop for long enough to be admired before slowly setting off again. The canal is emptied every fall and refilled in the spring— flooded with charm, according to schedule. You'll love it.

Art at the Shipyard

366

Arsenal, a shipyard that's been converted into an avant-garde space, presents works by Canadian artists with the aim to boost them onto the international stage. Pierre Trahan, the patron responsible for the site's renaissance, is a major collector himself. It's an amazing place—don't miss the boat [2020 Rue William].

The Iconic Tower

367

When I arrived in Montreal 35 years ago, **Place Ville Marie** was *the* building. As representative of Montreal as Mount Royal, it was part of the city's brand. I. M. Pei, who designed the Louvre Pyramid, is one of its architects. There's an exceptional view of the surrounding area from the rooftop. It's a legendary spot [1 Place Ville Marie].

AND MORE...

- **Mount Royal** (see Reason #165) is the top reason to love Montreal. The park was designed by Frederick Law Olmsted, the landscape architect who also designed New York City's Central Park.

- **The Underground City** (see Reason #61). Every time I go to Lucien L'Allier Metro station, I'm amazed that I've gone so far underground. They even managed to keep Christ Church Cathedral standing when Promenades Cathédrale was built underneath—a technological triumph.

- The **Quartier des Spectacles** (see Reason #52), a modern space that hosts screenings, shows and concerts during the many festivals held there throughout the year.

- The **kindness of locals**, who treat visiting tourists with respect.

- **Fashion in Old Montreal**. It's the neighborhood where I've done business for six years, alongside other creators from here like Philippe Dubuc, Rad Hourani and Lysanne Pepin. There's great shopping to be done there—a far cry from what you'll find at Zara and H&M.

Anne-Marie Withenshaw loves...

Pleasantville, the Montreal Version

368

With the winding avenues named after the trees that border them, and post-World War II homes that look like Swiss chalets, it's hard to believe you're in the heart of the city. I grew up in the **Cité-Jardin** neighborhood, where my parents still live. Halloween is unbelievable: Volunteers close the streets to cars, and people go wild with decorations. You'll find the peaceful countryside, just three miles (five kilometers) from downtown [east of Parc Maisonneuve].

A Gigantic Festival in the Middle of the River

369

A mere 10 days after giving birth, I was there: **Osheaga Music and Arts Festival** is one of the top reasons to love Montreal. I haven't missed a single one of the 12 editions of the festival. Arcade Fire, Eminem, Kendrick Lamar, Cœur de pirate, the Flaming Lips, Yeah Yeah Yeahs—so many unforgettable performances. It's also in a fantastic location. With emerging talents and established stars, both local and international, Osheaga has become one of the city's top attractions [Parc Jean-Drapeau, on Île Sainte-Hélène, in early August].

Chuck's Garde Manger

370

Garde Manger is one of a kind in Old Montreal. The restaurant is a star magnet, and it's always crowded. I met famous Canadian chef Chuck Hughes there, and we shot all the episodes of the Quebec version of the food show *Knife Fight* inside. A typical Montreal restaurant that's become a classic [408 Rue Saint-François-Xavier].

Montreal's Best-Kept Secret

371

It doesn't look like much from the outside: a basement in a garment district, near Rue Chabanel. But when you enter **Café Gentile**, an explosion of flavors awaits you. The coffee, the cannoli and the panini— *insanely* good. The biscotti are served right out of the oven. You can also play billiards and enjoy the 1950s decor. *Grazie!* [9299 Avenue du Parc]

The Bakery of my Youth

372

My mother would go to the bakery-pastry shop **Italia** in Saint-Léonard a couple times a week for the tomato pizza, the bread, the Italian cookies and ham. There are a few tables, and they make sandwiches to order: You can choose your toppings, like eggplant, hot peppers, etc. Authentic [5540 Rue Jean-Talon Est].

Club Sportif MAA

373

A Montreal sports club that dates all the way back to 1881, **Club Sportif MAA** has been my gym for 10 years. Athletes and stars train there, but the place also welcomes everyone from students to women in their seventies. Sports and tradition meet in a great setting, where you can practice all kinds of disciplines, including zero-gravity yoga and aerial acrobatics. They offer day passes, which is great for tourists. Let's go! [2070 Rue Peel]

The Best Bacon and Eggs on The Main

374

Leonard Cohen, who lived right across the street, liked to get a bagel and a *café allongé* at the bar at **Bagel Etc**. The old diner has truly become an institution. I like to go for the blintzes and the "Eastern European" breakfast (eggs, sauerkraut and knackwurst sausage). The decor is rococo. At the cash is an autographed album: "To the Bagel with Love, Leonard" [4320 Boulevard Saint-Laurent].

Stairways to Heaven

375

Princely mansions on the side of a hill, hundred-year-old trees, flower beds: all can be found in lovely Westmount, which is traversed by a **network of public staircases** that are unknown to the greater public. Designed to facilitate steep climbs, they're also a great way to stay in shape. Take the one east of 4835 Cedar Crescent or the one at Lansdowne Ridge. It's a great way to push your running routine or your dog walk to a new level.

AND MORE...

- **Hof Kelsten**, a bakery that ignores the trends and focuses on traditions. It supplies all the good restaurants in town; you'd be crazy not to try it yourself [4524 Boulevard Saint-Laurent; see Reason #157].
- The menu at **Kazu** is written on Post-it notes that are stuck on the wall. Their sauce is addictive: I can't live without it. At lunch, I order the bowl of tartare salad and ramen soup. My trick to avoid the lineup? Get takeout. [1862 Rue Sainte-Catherine Ouest; see Reason #86].

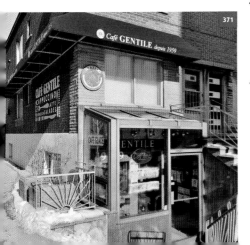

Index

The numbers in the Index refer to the Reasons to Love Montreal.

"no-name park" 148
#MTLGO, 68
1700 La Poste, 364
180 g, 265
357C, 352
À la Table des Jardins Sauvages, 293
Abreuvoir, 58
Accord, 15
Action 500, 224
Adamo, 108
Agrikol, 41
Alati-Caserta, 254
ALDO, 71
Aldred Building, 20
Alep, 268
Alexandraplatz, 264
Allez Up, 95
Alvéole, 261
Amaranto, 130
Amphitrite Fountain, 28
Anne-Marie Withenshaw, 368-375
Annex Vintage, 358
Anticafé, 54
Antidote, 197
Arcade MTL, 48
ArHoma, 202
Ariane Moffatt, 313-321
Arsenal, 366
Arte e Farina, 43
Atelier Make, 184
Atwater Cocktail Club, 357
Atwater Market, 100
Au Sommet, 68
Automne Boulangerie, 238
Avenue de Monkland, 345
Avenue Henri-Julien, 174
Avenue Laval, 174
Avenue McGill College, 73, 348
Bagatelle, 203
Bagel Etc, 355, 374
Bank of Montreal building, 21

Bar K Karaoke, 85
Barbie Expo, 64
Barré by Escif, 173
Beau Kavanagh (portrait), 126
Beauté Dee's, 267
Beaver Lake, 165
Bell Centre, 78
Belle et Rebelle, 246
Belvédère du Chemin-Qui-Marche, 14
Ben & Tournesol, 119
Berlin Wall, 28
Bibliothèque Maisonneuve, 211
Bibliothèque Marc-Favreau, 250
Big In Japan, 171
Bigarade, 200
Biiru, 65
Bily Kun, 166
Biodôme, 222
Biosphere, 12
BIXI, 72
Bleu Blanc Bouge skating rinks, 281
Blind Pig, 205
Bombay Mahal, 266
Boris Bistro, 27
Bota Bota, 3
Botanical Garden, 227
Bottega, 256
Boucherie Beau-bien, 201
Boucherie du Marché, 262
Bouillon Bilk, 45
Boulangerie Guillaume, 157
Boulevard Gouin Ouest, 291
Boulevard Gouin, 330
Bourgie Hall, 84
Boutique Room Service Loft, 25
Broue Pub Brouhaha, 232
Browns, 350
Brutus, 236

BUK & NOLA, 189
Buvette Chez Simone, 162
Byblos Le Petit Café, 188
Cà Phê Con Leche, 248
Cadet, 45
Café 8 Oz., 302
Café de' Mercanti, 131
Café Gentile, 371
Café Larue & fils, 269
Café Le Falco, 151
Café Milano, 282
Café Mucho Gusto, 230
Café Olimpico, 144, 327
Café Santropol, 172
Café Sfouf, 43
Café Vito, 273
Caffè Mille Gusti, 239
Caffè San Simeon, 254
Camellia Sinensis, 46
Campanelli, 108
Canadian Bank of Commerce building (Théâtre St-James), 21
Canal Lounge, 100
Capitaine Crabe, 208
Cardinal, 305
Carle Bernier-Genest (portrait), 214
Casa Bianca, 317
Casa do Alentejo, 248
Caserne Letourneux, 210, 213
Centre Phi, 354
Ceramic mosaic murals by Laurent Gascon, 204
Ceramic tile circles in the Peel Metro station by Jean-Paul Mousseau, 61
Chalet Bar-B-Q, 122
Champ-de-Mars Metro station (entrance glasswork by Marcelle Ferron), 60

Chapelle Historique du Bon-Pasteur, 53
Charles-Rudolph-Hosmer House, 82
Che Churro, 130
Chemin de Ceinture, 136
Chez Apo, 271
Chez Bong, 32
Chez Bouffe Café Bistro, 216
Chez Claudette, 178
Chez Ménick, 192
Chez Roger, 336
Chez Tousignant, 332
Chinatown arch, 33
Chocolats de Chloé, 179
Christ Church Cathedral, 66
Cinéma Beaubien, 231
Circuit Gilles-Villeneuve, 10
Cirka, 109
Cité-Jardin, 368
Citizen Vintage, 358
Cloakroom, 75
Clock Tower Beach, 8
Clos Saragnat, 244, 300
Club Chasse et Pêche, 15
Club Social, 144, 145
Club Soda, 58
Club Sportif MAA, 373
Cocoa Locale, 163
Cœur de pirate, 358-362
Cokluch, 273
Comme un Jeu d'Enfant by Seth (Julien Malland), 284
Comptoir Charcuteries et Vins, 159
Corona Theatre, 94
Cours Le Royer, 353
Cours Mont-Royal, 64
Crew Collectif & Café, 23
Croissant Monkland, 345
Crossover Comics, 116
Cul-Sec Cave & Cantine, 252
Da Emma, 343
Da Silva, 344
Damas, 142
Daou, 272
De Froment et de Sève, 230
Debout! by Roger Langevin, 181
Décalade, 6
Denis Gagnon, 25, 363-367
Dépanneur Le Pick-Up, 263
Détour Bistro, 230
Diabolissimo, 182
Dieu du Ciel!, 156

Dilallo, 110
Dinette Triple Crown, 257
Dinu Bumbaru (portrait), 51
Doggy Style, 312
Domtar Garden, 66
Dorchester Square, 66
Dr. Julien (portrait), 196
Dragon Flowers, 147
Drogheria Fine, 154
Dufresne-Nincheri Museum, 220
Duggan House, 82
Eastern Bloc, 313
Eaton Centre, 64
Ecomuseum Zoo, 296
Église de la Visitation, 286
Église du Très-Saint-Nom-de-Jésus, 215
Église du Très-Saint-Rédempteur, 198
Electrik Kidz, 200
Émile Nelligan, 136, 176
Encans Kavanagh, 126
Entre Ciel et Terre, 49
Épicerie 1668, 124
Épices Anatol, 259
Épices de Cru, 262
Escondite, 65
Espace Pepin, 25
Espace pour la Vie museum district, 222
État-Major, 216
Eva B., 56
Fairmount Bagel, 152
Farhat, 344
Farine Five Roses, 1
Fauna Foundation, 298
Female Landscape by Gerald Gladstone, 73
Fenêtre sur Kaboul, 177
Ferme Marineau, 292
Ferme Turcot, 292
Ferme Vaillancourt, 292
Fête des Neiges, 10
Fixe Café Bistro, 233
Fluke, 341
Fortune, 316
Foxy, 99
Frank + Oak, 350
Fridge de la Petite-Patrie, 340
Frigo des Écureuils Gourmands, 340
Frigo des Ratons, 340
Fromagerie Copette & Cie, 112

Garde Manger, 370
Garde-Manger Italien and Bistro Amerigo, 131
Germaine by Rafael Sottolichio, 173
Gia Ba, 128, 345
Gibbys, 16
Gibeau Orange Julep, 140
Gilles Beaudry (portrait), 214
Golden Square Mile, 82
Green alleys, 175
Greenspot, 101
Griffintown, 89
Grumman '78, 104
Gryphon d'Or, 129
Guaranteed Pure Milk bottle, 51, 79
Guy A. Lepage, 307-312
Hà, 164
Habitat 67 standing wave, 5
Habitat 67, 4
Havre-aux-Glaces, 262
Heavy Montréal Festival, 10
Henri Henri, 50
Herby Moreau, 352-357
Héritage Kalamata, 240
Héritage Montréal, 51
Histoire de la Musique à Montréal by Frédéric Back, 60
Hoche Café, 207
Hof Kelsten, 157
Hommage à René Lévesque by Robert Roussil, 299
Hommage aux Fondateurs de la Ville de Montréal by Pierre Gaboriau and Pierre Osterrath, 60
Hudson's Bay, see La Baie d'Hudson
Huguette Couture (portrait), 235
HVOR, 99
Il Bazzali, 253
Île Notre-Dame, 10
Île Sainte-Hélène, 10
Imadake, 118
Impact, 213, 221, 225
In Gamba, 335
India Beau Village, 266
Insectarium, 227
Isle de Garde, 238
Italia, 372
Jacques Cartier Bridge, 13

Jamais Assez, 160
James Ross House, 82
Jane Heller (portrait), 141
Jardin Iwaki, 125
    Mouton Vert, 127
Jean-Doré Beach, 10
Jean-Philippe Wauthier, 332-339
Jean-René Dufort, 322-325
Jean-Talon Market, 262
Jeans Jeans Jeans, 151
Joe Beef, 99
Joe la Croûte, 262
Just For Laughs, 347
Karl Mèche, 356
Kazu, 86
Kem CoBa, 154
Khyber Pass, 177
Kitsch à l'Os... ou Pas, 199
Kouign Amann, 167
L'Air du Temps by Phillip Adams, 49
L'Amère à Boire, 47
L'Entrepôt Mont-Royal, 183
L'Espace Public, 206
L'Esprit d'Été by El Mac, 243
L'Express, 363
L'Homme by Alexander Calder, 11
L'In-Time, 113
La Baie d'Hudson (Hudson's Bay), 64
La Banquise, 178
La Bête à Pain, 289
La Capital Tacos, 33
La Champagnerie, 27
La Cornetteria, 254
La Fermière by Alfred Laliberté, 210, 214
La Fournée des Sucreries de l'Érable, 262
La Graine Brûlée, 42
La Grand-Mère Poule, 230
La Grande Fonte by Robert Roussil, 2
La Guadalupe Mexicaine, 41
La Habanera, 65
La Joute by Jean-Paul Riopelle, 31
La Librairie de Verdun, 116
La Licorne, 328
La Maison de Mademoiselle Dumpling, 244
La Mère Créatrice by El Mac, 243

La Récolte, 241
La Ronde, 10, 346
La Salle à Manger, 159
La Tamalera, 333
Lachine Canal Bike Path, 102
Lachine Canal, 102
Lady Meredith House, 82
Larrys, 318
Lattuca Barbecue, 16
Le 4ᵉ Mur, 48
Le Belgo, 55
Le Bièrologue, 209
Le Boucanier, 310
Le Butterblume, 149
Le Caractère Chinois, 180
Le Cheval Blanc, 47
Le Fantôme, 97
Le Grand Jean-Paul by Roseline Granet, 31
Le Mal Nécessaire, 34
Le Marchand du Bourg, 234
Le Marché des Saveurs du Québec, 262
Le Mélomane by Jean-François Cooke and Pierre Sasseville, 281
Le Mousso, 45
Le Petit Alep, 268
Le Petit Coin du Mexique, 279
Le Petit Dep, 22
Le Port de Tête, 308
Le Richmond Marché Italien, 93
Le Roi du Smoked Meat, 245
Le Roi du Taco, 260
Le Sainte-Élisabeth, 48
Le Saut de l'Ange by Édith Croft, 136
Le Sieur d'Iberville, 191
Le Sino, 195
Le St-Urbain, 288
Le Valois, 203
Le Vin Papillon, 99
LeBer-LeMoyne House, 299
Leonard Cohen, 331, 355, 374
Les 400 Coups, 15
Les Affamés, 203
Les Beaux-Frères sur Beaubien, 230
Les Cavistes, 288
Les Conteurs by Richard Morin, 178

Les Douceurs du Marché, 100
Les Empoteuses, 237
Les Enfants Terribles, 68
Les Fermes Lufa, 287
Les Givrés, 270
Les Jardineries, 221
Les Jardins Sauvages, 262
Les Pervenches, 300
Les Petits Baigneurs by Alfred Laliberté, 212
Lester's Deli, 143
Life Association of Scotland Building (Le Place d'Armes Hôtel & Suites), 20
Ligue d'Improvisation Montréalaise, 58
Ligue Nationale d'Improvisation, 58
Lion d'Or, 58
Liverpool House, 99
LOCO, 276
Luciano, 253
Lucille's Oyster Dive, 345
Lutte, 198
m0851, 350
Ma Poule Mouillée, 178
Magasin Général Lambert Gratton, 306
Maison Birks, 69
Maison Coloniale, 174
Maison Descaris, 121
Maison du Jazz, 63
Maison du Ravioli, 283
Maison Indian Curry, 266
Maison Joseph-Décary, 121
Maisonneuve Market, 208, 210
Maisonneuve public bath and gymnasium (Bain Morgan), 212
Malhi, 266
Mamie chic by A'Shop, 173
Mandy's, 120
Mangiafoco, 17
Manitoba, 263
Marché 4751, 219
Marché aux Puces Saint-Michel, 280
Marché de Nuit, 264
Marché des Possibles, 320
Marché La Pantry, 105
Marie Saint Pierre, 80
Marie-Joëlle Parent, 301-306

Más - Penser à Prendre le Temps by Mateo, 243
McCord Museum, 70, 73
McGill University, 66, 82, 348
MELK, 129
Ménick (portrait), 192
Merchants' Bank building (Hotel Le St-James), 21
Mes Quartiers and *C'est Toi ma Ville* blogs, 214
Métropolis (M. Telus), 349
Mies van der Rohe, 342
Milano Fruiterie, 254
Mile-Ex (neighborhood), 263
Mile-Ex (restaurant), 263
Mitsou, 340-343
Mohamed Hage (portrait), 287
Moineau Masqué, 307
Moksha Yoga, 360
Moleskine, 315
Momesso, 123
Monkland Taverne, 345
Monsieur Smith, 206
Montreal Canadiens, 78, 351
Montréal Love by Nicolas Fortin, 243
Montreal melon, 121
Montréal Moderne, 199
Montreal Museum of Fine Arts, 84
Montréal Plaza, 247
Montréal Roller Derby and Montréal Roller Derby Masculin, 150
Monument-National, 339
Monumentalove by Jane Heller, 141
Mount Royal cross, 165
Mount Royal Park, 165
Mount Royal, 59, 135, 136, 165, 228
Moustache, 249
Mural Festival, 173
Murale Pop Art by D*face, 173
Musée d'Art Contemporain, 55
Must Société, 91
Muvbox, 3
Mycoboutique, 168
Myriade, 88
Nadine Jazouli (portrait), 91
Natatorium, 114

Nature Légère by Claude Cormier, 61
Nef pour Quatorze Reines by Rose-Marie Goulet, 134
Never Apart, 314
New York Life Insurance Building, 20
Nguyen Phi, 138
No-Name Bar, 321
Nolana, 17
Noodle Factory, 36
Nora Gray, 90
Noren, 170
Normand Laprise (portrait), 30
Notre-Dame Basilica, 18
Notre-Dame-des-Neiges Cemetery, 136
Nougat & Nectarine, 56
Nouilles de Lan Zhou, 36
Nuits d'Afrique Festival, 355
Off The Hook, 361
Ogilvy, 83
Olive & Gourmando, 24
Olympic Basin, 10
Olympic Stadium, 221
Orange Rouge, 32
Osheaga Music and Arts Festival, 10, 369
Oshlag, 226
Oui Mais Non, 275
Outdoor staircases, 186
Pagaille Café, 338
Palais des Chaussons et Pizzas, 290
Palais des Congrès de Montréal, 31
Pang Pang Karaoké, 85
Parc Dante, 254
Parc de la Cité-du-Havre, 7
Parc de la Merci et l'île Perry, 291
Parc des Bateliers, 291
Parc des Rapides, 115
Parc du Faubourg-Sainte-Anne, 92
Parc du Portugal, 331
Parc du Premier-Chemin-de-Fer, 106
Parc Jacques-de-Lesseps, 295
Parc Jarry, 275, 323
Parc Jean-Drapeau Aquatic Complex, 12
Parc Jean-Drapeau, 10

Parc Jeanne-Mance, 334
Parc La Fontaine, 181
Parc Luc-Durand, 250
Parc Maisonneuve, 228
Parc Molson, 230
Parc Morgan, 217
Parc National des Îles-de-Boucherville, 297
Parc-Nature de l'Île-de-la-Visitation, 285
Parc-Nature du Cap-Saint-Jacques, 294
Parc Nicolas-Viel, 291
Parc René-Lévesque, 299
Parc Sir-Wilfird-Laurier, 181
Pascal le Boucher, 276
Pâtisserie Bicyclette, 237
Pâtisserie du Rosaire, 169
Pâtisserie Harmonie, 35
Patrice Pâtissier, 96
Patsy Van Roost (portrait), 144
Pêche Vieux-Montréal, 7
Petite Maison, 337
Petite Rebelle, 246
Philippe Dubuc, 25
Pho Bac, 36
Pho Lien, 138
Piknic Électronik, 11
Piorra Maison, 160
Pista, 249
Pizzeria Napoletana, 303
Place De Castelnau, 269
Place des Arts, 359
Place des Festivals, 52
Place du Coteau-Saint-Louis, 185
Place Émilie-Gamelin, 52
Place Genevilliers-Laliberté, 210
Place Jean-Paul-Riopelle, 31
Place Montréal-Trust, 64
Place Roy, 324
Place Simon-Valois, 202
Place Ville Marie, 367
Plan B, 166
Planetarium, 222
Pointe-du-Moulin, 2
Pourquoi Pas Espresso Bar, 39
Premiers Vendredis, 221
Prenez Place à l'Orgue concerts, 18
Promenade des Artistes, 52
Promenade Luc-Larivée, 202

Promenades Cathédrale, 64
Prune les Fleurs, 91
Punjab Palace, 266
Quartier des Spectacles, 52
Quincaillerie Dante, 258
Quincaillerie Hogg, 119
Rad Hourani, 25
Rage, 42
Randolph, 311
Raoul Wallenberg Square, 66
Rasoï, 103
Rebecca Makonnen, 326-331
Red Tiger, 41
Régine Café, 233
RÉSO, 61, 64
   see The Underground City
Rhubarbe, 187
Ritz-Carlton, 81
River shuttle, 9
Rix Rax, 184
Robin des Bois, 161
Romados, 169
Rose balls, 38
Rouen Wall, 195
Rouge Gorge, 166
Royal Bank Tower, 23
Royal Montreal Curling Club, 87
Rue Adam, 218
Rue Berri, 185
Rue Coursol, 98
Rue de Bullion, 174
Rue de Grand-Pré, 174
Rue Demers, 158
Rue Gilford, 174
Rue Lagarde, 185
Rue Sainte-Hélène, 19
Rue Sainte-Rose, 40
Rue Somerville, 291
Rue Villeneuve, 174
Ruelle Beau-Dommage, 243
Ruelle champêtre, 175
Ruelle l'Échappée Belle, 193
Sabor Latino, 242
Sain Bol, 190
Saint Joseph's Oratory, 133, 326
Saint-Gabriel Lock, 365
San Pietro, 278
Santa Barbara, 233
Saputo Stadium, 225
Sarah B, 29

Sata Sushi, 194
Satay Brothers, 104
Self-serve mini-libraries, 229
Sen Vàng, 138
Shô-Dan, 74
Silo No. 5, 2
Simons, 64
Sir-George-Étienne-Cartier Square, 107
Snowdon Deli, 132
Société des Arts Technologiques, 57
Spoutnik, 44
Square Saint-Louis, 174, 176
Square-Victoria–OACI Metro station (entrance of a genuine Paris Metro station by Hector Guimard), 26
St-Viateur Bagel, 152
St. Lawrence Warehousing Co., 148
Station No. 1, 202
Street food trucks, 77
Style Labo, 160
Sugar Sammy, 344-351
Sumac, 103
Summit Woods, 135
Sun Life Building, 76
Sundial, 223
Système by Pierre Granche, 139
Ta Pies, 163
Tacos Frida, 107
Talay Thaï, 137
Tam-Tams, 165
Tamey Lau (portrait), 147
Tapeo, 274
TAZ, 284
Temps d'Arrêt by Jean-Pierre Morin, 230
Téo Taxi, 67
Terrines & Pâtés, 100
Thaïlande, 146
The four seasons, 153
The Illuminated Crowd by Raymond Mason, 73
The Underground City, 61, 64
The Urban Forest, 70
Théâtre Sainte-Catherine, 58
Thomson House, 82

Titanic, 24
Tommy, 22
Toqué!, 30
Tour de Lévis, 13
Trail du bas (the beaten path), 111
Trèfle, 205
Tri Express, 309
Trilogie, 277
Tuck Shop, 99
Tuk Tuk, 137
Tunnel Espresso Bar, 88
Uniprix Stadium, 319
Université de Montréal, 322
Upstairs, 63
Vague à Guy (Guy's wave), 5
VdeV, 160
Vélo Intemporel, 230
Venice MTL, 24
Verger Gibouleau, 292
Verre Bouteille, 329
Vestibule, 160
Viauville, 218
Vices & Versa, 255
Village au Pied-du-Courant, 37
Village Coteau-Saint-Louis, 185
Village Mammouth, 221
Vinum Design, 62
Votive Chapel, 326
Week-ends du Monde, 10
Wellington, 113
Westmount Conservatory, 301
Westmount Lookout, 135
Westmount Park United Church, 117
Westmount Park, 117
Westmount Public Library, 117
Westmount Square, 342
Westmount staircases, 375
Wilensky, 155
William Gray, 352
William J. Walter, 202, 262
Woonerf Saint-Pierre, 106
World Trade Centre Montreal, 28
Y Lan, 251
Ye Olde Orchard Pub, 345
Yokato Yokabai, 304
Youppi! (portrait), 78
Zébulon Perron (portrait), 59

Photo Credits

Photography : Olivier Ruel, except:

@**imac_27** (Instagram), page 124, bois Summit @**Photograph-i DrMartinPhoto.com,** page 174, Electrik Kidz **Alain Lefort,** page 276, 1700 La Poste **Alexandre Cv,** page 239, parc-nature de l'Île-de-la-Visitation **Antonin Mousseau-Rivard,** page 61, Le Mousso **Bénédicte Brocard,** page 45, Normand Laprise **Charlotte Lacoursière,** page 139, Montreal Roller Derby **Daniel Lannegrace,** page 273, Herby Moreau **Étienne St-Denis,** page 275, Cœur de pirate **Gabrielle Desmarchais,** page 202, Régine Café **Geneviève Laurin,** page 244, Clos Saragnat **Jane Heller,** page 127, Orange Julep **Jean-Marc Lacoste,** page 108, parc des Rapides **Jean-René Dufort,** page 263, Jean-René Dufort **Jimmy Hamelin,** page 279, Anne-Marie Withenshaw **Jo-Anne McArthur We Animals,** page 251, Quebec Fauna Foundation **Jules Bédard,** page 69, Ligue d'improvisation montréalaise **Julie Perreault,** page 267, Jean-Philippe Wauthier **Le_Pigeon,** page 261, Ariane Moffatt **Malina Corpadean,** page 277, Denis Gagnon **Marc Ménard,** page 253, Les Pervenches **Marie-Claude Viola,** page 26, plage de l'Horloge **Marie-Jade Côté,** page 108, Natatorium **Marie-Joëlle Parent,** page 256, Westmount Conservatory **MatDeRome,** page 273, Atwater Cocktail Club **Mathieu Dupuis,** page 251, parc national des Iles-de-Boucherville, Sépaq **Matthieu Roux,** page 8, Claire Bouchard and page 250, Zoo Ecomuseum **Maude Chauvin,** page 265, Rebecca Makonnen **Michael Vesia,** page 133, Damas **MK PHOTO,** page 103, Sumac **Myranie Bray,** page 19, Oshlag **Nancy Hinton,** page 248, À la table des Jardins sauvages **Nicolas Delucinge,** page 104, woonerf Saint-Pierre **Noémie Letu,** page 134, Champ des Possibles **Raphaël Beaubien,** page 4, Montréal la nuit, page 86, **Guaranteed Pure Milk,** and back cover, Place Ville Marie **Raymond Jalbert,** page 198, Botanical Gardens **Shanti Loiselle,** page 249, parc-nature du Cap-Saint-Jacques **Sophie Thibault,** page 259, Doggy Style **Stéphanie Lefebvre,** page 269, Mitsou **Ville de Westmount,** page 114, Westmount Park **Vincent Marchessault – Photographe,** page 232, Oui Mais Non **William Yan,** pages 6 et 257, Marie-Joëlle Parent **Yves Renaud,** page 259, Guy A. Lepage

Acknowledgments

Special thanks to Olivier Ruel and Myranie Bray: This guide wouldn't exist without your immeasurable help, and I'm eternally grateful for your extraordinary efforts. A special thanks to Liette Mercier, my superhuman editor, who completely astonishes me. Your curiosity, energy and love for art and architecture are truly inspiring. Thanks to Josée Amyotte and Diane Denoncourt for the wonderful layout and the subsequent beautiful book. Thanks to the whole team at Les Éditions de l'Homme for giving me the opportunity to set my love for Montreal down on the page: Judith Landry, Guylaine Girard, Jacinthe Lemay, Catherine Bédard, Fabienne Boucher, Dominique Rivard... Thanks to the English team: Matthew Brown, Louisa Sage, Robert Ronald, Reilley Bishop-Stall and Agnès Saint-Laurent. Thanks to Sylvain Trudel for your professionalism and constant rigor. Thanks to Sofia Duran and Chloé Lafrenière for the huge helping hand at the start of this project. Thanks to Matthieu Roux for everything you did for me. And to my sons, Ludovic and Renaud, for showing great patience while your mom had to write.

Thank you to everyone who shared the things they love most about Montreal; there's a whole lot of you in this book.

Thanks to Annie Trudel, who told me "When I read your writing, I can hear your voice." It was a sweet and simple comment that ended up changing the course of my life.

To Marie-Joëlle Parent, thanks for being you: generous, inspiring and full of great advice. And thank you for having created this collection: This book is my biggest professional achievement, and it all started with you.

And thanks to all the shops, boutiques, cafés, restaurants, artists and other Montrealers who make the city so wonderfully unique.

From the same collection:

French

English

Printed by Imprimerie Transcontinental, Beauceville, Canada